D0791007

Acknowledgements

I want to thank my wife, Cynthia, for her patience, her masterful editing, and, most importantly, her support for this very considerable project. This book would not have been possible without her participation. I also want to thank Philmer Bluehouse for making my experience in Navajo country possible.

Liberation from the Lie: Cutting the Roots of Fear Once and For All

Eric Gross

ISBN:1-4392-2160-X
ISBN-13:9781439221600

Foreword

The world is in crisis. We are in crisis.

The crisis that engulfs our world is made by human beings. It is a world with a few "haves" and innumerable "have-nots." It is a world whose very systems that allow human life to flourish are in rapidly accelerating decline. Science warns us that unless people change the way they live, these life-sustaining systems will drastically deteriorate and the world's chaos will greatly worsen. And yet we cling to our dangerous, throw-away habits, the "haves" lavishly splurging on world-debasing trivialities and the "have-nots" clawing, striving, aching to do the same.

Our world of endless consumption and ceaseless wanting is born of invalidation. When people operate from lack, they are living lives driven by fear. This fear, at its absolute root, is the product of our deep-seated belief in our own inadequacy. As times grow more uncertain, our insecurities about our world and ourselves loom ever larger, fueling a search for safety and happiness that is inevitably brittle and unsustainable.

Our identification with inadequacy is a direct consequence of the invalidation we have suffered from our earliest days, first by families who knew no other way and then by a culture whose values could create no other type of person. Living as isolated entities in an insecure world is the perfect recipe for a life of anxiety and strife with only brief interludes of fragile peace.

We are driven to fix ourselves, our spouses, our children. We hunt the world over for sources of power, in the vain belief that more power will allow us to control our threatening and uncertain world.

We seek healing outside of ourselves, whether through the balm of conventional religion or Eastern enlightenment or New Age spiritualism. Meanwhile, we overlook the beauty and balance that reside in our own beings.

This book shines a bright light on the forces that sustain our insecurity and identification with inadequacy and reveals them to be false. The task of true healing is one of understanding through seeing, and it requires the courage to be rigorously honest with our own selves. This truth will set you free.

In this way, even our deepest fears can become our closest friends, the gateway to connection with all our brothers and sisters throughout this world. For the ultimate truth is that we are directly connected not only to all of the people on this planet but to the animals, plants, air, and water. Our power comes from these connections.

This book is a call to wake up from the nightmare of lack, fear, and insecurity and reconnect with the abundance of our hearts. Hear the call.

Table of Contents

Introduction

The Hero Twins: A Navajo Parable

When the world was young, before the time of humans, the only beings who lived on land or in the waters were monsters and the twin sons of Changing Woman, the Great Spirit of the universe. Their names were Born-for-Water and Monster Slayer. Born-for-Water was introspective, calm, and pensive, while Monster Slayer was aggressive, energetic, and a god-man of action.

The Hero Twins, as they were called, were given the task of making the world safe for First Woman and First Man, our ancestral parents. With so many monsters roaming about, the earth was far too dangerous a place for people to survive. Born-for-Water reflected on the problem and came up with a plan: Monster Slayer should traverse the world and kill all the monsters so the time of people could arrive.

So Monster Slayer went out into the world, and with his power and energy he was able to kill nearly all of the monsters. Upon his return, he reported this great triumph to Born-for-Water. But the triumph was not complete: Even he could not kill the monsters of fear, frustration, hopelessness, and hunger. Born-for-Water accepted this proviso, proclaiming that each person would need to deal with those monsters on his own. This is the great challenge of our lives.

If Monster Slayer was so powerful that he could slay enormous demons and dragons with his arrows, why couldn't he kill the seemingly lesser monsters of fear, frustration, and hopelessness? The story tells us that we cannot combat these monsters with violence. Nor can we defeat them by running away from them. They require a different approach: that of awareness and wisdom.

What about the fourth monster, hunger? Like fear, frustration, and hopelessness, hunger is painful and ever-present in our lives. But it is also the gateway to liberation from the other three monsters. Down deep, all of us hunger for a pathway to true well-being and a life of strength and authentic passion. Hunger is the essential force that drives us to liberation from fear, frustration, and hopelessness.

When we accommodate the monsters by living an inauthentic life, we have agreed to live a life based on fear. When we feed our gnawing discomfort with acquisitions and accomplishments designed to impress others and ourselves, we are seeking only to shield ourselves from the underlying fear. This is the life of escape.

The only true path is the heroic path. When we travel the hero's road, we see through the illusions we have created out of fear, and we discover the gem of priceless value that glows in the heart of our authentic selves. This is the journey of liberation.

My Story

For me, writing this book was a voyage of discovery. It is a discovery that can transform your life as it has mine.

The seeds for this book were planted 30 years ago. I was a statistician for the New York City Department of Health, living in a small apartment on the now very chic Upper West Side of Manhattan. As a product of the Vietnam War era--I pulled a draft number of 1, but thankfully never was called to serve in the military—I had carved out an identity for myself as a kind of mild Marxist, writing book reviews for left-wing newspapers. Then a friend gave me a copy of a book called The Awakening Of Intelligence by Krishnamurti. The book opened my eyes to an entirely new way of being.

For the next three decades, I strove to possess the clarity expressed by Krishnamurti's voice. I started to write down some of my thoughts and experiences during this process, cobbling together a rather labored account of the innumerable approaches I had taken in my ceaseless attempts to experience Nirvana, enlightenment, infinite bliss.

I noticed that the more I searched, the more miserable I was. Happiness was like water. I could throw myself into it, but I could never hold it. Too much of my life was a waterless drought. The harder I searched for enlightenment, the more desiccated my life became.

It then dawned on me that my search for enlightenment, the "golden ring," was really no different from any other desire. Buddha said that the root of all suffering is desire, and I desired more, a lot more. In fact, I wanted it all. And in this wanting, I had really become almost an anti-Buddhist. How ironic, I thought.

I came to realize that my search for enlightenment was really no different from those who endlessly seek fulfillment through material possessions, romantic love, or power and authority. Like everybody else, I wanted to be happy and was willing to do pretty much anything to reach my goal. Yet I noticed that the more I searched, the more miserable I was. Happiness was like water. I could throw myself into it, but I could never hold it. Too much of my life was a waterless drought. The harder I searched for enlightenment, the more desiccated my life became.

But I continued to search. I read many books (you wouldn't believe just how many). I meditated at a Zen temple intermittently for many years. I did yoga. I attended Advaita satsangs. I spent several years living among and studying traditional Navajo healers. I scoured the world for that one little nugget of truth that would take me over the edge. I believed that I could have it all, if only I could discover the one final insight that would launch me from the boring world of humdrum existence and deposit me blissfully in Nirvana. But, no matter how hard I searched, the key insight eluded me. There were times when I thought I had it: I could grasp water. I dazzled myself. These were moments of great relief.

But within hours, if not minutes, I was back to my old, tired, seeking self, no closer to my destination than when I set out years before. I was amazed at how quickly life would respond with the exact event that would put me right back in the place where I started. My brief glow of attainment would then fade into the garbage heap of dozens of other similarly "brilliant" insights.

I looked back at my life and thought, what a waste. The more I searched, the more hopeless I became. Life often felt meaningless.

Then I had a breakthrough. I had read that the person we consciously believe ourselves to be is a construct--a self created out of fear. In my case, the person who was so disconsolate, so confused, so ceaselessly striving for answers was not, in actuality, the real me. But if he was not real, then who was this fiction? And if the self I believed to be me was not who I really was, then how could I find my true self?

Further reading and thinking led me to understand that the fictive person I took myself to be was actually a psychological projection with a life story all his own. He was the me that I recognized as myself—and that others recognized as me—but he was, in fact, a kind of overlay personality, or false being. I learned that this overlay personality, which we all possess, is an adaptation to the intense trauma that occurs when very young children are separated and invalidated from their parents. We will discuss this trauma and its after-effects in detail later in this book, but suffice it to say that the traumas of early childhood mark a decisive moment in our lives, laying the foundation for what I call the Wound. The Wound is the source of our greatest fears and self-doubt, even self-contempt. The purpose of the overlay personality, or Fear-Self, is to shield us from the pain and trauma of the Wound.

The person we take ourselves to be results from the interplay of the Wound with its Fear-Selves. Don't worry about the details just yet, but if one's Wound is expressed as "I am worthless," its corresponding overlay is a personality driven by the compensating motive, "I will show others how worthy I am." The 24/7 task of the Fear-Self is to strengthen itself against the negative pull of the powerful, fundamental Wound. Even the most well-adapted Fear-Selves are incomplete and vulnerable. The dark shadow of the Wound is always there, slipping through "holes" in the Fear-Self. The unconscious purpose of our lives becomes a ceaseless struggle to protect our psyche from the pain of the Wound. It is as if our psyches become frozen in this ceaseless struggle.

Liberation from the Lie seeks to bring healing light to this dilemma. The primary feeling of the Wound is lack. We have the feeling that we lack something vital to our well-being, and the Fear-Selves are created to overcome this sense of lack. Much of the self-help movement and renewed interest in Eastern philosophy has grown out of our search for help in dealing with the resonating pain embodied in the Wound.

The best teachings in this field seek to awaken us from the lie of who we believe ourselves to be. If you are interested in sustainable self-transformation--and reading these words shows that you are--then realize that a Fear-Self cannot be become a whole self. Because the Fear-Self is never complete, it always wants more of what it needs to sustain itself. If we are to liberate ourselves from its illusion, we must rupture our connection with it. This is a call to begin the journey of stepping back and taking a look at who we truly are. By seeing through the deceptive identities of the Wound and Fear-Selves, we can find our authentic selves and speak with our authentic voice.

Our ultimate destination is in the unfolding Now. This is where everything is and where everything happens. The Fear-Self, by contrast, lives in time, always looking ahead to its hoped-for goal that exists in a future that ceaselessly recedes. But truth resides only in the Now. It is the place where we are our original goodness. It is the place where our strength, our happiness, and our fulfillment are our authentic identity. This identity does not depend on other people, life situations, or the promises of a Fear-Self. It is exactly who we are. You may not realize it, but you are there already…. I urge you to try to feel it. This powerful current that underlies all thought and feeling is the authentic you prior to your identification with your Fear-Self or any self-image. Try feeling that part of your being which is not identified with any role.

I noted earlier that the Fear-Selves are porous. Gaps in their shells allow the emanations from the Wound to enter. This is why we can never be fully shielded by any Fear-Self, no matter how well-adapted it is. The Wound is also porous. It allows the light of your authentic being—your Original Core—to shine through the Wound's dark mist of pain and retreat. We experience our Original Core anytime we are uplifted by a child's smile, beauty in nature, a heartfelt touch, or the end of a wonderful novel.

The great self-transformative journey of our life becomes one of birth → separation → identification with the Wound → creation of the Fear-Self personalities → living life identified with who we are not

→ seeing the Fear-Selves for what they really are → returning to the Wound and coming to peace with it → returning to our authentic being, strong, happy, and fulfilled. This is the cycle of the Liberated Life.

Have faith in two truths: One, the Wound gives formation to all of our Fear-Selves (identities) and is more powerful than any of them. Two, our original goodness is more powerful and enduring than the Wound.

You might, at this point, be wondering what the "lie" in the title of this book means. The lie is simply this: What we think of as our primary identity is not our true identity at all. It is false; it is a lie. Until we experience, directly, the falseness of our overlay personalities, we will continue to live a lie.

Warning: Liberation from the Lie is not for the faint of heart. Our most personal beliefs about ourselves are ones that most of us are loath to question. Their familiarity is beguiling. That is why I call this a hero's journey. Our love affair with these beliefs is like living with an abusive spouse who is constantly promising to repair the damage caused by his or her violence. If we listen carefully, it won't take us long to discover that our inner voices are ceaseless critics. What we put up with from ourselves, we would never dream of putting up with from others.

The irony is that we are in love with our own abusive voices. The problem, contrary to the advice of many, is not that we fail to love ourselves enough, but that we love ourselves too much—or at least we love what we think is our self. Our authentic self is pure love. It remains deep inside, waiting for you to rediscover it. This book will not ask you to fall out of love with yourself, but to fall out of love with your many Fear-Selves. It asks you to tell that abusive spouse that you have seen through his false promises and empty protestations. It asks you to thank those thousands of advice givers you have previously turned to for their good intentions, but to proclaim that you now can stand on your own two feet, secure, finally, in your authentic self.

This book asks you, at its most basic, to suspend those beliefs through which you justify your self-image. You will also be asked to take a close and careful look at those beliefs without attempting to change, destroy, or let go of them. It is simply by looking through them that we can release ourselves from their compelling thrall. We can awaken from the trance of living in their shadow. We can, finally, find ourselves.

> *The problem, contrary to the advice of many, is not that we fail to love ourselves enough, but that we love ourselves too much—or at least we love what we think is our self. Our authentic self is pure love. It remains deep inside, waiting for you to rediscover it.*

Unlike many other books that share thematic similarities with this one, Liberation from the Lie will not ask you to drop your stories. We are human beings with preferences, judgments, and passions. The danger in much of Eastern philosophy is seeking to live life in extreme quiet where there is no apparent passion. I, for one, love passion! Take a stand. Get angry at what seems to you to be wrong in the world. If you are concerned about global warming, racism, sexism, or whatever, by all means act on your beliefs. Have passion. Claim your voice.

The one thing that will be asked of you is that you discern your authentic passions from false passions, which are statements of the deficient self. The difference is enormous. Liberation will help you navigate that process.

Sources

The content of this book is drawn from five sources: Advaita, a school within Hinduism; Taoism; Buddhism/Zen; the teaching of traditional Navajo healers; and, by far the most important, the observation and testing of these principles in my own life. After 30 years of studying and rigorously testing these ideas, I discovered the remarkable clarity of these life-affirming observations.

While much of this book is rooted in my own personal immersion in these philosophies, it is not my intent to add to the vast bibliography of Eastern thought. Rather my purpose is to communicate the tangible and visceral elements I have taken from these philosophies so that you, too, can observe them and test them in your own life. Take nothing here on faith or fear-based hope. Only one person can heal you, and that person is you.

The eminent psychologist Carl Rogers said, "The only learning which significantly influences behavior is self-discovered, self-appropriated learning. Such self-discovered learning, truth that has been personally appropriated and assimilated in experience, cannot be directly communicated to another. As soon as the individual tries to communicate such experience directly, often with a natural enthusiasm, it becomes teaching, and its results are inconsequential."

This is not a teaching book. Rather, it is a book that lays out the fruits of my own seeking, my own observations. Liberation from the Lie is a book that invites you to make your own discoveries. Only that which is directly experienced by the self can constitute authentic learning. Therefore, don't believe anything that is written here! Taking on even one more belief is just another form of accumulation, and that is what Fear-Selves do best. They always want more in their ceaseless drive to completion. The final goal is always over the horizon, just past that bend in the road. It is a place that is just out of reach in space and time.

I have often called this book a Liberation Manual, but it is unlike any of the manuals you've seen before. This is not a manual to help you construct something; rather it is purely a manual for deconstruction. Contained herein are your instructions for disassembly, and the person doing the disassembling is you. Your authentic being and voice are already there, waiting for you to discover them. I will show you how to feel them, even in—especially in—your most turbulent times. Anything you might do to construct or add onto the self would only contribute to one of your Fear-Selves. The only "doing" here is your undoing, and that needs to happen without any direct effort on your part. Only Fear-Selves believe in effort. Your radiant self is there, utterly without effort.

Liberation is a call to real revolution. Authentic revolution is not about achieving any state or believing in any ideology. It is the transformation of the self. If history proves anything, it is that we cannot rely on government, or any other entity outside of ourselves, to bring harmony and balance to the world. That task is yours exclusively. As you fall out of love with and lose your attachment to your Fear-Selves, your world will be truly transformed. This is revolutionary.

It took me 30 years of practice, experience, and patience to develop the message of Liberation from the Lie. While there is certainly more than one path to liberation from the wholly unnecessary pain and struggle of life, this book presents one of those paths: that of seeing clearly and testing experientially. By reading this, you can save yourself many, many years of therapy, reading, practice, and luck. You will be able to find your authentic self beneath the layers that have accumulated, as a kind of scar, over the belief in your own inadequacy.

I should also say what this book is not about. Liberation is not achieved by adding onto yourself. It's not about knowing more about who you are or who you should be. If you are seeking new and better thoughts about yourself, then you have picked up the wrong book. Finding the authentic you is not a matter of knowing more. Instead, it is a matter of seeing through the dense veil of thoughts that blocks us from experiencing our authentic selves. Liberation from the Lie is a lens through which we are able to see how we have unwittingly abandoned our true being and have adopted an array of secondary personalities to fill the gap. Therefore, I strongly suggest that you read this in the spirit of undoing and not of accumulating more information about yourself.

Truth cannot be wholly expressed in words; therefore, Liberation is only a signpost for you to use as a tool in your deconstruction. As the Zen Buddhists are fond of saying, all words are only pointers to elements whose subtlety cannot be captured by language. Discovery is more, much more about feeling than thought. Walt Whitman, William Shakespeare, Emily Dickinson, Lao Tzu, and many others have come close, but ultimately life eludes any verbal description of itself.

However, we can obtain a sense of the wondrous feeling Liberation from the Lie can bring through its depiction in literature (as well as film and other art forms). One of my favorite passages comes from Herman Melville's Moby Dick. Toward the end of that monumental work, Captain Ahab considers his life, its madness and ceaseless striving and suffering. Melville writes, "Slowly crossing the deck from the scuttle, Ahab leaned over the side, and watched how his shadow in the water sank and sank to his gaze, the more and the more that he strove to pierce the profundity. But the lovely aromas in that enchant-ed air did at last seem to dispel, for a moment, the cankerous thing in his soul. That glad, happy air, that winsome sky, did at last stroke and caress him; the stepmother world, so long cruel—forbidding—now threw affectionate arms around his stubborn neck, and did seem to joyously sob over him, as if over one, that however willful and erring, she could yet find it in her heart to save and to bless. From beneath his slouched hat Ahab dropped a tear in the sea; nor did all the Pacific contain such wealth as that one wee drop."

Open your own heart to that same "one wee drop" in yourself and you will have started your own journey toward liberation.

Section One:

The Sources of Fear and Insecurity

1 - Portraits of the Fear-Self

Before we explore the roots of the Wound and its compensating personality overlays, let's take a look at some of the common Fear-Selves. Remember that the Fear-Self is an identity we create to shield us from the pain of the separation trauma. Fear-Selves are also molded by the social institutions that make up our society and culture, particularly our families of origin and schools.

The examples below are intentionally simplified. No one is a single, pure type; rather, we are combinations of many Fear-Selves, some of them very subtle but quite powerful in their impact. In fact, the subtler Fear-Selves are likely to be more important, in the long run, to identify. Often we are so closely identified with our Fear-Selves that we need the help of others to recognize them.

No one is a single, pure type; rather, we are combinations of many Fear-Selves, some of them very subtle but quite powerful in their impact. In fact, the subtler Fear-Selves are likely to be more important, in the long run, to identify.

For clarity's sake, the "Fear-Self" label is predicated on four conditions:

- The person becomes attached to the identity in order to counter the negative feelings of the Wound;

- The person has an irresistible need to be identified in this way, and the resulting thoughts, feelings, and actions are compulsive;

- The person seeks validation through this identity; and

- The person believes that being identified in this way will result in enduring happiness.

Each Fear-Self type is listed by name, common social roles represented by the type, predominant characteristics, underlying Wound, the resulting life view, and common personality variants.

The Achiever

Common social roles: Salesman; physician; attorney; executive/manager; politician.

Predominant characteristics: Driven to succeed, achievements must be visible, always preparing for what's next. He is addicted to others identifying him as a powerful person, one to be reckoned with.

Fears/Insecurities: Fear of failure; resentment of competitors, especially those in the same field whose achievements have outshone his own. Any event in which success is threatened may result in high levels of anxiety. May become isolated, bitter, and self-critical if failure is experienced.

Wound: I am incompetent, worthless, and powerless.

Life view: The story of his successes and the brilliant way he has addressed challenges dominates his view of life. Believes that increased achievement will lead to a stable sense of fulfillment. Often unaware of his own need for adulation. Often a conspicuous spender.

Variations: The Patriarch, often seen in bosses and political leaders. This type can be prone to violence when challenged and depression when not validated. In extreme form, The Achiever can become a sociopath (Hitler, Stalin).

The Pleaser

Common social roles: Housewife; not-for-profit or volunteer worker; social worker.

Predominant characteristics: Perfectionism, needs to do everything "just right," keeps tastes and activities neutral to avoid offending others.

Fears/Insecurities: Fear of isolation, broken family, ache of inner emptiness when the party's over, haunted by fear of not pulling off her social persona properly. Without social accolade, she is nothing. Fear of not being liked, of losing social status, of being ostracized.

Wound: I am unlovable.

Life view: Her personal history tends to be inconsequential, but she is proud of her orderly way of living (well-maintained home, manicured lawn, loving, "normal" family). Likes to host social events, but only if the conversation remains polite and generally insincere; she is embarrassed by loudness or raucousness. Sexual expression is reticent, highly controlled. Can't say "no" to any request, and will manufacture reasons to help people even when help is not requested. Addicted to compliments and acknowledgment. Hypersensitive to others' opinions, interpreting others'"looks" and comments as innuendo and criticism. Responds to others' failure to express appreciation for her efforts with covert or overt hostility.

Variations: The "Do-Gooder," who loves to be associated with helping the "less fortunate," but whose underlying motivation is public accolade.

The Body Person

Common social roles: Found across all classes and work positions, but especially among actors and other performers.

Predominant characteristics: Compulsive focus on the body, face, diet, and health.

Fears/Insecurities: Fear of physical decline, disease/sickness, death, social rejection on a physical basis, and time.

Wound: I am ugly, I am unwell, I am fragile.

Life view: I must look and feel good. Time, as expressed in aging, is a constant enemy. Frequent obsessive fear of germs (see the Terrified One), excessively self-conscious with respect to body image. Feels superior to people not focused on their physical appearance and/or strength/flexibility. This type will often focus on accessories, make-up, perfumes, and other items that enhance their physical attractiveness. Likely to be uncritical of cosmetic surgery or other modification of body parts. Self-appraisal is often highly unrealistic (in either direction – positive or negative).

Variations: The Body Person shares many characteristics with The Terrified One (below).

The Expert

Common social roles: Professor; physician; attorney; engineer; mechanic; geek.

Predominant characteristics: Utterly knowledgeable on all subjects, full of information and expertise and eager to share them with anyone and everyone.

Fears/Insecurities: Fear of being seen by others as incompetent, irrelevant, inconsequential; fear of being ignored. Can't tolerate being trumped by a "superior" intellect or expert.

Wound: I am stupid/incompetent; I am not worth being seen or heard.

Life view: Loves to pontificate, always assuming a tone of authority. Sees other people as stupid and seeks every opportunity to demonstrate his authority through knowledge. Belittles others' intellects and becomes indignant when confronted by an adversary. Believes that the acquisition of knowledge can ultimately fulfill his desire for happiness and contentment, which manifests in the acknowledgment of his knowledge and authority by respected others.

Variations: The Critic and Competitor, who loudly proclaims that he knows the best restaurants, films, vacation spots, sports tips; The Cynic, who covertly assumes superiority over others and sees most people as dumb and naïve.

The Spiritualist

Common social roles: Student; academic; artist; social activist.

Predominant characteristics: Perennially seeking higher truth, enlightenment; tending toward elitism in spiritual matters.

Fears/Insecurities: Fear that he will never reach his goal, will never be among the chosen ones; over time, he sinks into existential despair as the knowledge that he will never attain his goal becomes increasingly apparent to him.

Wound: I am ordinary; I am not special.

Life view: Is very vested in the story of his "holy journey." Amasses mountains of books focusing on spiritual issues; endlessly attends workshops, satsangs, retreats. His sense of well-being is dependent on seeking. Tends to reject the world around him, which is seen as pervasively crass, as well as his perceived self, which he believes to be an illusion.

Variations: The Self-Help Fanatic, prone to melancholy and hopelessness as the answers perpetually elude him.

The Tough Guy

Common social roles: Police/military officer; prison guard; bartender; executive/manager; construction worker; tradesperson (electrician, plumber, etc.).

Predominant characteristics: Stoic yet easily angered, domineering, emotionally distant, adheres to traditional/patriarchal values (either gender).

Fears/insecurities: Fear of being seen as soft or weak, effeminate, self- conscious.

Wound: I am weak, vulnerable, unprotected.

Life view: Nobody is going to push me around; I can protect and stand up for myself. Not willing to allow others to get to close to him emotionally, although he cultivates mutually validating, usually same-sex friendships with similar types. Enjoys confrontation because it gives him the opportunity to demonstrate his toughness. In its milder form, The Tough Guy can simply be prim and proper and know what's best for everyone else.

Special comment: The Tough Guy's Wound lies just beneath the surface. If his defenses ever fail him, tears and weakness surge forth with heart-rending intensity. This is a scenario often favored in movies. For example, in the film "On the Waterfront," when Terry Malloy (Marlon Brando) tells his brother (Rod Steiger) that he "could have been somebody," the audience is deeply touched by his immense sadness.

Variations: The Loner, who similarly needs to protect himself but who generally retreats from confrontation (see below).

The Loner

Common social roles: Any position that accommodates his preference for low visibility, such as low-level office worker, writer, artist, specialized consultant.

Predominant characteristics: Needs to stay separate, removed from others, both emotionally and physically; feels safest when emotionally unconnected with others.

Fears/insecurities: Fear of intimacy and commitment; expends a lot of energy on avoiding relationships and maintaining a life alone.

Wound: Generalized pain from separation; "I was hurt too badly to risk being hurt by others again."

Life view: Getting involved with others can only lead to disappointment and heartache, so he remains apart. Other people are the source of trauma, and anyone who gets close to him has the potential to hurt him. As people become close to The Loner, they are projected as mother substitutes. The Loner will inevitably have difficulties with issues of intimacy and commitment. He pays for his isolation with loneliness, but this is typically a cost he is willing to pay.

Variations: The Loner is a close relative of The Tough Guy, but is not invested in possessing authority over others.

The Imitator

Common social roles: Found in all walks of life.

Predominant characteristics: Very unassertive, indecisive, prone to following authority without question.

Fears/insecurities: Fear of making the wrong choice, so always deferring to the opinions and choices of others.

Wound: "I'm nobody; I'm nothing."

Life view: The Imitator distrusts her own being; to get along in the world, she finds models for personality traits and co-opts them for her own use. She is motivated by self-loathing. This type tends to become involved in relationships that result in her abuse and humiliation. In its milder form, The Imitator cannot make decisions until she consults with external "experts." She has no opinions of her own; books, movies, clothing are selected on the basis of trusted reviewers or friends. The Imitator is uncomfortable with spontaneity; everything is checked and considered. She is very uncomfortable expressing herself in public.

Variations: The Victim, who feels she deserves her suffering.

The Terrified One

Common social roles: Varied, but this type is preponderantly represented by women.

Predominant characteristics: Compulsive need to be safe.

Fears/insecurities: Fear of danger, chaos, violence; fear of becoming a victim.

Wound: "I am helpless; the world is a dangerous place." This type often grew up in a turbulent, chaotic environment that left her with the belief that she is incapable of providing herself with enough safety.

Life view: The Terrified One must have safe places as havens where she can hide from the ongoing trauma of life. This can come in the form of an unchallenging workplace or a highly controlled relationship. She projects her terror onto those she cares about and often imposes her seemingly well-intended, but usually unwanted, obsession with safety oppressively onto others. Over time, others begin to resent her, and then ignore her. The Terrified One is expert at finding justification for her fears. Whether it be germs, crime, career failure, or historical events, she can point to any number of facts or experiences to justify her terror projections. She tends to view those who do not share her fears as naive. In its milder form, this type often has an air of grave maturity, looking down their noses at those who take "foolish" risks. In its most evolved form, this Fear-Self is smug and self-satisfied, an overbearing caretaker of the others in her life.

Variations: Every False-Self contains an element of the insecurity that underpins The Terrified One. The difference is that this type amplifies and centralizes fear to a far greater extent than others.

The Resilient One

Note: The Resilient One is not really a Fear-Self. She has overcome separation and social wounding. This is can be achieved in three ways that may act together or separately. One, her family of origin was unconditionally loving and consistently validated her innate selfhood. Two, she encountered powerful mentors as a young person who enabled her to be resilient in the face of powerful social pressures to conform and to acquiesce to external authorities. Three, she was born with a more vibrant Original Core, which allowed her to overcome separation traumas and social conformity pressures.

Common social roles: This is a very uncommon type, tending to occupy caretaking roles. They may provide care to people, animals, or the planet (nurse, social worker, veterinarian, ecologist).

Predominant characteristics: Even-tempered, generous, patient.

Fears/insecurities: Very mild.

Wound: The Resilient One experienced the pain of separation in infancy, like the rest of humankind, but does not need to rely on a Fear-Self to compensate for the trauma. Why? First, resiliency may have some inborn or genetic component; and second, the unconditional love expressed for her as a child may have been powerful enough to overcome the separation trauma and provide protection against spirit-defeating social institutions.

Life view: Some people have the resources to give and expect nothing in return; can love unconditionally; do not feel the need to defend themselves; and can address conflict with equanimity. The Resilient One does not escape the trauma of separation, and so even she has a Wound. However, the need to counter its pain with an array of Fear-Selves is greatly reduced.

Variations: Not applicable.

Portrait Summary

Each of us has an identifiable personality. Even the Buddha, Jesus, and Lao Tzu had Fear-Selves. While I have listed the most obvious, overriding personality types, it is important to remember that most expressions of the Fear-Self are subtle and can easily escape attention. The differentiating feature in individuals such as the Buddha (who said "I am only a man") is that, over time, these individuals are able to become largely disengaged from their attachment to their Fear-Selves. They have had life experiences that enable them to see through their manufactured, yet real-feeling, identities. By disengaging from their Fear-Selves, they can come into direct contact with their Wounds. This is the decisive step that allows the glow of the Original Core to shine through and, literally, enlighten us.

This is the first leg of our journey towards our final destination: liberation.

2 - Trust and the End of Trust

"In my solitude I have seen things very clearly that were not true."

~ Antonio Machado

Is it possible to live life without emotional insecurity? Historians and anthropologists say "yes."

Modern human beings have been around for about 150,000 years. For about 140,000 of those years, survival depended on hunting and gathering. The time of the hunter-gatherers in the human cultural story is over; these societies, isolated from modern influences, have all but disappeared. However, scientists and explorers have studied and left detailed descriptions of what these societies were like prior to their demise. These observations show us a world that is very different from our own—a world in which individuals trusted life.

It must seem paradoxical to point to hunter-gatherers as models of security. To us, they lived in a world utterly lacking in the most rudimentary elements of security. Imagine waking up tomorrow with no food in your home. All the food stores have disappeared. You are living in a pure wilderness, without any ready source of sustenance. You are facing your own death and the deaths of everyone in your family from starvation. This is the world the hunter-gatherers faced every day!

Hunter-gatherers were nomads, possessing only the food they collected or hunted each day. Their societies lacked any form of food storage. And yet they survived, purely through their daily labor and ingenuity, even in the harshest climates on the planet.

Did the absence of food fill them with dread? Did their daily confrontation with starvation and death terrify them? Did their deep and persistent anxiety compel them to beseech the supernatural for good fortune? The answer is no. These societies had little apparent insecurity. They had no specific gods they felt the need to turn to for protection. They trusted nature implicitly, confident that it would provide for them.

Hunter-gatherers differed from us less in the shapes of their bodies and the development of their intellect than in the way they related to the world around them. While they had every reason to live in fear—fear of wild animals, illness, starvation, fear of competing groups, fear of natural phenomena like storms—the vast preponderance of evidence shows us that they trusted the world to provide for them and keep them safe. We, in contrast, have nearly every reason to trust our world.

Hunter-gatherers differed from us less in the shapes of their bodies and the development of their intellect than in the way they related to the world around them. While they had every reason to live in fear—fear of wild animals, illness, starvation, fear of competing groups, fear of natural phenomena like storms—the vast preponderance of evidence shows us that they trusted the world to provide for them and keep them safe.

For most of us, food is abundant; our living environments are sheltered from the elements and from hostile competitors; medical care is available if we become sick or injured, and we can expect to live into old age. Yet our actions demonstrate the belief that we face ruin unless we do exactly the "right" thing. Ironically, in our relatively safe world, we see danger everywhere.

The hunter-gatherers believed that their world would always take care of them. They returned this care with ceaseless appreciation and wonder at the world's abundance and benevolence. They sang songs, fell in and out of love, laughed, and played, confident that their world would always provide for them.

Studies show that hunter-gatherers worked an average of four hours a day to sustain their lives. While each day's physical survival depended on their well-honed skills, their working lives, compared with ours, were far less demanding. While women labored for more hours each day than men (some things never change), their work was made lighter by singing and talking side by side with friends and family as they made clothes, gathered seeds, plants, and herbs (the core of the Neolithic diet), and supervised their children. If the children were young (under the age of 4), they were strapped onto their mothers' bodies and carried about throughout the day.

This lightness of being extended into their world view. In contrast with our culture's obsession with achieving transcendence (for many through religion, but for others through meditation, mind-altering substances, public accolade, or material success), hunter-gatherers did not invest faith or fear in an overarching life goal or all-powerful deity. In fact, there is little evidence supporting any notion of the sacred in their world. Morris Berman, one of the world's foremost experts in Neolithic culture, points out that when "Native Americans refer to the Great Spirit, they often are talking about the wind. This spirit is the creation itself: water coming off a leaf, the smell of the forest after rain, the warm blood of a deer." No great god rules supreme. There is only creation unfolding.

Hunter-gatherers did not invest faith or fear in an overarching life goal or all-powerful deity. In fact, there is little evidence supporting any notion of the sacred in their world.

This was a culture that lived, as Virginia Woolf put it, "between the acts"; alertness, not escape, is the *sine qua non* of a hunting society. The great anthropologist Paul Radin, who did extensive fieldwork among the Winnebago Indians, argued that for such peoples, reality was heightened to such a pitch that the details of the environment seemed to "blaze." This, he points out, was not a sacred event. It was imminent, but not transcendent. It involved heightened awareness. In this world, the secular is the sacred, which is all around us.

In some small pockets of the world, this way of life has persisted into the current era. As observed by Colin Turnbull, author of the classic <u>The Forest People</u>, the Mbuti of Tanzania still today live within a "sacred reality" that is "no more sacred or esoteric than the forest in which they dwell." There is a notable absence of any preoccupation with political power, magical rites, or "hidden realities." The Mbuti regard all of these as superstitions. To the Mbuti, writes Turnbull, the forest alone is "presence" or "God."

Child-Rearing and the Origins of Invalidation

While the hunter-gatherers lived in a world fully connected with nature and other members of their families and tribes, we live in a world of profound disconnection, set apart from both nature and the other people in our communities. While hunter-gatherers were an integral part of their environment, we are like visitors in a hostile land. Somehow we have migrated from a place of apparent peril where people felt safe and secure to a place of apparent security where we feel unsafe and insecure. How, then, can we account for the paradigm shift that has occurred in the modern era?

An explanation can begin by examining the differences in central beliefs regarding children and the role of parents. Hunter-gatherers regarded new human life as perfect in and of itself. Each child was seen as a unique being intended to follow his own, distinct journey through life. On the other hand, modern civilization sees children as flawed even at birth, requiring constant discipline and education in order to become fully functioning adults. In hunter-gatherer societies, children remain physically connected to an older person, most of the time their mothers, throughout most of their first three or four years. In today's homes, most children are physically separated from their mothers from the very day of birth. Their life of partial isolation begins on day one.

> *Hunter-gatherers regarded new human life as perfect in and of itself. In contrast, modern civilization sees children as flawed even at birth, requiring constant discipline and education in order to become fully functioning adults.*

The separation and endless correction that a child undergoes in modern times results in invalidation—the negation of ourselves as we are.

Our sense of self is most vulnerable when we are very young, well before we can understand words or express ourselves. Thus is the origin of what I call the Wound, our conviction that we are innately inadequate, insufficient, and worthless. This angst is the very signature of modern life. It is the source of our disconnected selves, those parts of us that struggle for completion and wholeness only to find persistent frustration.

The hunter-gatherer did not carry the burden of invalidation. He knew he was "as he is supposed to be" prior to any action or doing. He was not expected to prove anything; he didn't have to justify his right to be just as he was.

Child-rearing philosophies tend to develop in order to reproduce a particular personality type that will be functional for adult life in the society at hand. Consider these differences between the way children were raised by hunter-gathers and how they are raised now:

- Hunter-gatherer children were raised without overt discipline; we "civilize" our children through punishment and other consequences levied when "rules" are broken;

- Hunter-gatherers perceived children as a creation of the same nurturing universe that supported and took care of the tribe; we see children as "little savages" who need to be domesticated;

- Hunter-gatherer children remained physically close to their mothers for up to four years, constantly held and carried; modern children are separated from their mothers at least for periods of time each day from birth onward;

- Hunter-gather mothers breastfed for three to four years; we usually wean within a year;

- Hunter-gatherer children slept with their parents for up to five years; most modern children sleep in a separate bed, if not a separate room, from their parents from the day they arrive;

- Hunter-gatherer children possessed the same power as anyone else; modern children are told in no uncertain terms that they are powerless and are often punished if they try to exert power;

- Hunter-gather children were raised in groups or clans, with many adults taking responsibility for parenting duties;

modern children are usually raised by their biological parents alone, or with the help of a very few trusted relatives or hired caretakers.

The differences are many, but the most profound is this: Hunter-gatherer children were loved and respected just as they were. Modern children must earn the love and respect of their elders, on their elders' terms. This is the origin of the fundamental invalidation that nearly all of us experience in our very first months of our lives. We are left alone at times; we are constantly corrected. We get the message that we are deficient burdens. Expressions of parental love are undermined by angry words, harsh expressions, indifference, distance, and punishment.

Let me elaborate on some of the differences outlined above. While a personality is shaped by genetics, upbringing, and socialization, one of the most potent ingredients in that mix is one's earliest relationship with his or her mother. For the hunter-gather, that relationship was extremely close, both physically and emotionally. Among the !Kung (and many other non-Bantu tribes of southern Africa), Australian Aborigine groups, the Berbers of the Middle East, and most Native American tribes of the Plains and Plateau region, children were virtually attached to their mothers for most of their first 18 months. When not in the arms or on the back of her mother, a young child was passed on to other people in the community who held her for extended periods. This provided contact and bonding with a much more diverse array of adults than would be found in an American household today. In the parlance of the well-known African adage, it takes a village to raise a child.

We, on the other hand, typically place children into their own rooms early in life, where they experience isolation and terror from being alone; often in the dark. This occurs at a time when a baby is utterly vulnerable and powerless to affect her fate. She screams in protest, but parents close their hearts to these cries in order to allow the child to habituate herself to pain and fear. Over time, as the child begins to cooperate, she is praised and rewarded for her compliance. This early trauma is relatively new to our species; the children of hunter-gatherers were touched, held, and comforted almost continuously for the first few years of their lives.

> *We, on the other hand, typically place children into their own rooms early in life, where they experience isolation and terror from being alone; often in the dark. This occurs at a time when a baby is utterly vulnerable and powerless to affect her fate.*

Consider another difference. While the hunter-gatherers considered each child to be unique, to be loved and respected for the individuality of his talents, life path, and story as it unfolded, modern parents seek to produce children who become "special" by dint of their accomplishments. But when some in a group are considered special, others, of course, will NOT be special. Indeed, the special ones continually run the risk of losing their special status. Children soon absorb this lesson and sever themselves from their innate, unique identities; instead, molded by external rewards and punishments, they strive to achieve the standards of "specialness" defined by their parents and society. In this competition for attention and esteem, children disown their inherent power of self and bow to the authority of those who can confer on them the coveted "gold star." We innocently participate in our own powerlessness making.

The extreme pressure modern children feel to compete for accolades—indeed, for love itself—adds additional trauma to that already inflicted by separation and isolation. The Wound, source of our persistent sense of inadequacy and incompleteness, is deepened. And the resulting anxiety, turbulence, conflict, and unhappiness on an individual level is mirrored by our culture at large.

The World Cut in Two: The Development of an Invalidating Society

The dawn of civilization heralded the end of the nomadic life of the hunter-gatherer. The transition to settled village life was perhaps the most decisive moment in the human story. Everything changed. The egalitarian life of the hunter-gatherer ended; hierarchies and classes were born. Rulers took control over the masses, creating rules to govern all aspects of existence. Obedience, a trait with little meaning to the hunter-gatherer, emerged as central to the establishment and maintenance of order in our world. The world of the "haves" and "have nots," with the inevitable few winners and countless losers, arrived and was here to stay.

Obedience, a trait with little meaning to the hunter-gatherer, emerged as central to the establishment and maintenance of order in our world.

In hunter-gatherer societies, where little was accumulated, there was little to demonstrate one's superiority over others. There were very few rankings and no sustainable positions of prestige people could exploit to proclaim their success. (An important exception was success in hunting.) Conversely, there were few who felt inferior to or were forced to live with less than others. The harmony and balance that existed between people and the natural world was mirrored in the relations among individuals and groups of people. Conflict, especially lethal combat, was very rare. But as sedentary society developed, with its value placed on wealth as a symbol of superiority, conflict over material possessions and positions of power became frequent and severe.

Our age-old trust in the beneficence of nature began to disappear. Nature morphed into a distant god that demanded reverence and sacred offerings in order to ensure its bounty. Not content with what nature produced in and of itself, people seized on agricultural technology to influence its output. Just as rewards and punishments began to be used to shape children into the beings their parents desired, nature became an entity to be cajoled, worshipped, and manipulated. Humans and their fledgling city-states split from the natural world, which was now seen as unpredictable and foreign.

The decisive break that separated the hunter-gatherers from sedentary farmers represents the collapse of the trust relationship between people and their world. People began to depend on the technology of agriculture to survive. Crop failure meant death. The outcome of our alienation from the world was chronic anxiety. This fear required a powerful management structure in order to minimize social chaos. Enter the sacred and political elites as the new class of social managers. The elites needed armies to maintain their hold on power and to extend the range of their influence.

The decisive break that separated the hunter-gatherers from sedentary farmers represents the collapse of the trust relationship between people and their world.

As the rift between nature and human beings widened, people also split with one another as classes formed. Rulers separated themselves from the ruled. Priests, with their sacred authority, were set apart from the mass of believers who were expected to show deference and obeisance. Where they once believed in themselves and in life, people of all classes and ranks suffered from their collective disempowerment, for even rulers must constantly look over their royal shoulders for those who would use force and violence to wrest away their treasured status.

The social revolution set off by organized agriculture, city building, and, eventually, empire creation demanded a very different kind of personality than that of the hunter-gatherer in order to fill its need for laborers, fighters, artisans, scientists, and homemakers. The essential psychological requirement was submission. Tribal groupings that were classless and landless, whose individuals were autonomous, were simply not the right human material for civilization. What civilization needed more than anything else was a populace that would be obedient, fearful, and reverent of the small class of aggressive power elites. Therefore, models of child-rearing developed that could assure the creation of social classes who would want and need to comply with authoritarian structures.

Civilization was not, of course, something that a group of cunning social scientists concocted in the back room of their tent. It was a natural outgrowth of the organization of food production, which was already occurring toward the end of the Paleolithic era. As diets changed from that which was hunted and gathered to that which was cultivated on farms, the roles of men and women changed. Instead of hunters, men became laborers; instead of gatherers who bore children, women became, first and foremost, mothers who augmented the labor supply. Family structure was inexorably altered to serve the needs of production and maintain the power and stability of the ruling elites.

It was necessary for people to be discontent with who they were so they could strive for what they could be. Human beings had to migrate from a place of sufficiency to one of deficiency. Without this pivotal change, the world of mass production and endless labor could never have gotten started.

The development of new social institutions was a process that worked with modifications in family structures. They are two sides of the same coin. One could not exist without the other. Civilization could not have existed were it not for a family structure that produced discontent and the urge to heal this discontent through an array of responses, including egoistic achievement, and for the masses of people to identify as members of the culture of achievement, even if they were not in a position to create such public achievement themselves. In visual terms, the background of civilization is self-discontent; the foreground is the glitter of cities, the might of armies, and the power of science and technology.

Civilization requires order, discipline, and obedience. Pre-modern societies were mostly matriarchal, with the emphasis on connection with broad and diverse networks of association. With the advent of civilization, matriarchies were supplanted by patriarchies, emphasizing power and control. Authority concentrated, on a family level, in the father, and on a societal level, in a patriarchal ruler. Children were punished, often severely, for disobeying their parents, as were citizens who defied their leaders.

In order to sustain the evolving system of agriculture (and later industry), men whose forefathers worked perhaps four hours a day now toiled in the fields (and later in factories) from dawn to dusk. To reduce costs, many people were enslaved as the property of powerful rulers and landowners. An ever-growing and compliant work force became essential.

The hunter-gatherers had small nuclear families. Births were spaced about four years apart, aided in large part by the natural contraception provided by prolonged nursing of toddlers. But as organized agriculture and industry demanded more and more workers, birth spacing was reduced to as little as one and usually no more than two years. Families had children for the sake of providing cheap labor, conceiving their offspring out of need rather than love.

Mothers who previously were able to lavish individual attention on each of their children found themselves torn by the day-and-night demands of a large family and additional responsibilities in the fields. The sustained and relaxed bonding once supported by other villagers disappeared. Those villagers, in fact, were overwhelmed by their own burdens of multiple children and workload. Children, exposed almost exclusively to their mothers, received far less notice from others as well as from their own mother. Sibling rivalry began to rear its ugly head as attention-starved children experienced the despair of new babies being introduced into their already crowded households. Compared with the emotional harmony of the hunter-gatherer household, where children tended to be far more placid, where temper tantrums were all but unknown, and where insecurity was essentially nonexistent, the civilized family became fraught with conflict, insecurity, emotional domination, clinginess, and imposed hierarchies.

Children became workers in training, needing discipline. They had to abandon their own natures and assume the responsibility of providing basic, unquestioning labor for their fathers and their rulers.

When they grew older, they could then be used as obedient soldiers to advance the power of the elites.

The culture of patriarchy thus was firmly established. Nature, rulers, and gods—all of them demanding and unreliable—needed to be amply placated. The anxiety that beclouded households could be held in check only by the unquestioned authority vested in the father, replicated in time by the patriarchal structure of religion. The engine of civilization therefore became one of productivity. As populations continued to grow, new lands needed to be opened up to cultivation and new technologies employed to take advantage of limited resources, such as water for crops and domesticated animals to share labor and provide an additional food source. In this competitive environment, war and conquest became the policy of the strong against the vulnerable.

These changes in family structure, child-rearing, and social organization formed the crucible in which an entirely new kind of human being was burnished. The eminent psychologist Erik Erikson presents one way of understanding the very different emotional makeup of the modern individual: Children are born bound to their mothers in a blissful and almost mystical relationship of adoration. When these relations are severed relatively early in life, narcissistic injury occurs, and people later seek to recreate the lost relationship, through worship of religion or the cult of a leader. The adult needs others to fulfill his narcissistic needs: "I, myself, am nothing (inadequate), but I can become something by securing status or by being close to others who have status. We compensate for the love we failed to get (or which was cut off early) by obtaining love or its substitute, through visible achievement." Berman notes, "It's all hype, of course; prestige in either direction, up or down the vertical ladder, will not heal the narcissistic wound suffered in childhood, and that is why there is no end in chasing it."

There is some benefit to narcissism: These personalities over the centuries have produced great art, technology, and a large body of knowledge in their attempts to compensate for the love they failed to receive (or which was truncated early). But the suffering on an individual emotional level is correspondingly great. The eminent historian Philip Slater notes, "This degree of narcissism means that life is never savored, that the joys of the many are sacrificed to the achievement of the few." The majority of people in our culture are embittered by their inability to achieve heroic status. And even heroes don't get to enjoy it very much because they have channelled sensual pleasure and experiential immediacy into "transcendent" realms, such as mastery and glory. Eliminating narcissism altogether may not be our desired goal, considering the gains it has produced for us, but seeking to return the narcissistic pendulum from the extremes reached by ancient Greece, Rome, or modern-day America is probably a worthy objective.

The overarching problem with the emotional life of civilization is that one can never get enough of its "vertical" energy. There is no end to the pressure to achieve, to compete, to wage war (an important source of excitement and a distinguishing characteristic of civilization from its outset). The magnificent achievements of civilization are in large part the outcome of behaviors and modes of living designed to mask fear and insecurity. Those in the aggressive subgroups mask their fear and inadequacy and become rulers; those who acquiesce in the political process mask their fear and inadequacy by becoming the ruled.

Our purpose here is not to condemn modern civilization. One would need to be blind not to acknowledge its extraordinary accomplishments. But these accomplishments have come at a high price. War, starvation, destruction of the natural world, mass species extinctions, pervasive fear and insecurity, and many other hardships stand in the shadow of its many achievements.

We have, for better or worse, moved a very long distance from the world of the hunter-gatherers, and there is no turning back. It is not the purpose of this book to argue for a nostalgic return to some lost time prior to the inception of civilization. Instead, the point is to remember that it is possible to be a human being and to live without overt insecurity and fear. (People lived that way for well over 100,000 years.) An important step towards regaining stability is to examine how the evolution of our culture has brought about a way of life that is, at heart, unstable, threatening, and ultimately unfulfilling.

One of the key questions we need to address is: Can we continue to evolve as a civilization beyond our culture of inadequacy, insecurity, and fear? Could it be that the many wonderful accomplishments of this world require a compulsive need to prove self-worth? Can we continue to achieve without the psychological motivation to compensate for the belief in our own worthlessness?

We are a product of our culture, but the soul of our hunting-gathering ancestors—the essence that enabled them to live in trust with life—still lives within us. Our task is to discover who we were prior to our invalidation—to find the way back to our authentic selves. We will never live the life of the hunter-gatherer (and I'm not so sure we would want to), but we can regain their heart. After all, their blood continues to run through our veins. The core of our being is no different from theirs. We are connected, directly, through the humanity we share.

I am asking you to inquire deeply into the truth of our being. If we can understand the roots of our self-negation, we can obtain a new vision of what we can be and what our civilization can create. Together we can reverse the damages of invalidation to ourselves and our social institutions.

Like the famous Robert Frost poem, we have come to a place in the forest where a road less taken becomes visible. We can continue moving along the path of fear and insecurity, which is the easy choice, or we can pause for a moment and consider the alternative. We can look beyond invalidation towards our true identities. We can take a fledgling step into the unknown world of our own authenticity.

3 - The Child as Savage

Beyond living and dreaming
Is what matters most
Coming awake."
~ Antonio Machado

Are we born fundamentally perfect, or are we born wild and imperfect, requiring the graces of civilization to become good, productive human beings?

One advocate of the theory of primal inadequacy is Aristotle. In his treatise <u>Politics</u>, the Greek philosopher argues that we are born as savages. People without laws and permanent settlement need to be subjugated and ruled over, he claims; they are like children who are not habituated to civilized society. Our goodness, if it is to manifest in our lives, is solely a consequence of our exposure to the fruits of moral and ethical culture. We are, in other words, born insufficient. Most of us have accepted this belief without exploring our own childhoods, our relations with our children, or our view of humanity.

If we believe that all children are savages, then their transformation into civilized, moral beings should simply be a matter of teaching them the ways of civilization. Do our observations of everyday life and our knowledge of history support this statement?

When the "civilized" nation of Spain landed on an unknown island in the eastern Caribbean in 1492, Columbus noted the remarkable grace, positive spirit, and extraordinary kindness of the "savages" he encountered. He also noted that they would make excellent slaves.

When the Pilgrims were starving during their first, long New England fall and winter, not only did the "savage" Wampanoag Indians feed the "civilized" European newcomers, but they taught them how to plant and grow maize and beans, enabling them to survive future winters. When the "civilized" Portuguese first entered sub-Saharan Africa and encountered the "savages" who lived there, it took them less than 10 years to organize the first slave trade by paying off tribal leaders.

Earlier we examined the lives of hunter-gatherer children. Contemporary anthropologists consistently describe their placid but alert natures, their deep connections to their communities and the natural world, the absence of sibling rivalry and temper tantrums, and their easy smiles. These children possessed a sense of stability and balance that has attracted note from observers from the 17th century to the present.

When Europeans first landed in North America and Africa, they were greeted with kindness, curiosity, and care. They responded with ruthless violence, including genocidal massacres, cultural intolerance, and total subjugation of the native peoples who had lived on those lands for countless generations. Invariably, they used religion and God to justify their murderous intents and actions.

Who, exactly, is the savage?

Certainly these painful interactions occurred between two very different peoples. The Native Americans and Africans were relatively content. The Europeans, in dramatic contrast, were not. Their discontent was rooted in their sense of inadequacy, a quality the natives did not share. The Europeans sought to fill their empty feelings of "lack" with power and possessions. But their insufficiency was a bottomless abyss. It could never be filled. And the very actions through which they sought to fill the void inadvertently sustained its gaping emptiness. This is why the Europeans related via force, while the natives related through curiosity and care. The Europeans were already wounded by their culture. They were a restless people, always on the lookout to augment their riches and control. Their response to the gentle, satisfied souls they encountered in their explorations was to kill or enslave them. The taste of power created a rapaciousness for more power and possessions, a quality of imperial civilization from the dawn of history to the present.

> *The Native Americans and Africans were relatively content. The Europeans, in dramatic contrast, were not. Their discontent was rooted in their sense of inadequacy, a quality the natives did not share. The Europeans sought to fill their empty feelings of "lack" with power and possessions. But their insufficiency was a bottomless abyss. It could never be filled.*

Invalidation is born of a significant imbalance in power, and the consequence of that imbalance is violence. Secure people are not motivated to apply force against others as a way of expressing their inadequacy. The European settlers' attitude and actions toward indigenous populations were paralleled in the relationships between parents and children in their "civilized" society. When adults see their children as "savages," they project their own experience of self-contempt onto their children. In this way, the wound of invalidation is passed down through the generations.

Aristotle correctly points out that children act in a way that could be described as "deficient." But he fails to understand the source of the deficiency. The "savage" children he observed had already experienced their infantile trauma, their emotional separation from their mothers, and pressures to change; thus they were already insecure in their standing with their parents and had begun to exhibit behaviors to compensate for their internal feelings of low self-worth. These characteristics are part of the price of civilization.

Because this phenomenon is both unintended and little understood, it is not surprising that we have adopted a belief system that seeks to explain what we think we are observing. By accepting the belief that children are savages, we justify the role of civilization to transform their "savageness" into more manageable personality traits. We do this through coercion, hard and soft. We remake people into the images projected onto them by civilization.

The collapse of our original sense of self occurs at a time before communication can occur between child and parent; the original person is already covered over by the Fear-Self before the child is able to protest. Children develop a sense of their inadequacy well before they can ever express their dissatisfaction in words. The child's "savage" behavior is simply his expression of his despair. Some children will really persist in their "savagery," acting out with "unacceptable" behaviors. But even the most docile child will express her anger and frustration in some form. The family uses the power of repression to control this anger and frustration, just as the larger society later uses its authority to manage her as an adult.

It's time that we moved on to a more loving and accurate understanding of who our children are and who we are in relation to them. Children are not savages. They are human beings who already have been cut off from their Life Force. A child's anger and frustration come from the struggle to learn new abilities in order to establish an identity designed to mollify the emotional pain she has experienced.

Keep in mind that not all children display in this way. Resiliency varies greatly from child to child, as does the fear of expressing one's true feelings to parents who might be perceived as threatening or whose connection to the child is so tenuous that he fears loss of love if he is honest. Most of us become experts in the fine art of repression early in life. The problem of repression becomes much more serious when we begin to regard it as normal and rational—which is, of course, what most of us do.

Savagery, therefore, is in the eye of the beholder. The term "savage" is useful mainly to those who would like to manage another person or group through the use of the pejorative.

4 - The Wound and the Lie

Beneath our public and apparent selves thrives a lie. This lie is the mark of our invalidation; it is the belief that our authentic being is the invalidated, hurting self. Belief in this lie keeps us locked into self-contempt, self-improvement, therapy, and addiction to achievement. As long as we buy into this lie, we can never live as our authentic selves.

In ancient times, people would look around and perceive the world as flat. This was, and continues to be, an obvious "reality." Try it out for yourself. Go outside and look around. Decide for yourself whether the world does indeed appear to be flat. For tens of thousands of years, this belief persisted. The most seasoned sailor was filled with the palpable fear that if he sailed far enough, he would eventually fall off the world's edge. Yet when the boldest explorers finally did set out across the oceans, it became clear that our planet is not at all flat. Contrary to everything our senses and mind tell us, the world is, in fact, a sphere.

Our perception of the visible world also led to the longstanding belief that the sun, stars, and, indeed, the entire universe must revolve around our vast, magisterial Earth. Questioning this empirical observation was regarded as an act of madness—at least until Copernicus proved that our planet, in fact, revolves around the sun. We now know that not only does the tiny fragment of rock and water that we call Earth revolve around our sun, but that our whole solar system revolves around the Milky Way—which itself revolves around a larger immensity consisting of many thousands of galaxies. Instead of commanding the center of the universe, our little Earth is at the periphery of a periphery.

The truth about the shape of our world and our place in the cosmos contradicts everything that we perceive. We live in a physical universe that is very different from the way it appears to us.

The same principle applies to how we perceive ourselves. Who we believe ourselves to be is not who we are.

We perceive ourselves not as the perfect and complete beings that emerged from our mothers; instead, our self-identities are inevitably shaped by invalidation. The inadequate and incomplete person we take ourselves to be (on a largely subconscious and core identity level) is a fiction, a construct that is born of pre-verbal emotional trauma. It is the stigma of modern civilization that each of us carries in the core of our being. The invalidation we experience even as infants cuts us to the quick; the pain that results is our Wound.

The inadequate and incomplete person we take ourselves to be is a fiction. It is the stigma of modern civilization that each of us carries in the core of our being. The invalidation we experience even as infants cuts us to the quick; the pain that results is our Wound.

The assault of invalidation results in the development of a battered self, which assumes blame for its own negation. We hold ourselves responsible for our Wound. Then we begin the second stage of our lives, in which we respond to the knot of self-contempt that has taken root in our souls. Our response is the creation of the Fear-Selves, our adaptive, secondary personalities that refute or counter the veracity of the Wound.

Our pain is revived each time we personally identify with the Wound—each time we view and experience the world through the lens of worthlessness. We respond to people and events from a place of unchallenged inadequacy. As with any pain, we seek healing with all our strength. At first, most of us do so by trying to heal the rift between our parents and ourselves. We want to be cared for, so we act in ways that we hope will garner their love. As we get older, our stigmatized self can spend a lifetime seeking to prove its value and worthiness of love.

Like all great challenges worth their salt, understanding, approaching, and addressing the Wound is the ultimate heroic journey. This journey asks us to question everything that we have assumed to be true of ourselves. It requires us to shed everything that is designed to hide our invalidation. If the healing is to last, it must bring the light of understanding and compassion to what was covered over by darkness. If you are willing to take on this challenge, we can begin by learning more about the nature of the Wound.

The Wound Explained

I use the term "Wound" to refer to the consequences of invalidation each of us experienced as we were growing up. The Wound spawns our belief that we and our world are inadequate, insufficient, worthless. This belief—which I call the Lie—is very much like an iceberg, with most of its mass invisible, below the level of conscious recognition. The vigor with which we seek to prove our value to ourselves, our friends, our family, or anyone else is equal to the extent to which the mass of our Wound is hidden. It is the engine that produces the fuel of our insecurity and endless and hopeless seeking.

How does the belief in our own inadequacy come about?

The Wound is a product of invalidation and negation of the self. As we discussed earlier, each of us is invalidated by our family, society, and culture. No one is spared. However, the amount and impact of the invalidation experienced by individuals varies. Also, the capacity of resilience among individuals varies. Therefore, every individual's response to invalidation is unique.

All families invalidate their children. Every day that a mother separates her child from herself and the child experiences pain on account of that separation, invalidation occurs. Such separations are bound to happen multiple times each day; each time, the child receives the message that there is something wrong with him. On the level of preverbal feeling, the child asks, "what have I done to create this pain?"

Most behaviors that parents interpret as "bad" are the child's attempt to express his pain. He often does so simply by drawing attention to the pain of his negation. He will also seek to restore the loving relationship he needs and deserves by trying to please the all-powerful parent. Attention-getting actions and manipulative compliance are a child's response to invalidation. Inevitably, these methods arouse countless more invalidating events as parents and other authority figures react negatively to the child. In this way, the Wound deepens over time, and the methods used to seek power and manipulate others become fixed as a person's lifelong model for dealing with the world.

From the time she was born, my daughter Julia had problems getting to sleep (she is now an adult and still has this problem). Her mother and I would put her in her crib, bribe her with apple juice, and hope for the best. In absolute silence we would go downstairs and wait, in almost comical fear, for the inevitable cries. We were never disappointed. Eventually, Julie would be hysterical, crying her head off, and we would rush upstairs to comfort her. When I described this problem to my parents, I clearly remember their reply, which also revealed important details of my own childhood.

First, they laughed at our ineptitude as parents and then scolded us for spoiling Julia. They said we needed to simply put her down without any comforts, close the door and ignore her cries. The comforts, like apple juice, were just a crutch. We had to go cold turkey and endure the agony of sitting through what seemed like hours of raging despair upstairs.

My parents also told us of my own unceasing "crying and complaining," which, as good parents, they were compelled to ignore.

Julie cried and cried, while we sat in horror in our living room, our stomachs rolling over in uncertainty about what we were doing.

My parents were right. The length of time she cried did decline as the nights passed; eventually, her periods of tearfulness were quite short and bearable. The lesson had been learned: Even in our most innocent despair, those whose love is most essential and whose bodies are so nearby are not necessarily available to us. Their love and attention are conditional and arbitrary. Their power is, at times, unapproachable. Julia's Wound was established and, over time, descended below the level of consciousness. An angry and resentful Fear-Self was born in its wake.

A child's early separation experiences can be potent, particularly when they occur in the frightening darkness of evening when the child is placed in her own crib apart and alone from her parents. These separations are, at first, terrifying for children. But despite the obvious trauma, separation is normalized within most families as not only appropriate but essential for the proper maturation of the child.

The younger the child, the more vulnerable she is to experiences that have the capacity to mold her personality for a lifetime. Many children in our society are removed from the care and touch of their mothers within minutes of birth. When new parents return home from the hospital with their newborn, the child may be placed that very first evening into the dark, unknown confines of a separate bedroom in a crib with tall, prison-like slats that separate him from the warmth and unconditional love he needs.

The parents hear the cries of their child, but believe that "toughing it out" is a necessary step towards the child's ultimate well-being. They believe they are doing the right thing; after all, they learned about correct parenting from their parents, their friends, or the proliferation of parenting books available today. The child's cries may be desperate, but parents know they will eventually stop and believe their child will eventually be the better for it. The irony is that the quiet child only appears to be strong; compliance is the quiet side of fear. Instead, the fear-scarred child grows up to be insecure, doubting, and uneasy.

The quiet child only appears to be strong; compliance is the quiet side of fear. Instead, the fear-scarred child grows up to be insecure, doubting, and uneasy.

The impact of the separation trauma is immense; it is the origin of the Wound, which becomes a hole inside the person. The hole is experienced as a sensation of "lack." This inner emptiness becomes a large part of our self-identity. What we are and what we have is never enough. Psychologically, we become "feelings" junkies: We are constantly calling out to the world, "Fill me—I need another hit!" People try to fill the void with accomplishments, acquisitions, hopes, and dreams. But our holes are bottomless. No amount of material goods or achievements can ever remove the painful identification with lack that will always return in moments of doubt, boredom, crisis, or fear.

Over time, children adapt to separation. Their crying becomes less vigorous, their protests less hysterical. Parents know that a boundary has been crossed. The child has accommodated herself to her own negation. The mother, thought to be the ever-available source of unconditional love, is now understood also as a source of unease and love that must be earned. We learn that our attempts to regain power will result in punishment and the withdrawal of love.

Over time, children adapt to separation. The child has accommodated herself to her own negation. The mother, thought to be the ever-available source of unconditional love, is now understood also as a source of unease and love that must be earned. We learn that our attempts to regain power will result in punishment and the withdrawal of love.

Mother and child now live on different sides of a chasm. Love between them now is likely to manifest as neediness, with its ancillary qualities of anxiety and fear. There is, always, the threat that love can and will be withheld, unless the child is compliant and loving without any conditions on her part. This way of relating imposes its signature on all of the child's intimate relationships as she grows and begins to live more independently of her parents. She will look to others as sources of both validation and invalidation. As she projects her need to be cared for, her capacity to be content and balanced within herself is severely reduced.

The Realization of our Innate Powerlessness

Perhaps more than anything else, the Wound is founded on an assault upon our power and independent integrity. It is the inevitable consequence of physical separation and negation from our parents, but as time passes, our schools and society exacerbate it with the imposition of demands for obedience. From the very outset of our lives, we learn that we must suppress our authentic power and surrender to the far greater and more dangerous power of others.

Yet our power cannot be completely suppressed. Young children try to express their power in passive-aggressive ways through crying, recalcitrance, and, when those tactics don't work, goal-directed compliance.

When separation is interpreted as evidence of our unworthiness to deserve love, we begin to deny our innate goodness. We see that we cannot, through the simple act of being, cultivate the love and acceptance we crave. This is our initial and decisive projection that we are powerless and unworthy. From this point forward, we learn that we must <u>earn</u> love.

Children today are expected to act as if they are without power. Power suppressed will always emerge in a form that is ugly and distorted—tantrums, whining, wheedling. But these expressions of power by children are, in nearly all cases, considered undesirable behavior requiring swift and often severe punishment—which redoubles their invalidation. The child must thoroughly divest himself of his innate sense of self as powerful if he is to be loved and accepted. The cost of love is the death of the self.

While children are discovering the price of their parents' love, they are simultaneously learning that they are expected to love and respect their invalidators. They must love those who are negating them; without compliance, their parents' love will be withdrawn. We learn that to deserve love, we must meet the expectations of others. Just as our invalidation comes from external sources, our validation is forever sought externally—that is, we only find our worth through the strokes of others. In the process, we lose our center and live our lives out of balance.

Children are expected to love and respect their invalidators. They must love those who are negating them; without compliance, their parents' love will be withdrawn. We learn that to deserve love, we must meet the expectations of others.

A child who is vulnerable and anxious has replaced the natural child. Thanks to the Wound, he already understands that in comparison with his parents, he is inadequate and insufficient; now he must consider that he perhaps does not demonstrate enough love for his invalidators. Our inborn integrity is forever compromised by our need to achieve goals through compliance and using phony affection and flattery to manipulate others.

The invalidating processes observed in families are mirrored in our social institutions. Just as love is the reward for obedience in the "responsible" family, success is the reward for obedience in the educational and work worlds. Winning is a function of compliance. Dissent is stifled. The world of winners and losers is created and is, largely, a measure of social compliance.

Creative children are often punished or corrected for their unwillingness to submit to authority; they either learn to suppress their authentic selves or wind up on the fringes of life. Success at school is predicated on testing in which merit equates to correct recapitulation of lessons. Educators enjoy speaking about the "uniqueness" of every individual, but, in fact, regimentation is the order of the day. Deviance from the standard curriculum results in failure. This enforced regimentation is a form of negation. And so it goes through life: We play our assigned roles, and in the process lose touch with who we are.

When we lose our original selves, we seek to regain our power in convoluted ways designed to draw attention to ourselves. The Wound assigns that role to our Fear-Selves. This is one of the primary ways in which we seek solace once our original power has been negated. It recreates, in our adult lives, our primal relationship with our parents. But the power exerted by our Fear-selves is fear-based and false. That is the cost of losing our original integrity.

Just as the young child draws attention to herself in an attempt to regain parental love, we replicate that same dynamic in our adult lives. Thus the Body Person asserts her power through the beauty of her physical appearance; the Spiritualist seeks power through personal enlightenment; the Expert feels powerful when lording his expertise over others; the Achiever shows the world his power through his accomplishments; and the Pleaser displays her power by winning the acceptance of others. Through religion we seek to recreate the breached relationship with our parents in our relationship with God. In each of these examples, the powerless seek power through external entities. Because our original selves can never be enough (the Wound), we must find "opportunities" for self-completion outside of ourselves. It is a journey without end or enduring success.

Adult life in modern society offers myriad opportunities for invalidation to be continually foisted upon us. In the workplace, production and productivity demand strict organization, controlled labor, efficiency, and compliance. The natural, unfettered person cannot easily fit into this regulated world. To be a person of standing, the authentic self must be subsumed by an invalidated self. We are awarded for our docility, our domestication through vapid "success."

Settled into our belief in our own inadequacy and worthlessness, we become models of social duty. Our spirit is already broken and we take on the mantle of modern humanity: to cooperate in the process of our own negation, to be blind to hypocrisy, and to play the game of being mature and false with our peers. We also nurture the engine of invalidation by replicating our own negation experiences with our own children.

We thank our oppressors and make obeisance visible to those who have power over us. We are thoroughly debased. In fact, we are so debased that we must push the nature of our Fear-selves below the level of critical awareness and come to believe that our docility and willingness to please are essential human attributes. We become compliant players of the game. We cut the cord that connects us to our souls. The "savage" child has indeed been tamed.

All of us are born and raised within a class and a race. These are potent forces for both invalidation and false validation. A straight man may seek to elevate himself when he calls a gay lifestyle "abnormal" and justifies his hate with a single line taken from the Bible. A black person may use his race's "innate soulfulness" to inflate himself over people of other races. The well-off may use the poverty of others as a sure sign that something is wrong with them as individuals, as families, and as a community. Ironically, for some who grow up rich, shame in wealth unearned can also become a source of invalidation, particularly in societies such as the United States, which pretend not to have rigid class distinctions. Propelled by our fear of the ever-present threat of re-experiencing our Wound, we will use anything to compare ourselves favorably with others.

Every time we compromise our innate, heart-centered values for the sake of social standing, we pay with the loss of our souls. The doctor whose time is more important than the electrician's, the religious man who belittles the non-religious for their godlessness, the church member who takes pride in her high standing compared with other congregation members, the professor who arrogantly uses his formal learning to demean those less educated—all these people are using their positions in society as a filter to protect themselves from their underlying Wounds.

Wealth, beauty, and authority are alluring, but when we are attracted to any of these qualities out of fear, compulsion, or need, we are directly participating in our own self-negation.

Wealth, beauty, and authority are alluring, but when we are attracted to any of these qualities out of fear, compulsion, or need, we are directly participating in our own self-negation. For most of his life, my grandfather wanted to be an official at his synagogue. He craved the respect of the congregation. His failure to achieve this status was always a source of sadness for him. Looking back, I suspect that his motivations were mixed. He did have an authentic connection with Jewish practice that stimulated his desire to participate actively in the Temple. But he was also prompted by the need for external acknowledgment in an arena that meant a lot to him. Anything we "show" to the world to demonstrate our value or worth, whether it is the latest luxury car or a cool tattoo, becomes our badge of the negated self.

The Wound covers over our authentic selves with a layer of personality that is very nearly opaque. On account of the Wound, we only very infrequently experience our Life Force, the true self that underlies the Wound. But at those precious moments when we are disarmed by a beautiful moment in nature, when we feel the oneness of love-making, when we bask in the innocent smile of a child, our Life Force shines through.

Our Life Force does not hearken back to some prior time in our lives; it is our authentic self as it is now. So when we connect with our Life Force, we are living as our authentic selves, without ulterior intent or purpose. This is the polar opposite of our typical intents and purposes, when we seek to show, yet again, our worth and value. The mind ceaselessly posits something we need to be, because we can never be comfortable as we are.

One way the Wound presents itself over and over again is in our projections of a catastrophic future unless we "do" something to prevent it. This is how the threat of coming face to face with our own inadequacy and worthlessness becomes our primary motivator. The subtle, anxious energy that results is essential to nurture each and every one of our Fear-Selves. Until we address this vital issue, we can never have sustainable contentment in our lives.

This dark energy also blocks us from our inherent capacity to trust life. Instead, life becomes something we need to fear and overcome. Living life without feeling the need to change anything is alien to our fear-based nature. We can spend a lifetime telling ourselves how wonderful we are, but the Wound will always win out. Therapy, meditation, the positive mantra are all empty strategies because they fail to dissolve the unquestioned, underlying beliefs about ourselves which are born from the Wound. In fact, our flailing attempts at self-improvement are a direct expression of the belief in our own inadequacy.

We can spend a lifetime thinking about the past, but such thinking does not offer a pathway to liberation. Instead, it devolves into a fascination with the Fear-Self, which thrives on therapy and self-examination. These are forms of self-inflation.

The Wound is always alive in us. It becomes our puppet master, and the Fear-Selves are the puppets it directs. We can never become the actual puppet master. That position is occupied by the Wound, whose ongoing mastery is never seriously challenged. This is the life of the slave.

Long ago, when we established our primary identities as inadequate, we relinquished ownership of our own lives. And, for most of us, that is the end of the story—the details of our day-to-day existence are mediated by the Fear-Selves, and only rarely are we touched by our authentic selves.

Ultimately, down very deep, the Wound is naked self-contempt. This is the agony of invalidation unchallenged. It is the limitless source of our resistance to life. It is the hard side of the superego, which can never accept our authentic selves. It is the voice of doubt and distrust. It is the core of our seriousness, even that seriousness which drives our addiction to happiness and fun. But it is not our enemy. Ultimately, as we will see, it needs to become our closest and most intimate friend.

When the mind hears about the Wound, it will do exactly what the mind will always do: ask, "What should I do about it?" The answer, short and long, is—nothing. The seeing is the understanding, and the understanding is the seeing. We need to see and experience the Wound exactly as it is. We have spent most of our lives hiding from it. Now the time has come to bring the light of day to this Wound that has been buried within us since our very early childhood.

5 - The Development of the Fear-Self

A cage went in search of a bird.
~ Franz Kafka

As young children, our individual personality development begins with the Wound. We have absorbed the most potent belief we will ever experience: the belief in our own inadequacy. This belief that we are fundamentally flawed, which arises from the immense pain of separation and invalidation, leads us to a place of powerlessness; a powerlessness that is hungry for the power it lacks. The pain is too deep, the impotence too intense, to live with. As we grow towards adulthood, we constantly seek to refute the Wound and ease our pain by securing power. We do this by covering over the Wound with a public persona called the Fear-Self.

The Fear-Self and Power

The child experiences power as force—being forced to be and do what others wish. She also discovers early on her own capacity to exert influence through force. At first, her repertory is very limited— crying, screaming, tantrums, recalcitrance, and intentional misbehavior. Soon she learns the force of pleasing parents through accomplishments approved by them. Expressing power through forceful tactics becomes the *de facto* approach to conflict resolution for most of us. The tactics we choose to use become core elements of each of our Fear-Selves.

Some Fear-Selves are designed to please—at first the child's parents, and later others outside the family. These are compliant Fear-Selves. Recall that children often believe that they have created the breach between themselves and their parents. Compliant Fear-Selves evolve as children seek to heal the failure of love for which they have taken responsibility. Thus develops the compliant child—the good little boy or girl.

The incipient compliant Fear-Self needs always to be checking how well he is doing. Displeasure from a parent can potentially signal failure. The child launches into what will become a lifetime of insecurity. Any absence of approval from a parent or other authorities revives the pain and suffering of the Wound. Fear of reopening the loveless breach between parent and child haunts the child.

From the child's perspective, she now shoulders responsibility for the psychological and emotional well-being of her parents. The compliant Fear-Self is endlessly saying, "Look at me; look at how good I am; aren't you happy with me? Don't I make you happy? Won't you love me now and forever?" Notice how the child's concern migrates from her own well-being to that of her parents. From this point forward, the Fear-Self relies on external sources of demonstrable love.

Fear-based compliant types will transfer their neediness for reassurance from their parents to any authority figure. Their happiness and fulfillment depend on their ability to figure out how people and situations will allow them to achieve their goals by pleasing others. They are always on guard, evaluating situations, monitoring their level of success or failure.

Fear of failure is a guaranteed source of emotional pain and turmoil. For all Fear-Selves, failure results in fresh contact with the Wound: The mask of the Fear-Self drops to reveal the Wound's unspeakable misery. The Fear-Self establishes itself as a person's most enduring and consistent identity because of the protection it promises. For the compliant type, failure means that he must now redouble his efforts to please in order to mend whatever relationship he believes has been frayed on account of his inadequacy as a pleaser.

Ironically, all Fear-Selves designed to counter the Wound actually work to sustain its vitality in a person's life. The need to cover over the Wound with a Fear-Self actually validates the Wound's potency. In this way, we live, always, in intimate contact with the Wound.

Of course, compliance is not always self-motivated. Some compliant Fear-Selves, induced by fear, use fake deference and conformity to avoid punishment. Families who use frequent punishment to coerce "good" behavior will create a child who must not only suppress her authentic self, but must also suppress her anger. The child learns that faking obedience becomes his ticket to successfully avoiding violence. He also learns that he can get what he wants from others through the force of manipulation. This type of Fear-Self has a significant achievement and manipulation orientation. This is the perfect politician.

Families who use frequent punishment to coerce "good" behavior will create a child who must not only suppress her authentic self, but must also suppress her anger. The child learns that faking obedience becomes his ticket to successfully avoiding violence. He also learns that he can get what he wants from others through the force of manipulation.

Other Fear-Selves are rebellious. They counter the pain of the Wound by actively rejecting those who they believe rejected them—first parents, then other authority figures. The Loner, for example, tells the world, "I don't need you or your rules. I'm fine all by myself." The Tough Guy swaggers through life, bullying others to demonstrate his own power. The Expert lets others know in no uncertain terms that he doesn't need to consider anyone else's opinions or thoughts; he knows everything he needs to know already. Rebels, it seems, have given up on trying to repair their breach with their parents, and replicate that attitude in their relationships with others.

It is important to note that any of the Fear-Self types can be either compliant or rebellious. Even the Pleaser, which on the surface would seem clearly to be compliant in nature, can harbor a rebellious streak: "My guests are going to enjoy this party the way I want them to." The Achiever can rack up accomplishments in hopes of winning the approval of a loved one—or to flaunt them in the faces of those who doubted their abilities. Either way, the objective is to regain the power lost in early childhood.

The Fear-Self and Desire

To be human is to have desire. What brings us pleasure and happiness may vary, but we all experience the hunger of wishes unfulfilled. And our desire expands in proportion to the size of our Wound.

If we observe our desires carefully, we can see that all of them are ultimately about being taken care of. Some of us believe we'll find happiness by being cared for by another. For others, the satisfaction lies in being the caretaker: We take care of ourselves by connecting to others through the emotion of providing care.

A Fear-Self desire is one that is compulsive; it is one that we must indulge. To the extent that we believe ourselves to be insufficient and/or inadequate, our desires will inevitably organize around those things we feel that we lack most, or the ways in which we feel we most fall short. We believe we need more love, so we desire people and experiences that will provide us with that love. We believe we need more money, so we desire situations and relationships that will provide us with that financial power. We believe in enlightenment, so we desire esoteric knowledge to achieve transcendence of the real.

Liberation is the recognition that we are exactly as we should be. The only obstacle to our personal liberation is the belief that we are inadequate. As long as we believe that we are lacking, we will live in fear and desire. No external knowledge or possession can possibly ever save us from this dilemma. We need to discover the one who lives beneath the level of the Wound and the fear it arouses. We need to realize that we are not who we believe ourselves to be. It is the belief in the needy self that is both self-sustaining and self-defeating. It has no remedy outside of the understanding that it is not who we are.

When we identify ourselves with a belief—any belief—we live fragmented and confused lives. We struggle to think our way through each moment of the day. But life surges forward without any reference to our thoughts! Try to observe this in your own life. All of our desires for self- improvement are a consequence of our deep sense of personal inadequacy. They are our core fear. They are not who we are!

But as we persist with this false identification, we sustain our endless suffering. The Terrified One seeks out places, people, and things to flee—the desire is for safety. The Spiritualist yearns to escape both the world and himself through enlightenment—the desire is for peace. The Expert looks for opportunities to expound—the desire is for recognition. The Achiever asserts himself ever more aggressively—the desire is to prove his image of worth and value.

For the Fear-Self, desire unfulfilled is pain. The Fear-Self lives in a world of unrealized desire and is, therefore, always seeking more to meet this gnawing need. He is a restless being, always on the lookout, never comfortable with himself or his world. Contentment is not something we can achieve. It is what we are when the thought/desire/pursuit of it ceases. Then an entirely new sensation of self is allowed to arise.

The problem lies not in the expression of desire. It comes from predicating one's value and worth on the fulfillment of that desire. Can you see that in your own life? Liberation from desire is simply being able to acknowledge our value independent of the fulfillment of any desire.

By observing desire, we can see the Fear-Self in stark terms. It is often most clear when desire manifests in its negative form—fear. The Achiever fears failure more than anything else; the Pleaser fears rejection. The Body Person fears time; the Spiritualist fears not achieving enlightenment. If you are ever uncertain of what your Fear-Self is, take a sober look at your fears. The answer will be found there.

The Fear-Self and the Wound

The exact content of the Wound is vague. It is a generalized belief of unworthiness. How that unworthiness is interpreted by the evolving mind as it forms Fear-Selves depends largely on one's life circumstances. In this way, the Wound can spawn a variety of different Fear-Selves in the same person. If the young mind believes that the primary cause of its familial rejection is a function of appearance, it will develop a Fear-Self that emphasizes the physical. If it believes that its rejection was a function of its stupidity, it will develop a Fear-Self emphasizing expertise. If it believes that it was spurned due to its carelessness, it will become compulsive around the issue of order.

Often, the parental rebuff is traced to one's lack of success. In such cases, Fear-Selves evolve that emphasize our capacity to achieve.

Each Fear-Self carries an element of the Wound within it. The Wound and the Fear-Self are two sides of the same coin. When things are going well, the Fear-Self side of the coin shows. When things are going poorly, the Wound side of the coin appears. Because Fear-Selves are incomplete artifacts of circumstance, they are never free of their implicit insecurity. It often manifests as a faint feeling of unease in the pit of our stomachs.

We fail to understand ourselves when we believe that a Fear-Self is not only who we are, but is our only identity. When we believe this to be true, we also assume that we need our Fear-Selves to meet our most fundamental requirements. We take the Fear-Self to be natural and right, no matter how much anxiety and frustration it arouses in our daily lives.

Fear-Selves are deeply entrenched within nearly all of us. We hold onto our Fear-Selves like we would hold onto life rafts in a stormy sea. After all, we developed and adapted these selves as an essential shield from the pain and defeat of the Wound. The Fear-Self is defended by many years of testing in nothing less than the "real world." But there is one question we don't ask ourselves: Is it possible that the person I unquestioningly assume myself to be is not the real me?

The Fear-Self is a clever device whose primary purpose is to make us feel safe. The obvious irony in all of this is that it actually makes us feel unsafe. Life within the Fear-Self is persistently uncertain. We must constantly be on our guard for both failure and threat. The Fear-Self must labor tirelessly to sustain itself against the pressing weight of the Wound, as well as against obstacles that continuously arise in our everyday life. This means, in practical terms, that we must work ceaselessly to maintain the declining beauty of our body, to yet again prove our expertise, to impose our authority, to compete against others to maintain our standing, to find new ways to please, to work harder to reach enlightenment, or to find ever more excitement in our lives. Under the command of the Fear-Self, life can often feel like drudgery.

The Fear-Self is a clever device whose primary purpose is to make us feel safe. The obvious irony in all of this is that it actually makes us feel unsafe. Life within the Fear-Self is persistently uncertain. We must constantly be on our guard for both failure and threat.

Many of the accomplishments of our civilization are a direct result of the Fear-Self. We have already seen that the Wound is considerably more powerful in civilized society than in hunter-gatherer cultures. The fear-based drive to achieve which results from the Wound is one of the great engines of creation in our modern world, but it is not, by a long shot, the only mechanism for achievement. As we will discuss later, there are other avenues to invention and accomplishment. Unless our achievements are expressions of our authentic selves, they are likely to be linked with expediency and compulsion. They will be designed to impress rather than inform; they will result from external pressures; and they will be predicated, ultimately, on the fear of not achieving them and the consequences of that failure. In fact, because achievement based in the Fear-Self will inevitably possess a quality of self-centeredness, as opposed to life-centeredness, we can assume that the most destructive "achievements" of civilization—those achievements that have impoverished millions, destroyed natural habitats, polluted the air and water, and greatly enhanced the capacity to wage massive wars—are precisely those achievements linked to the Fear-Self.

The Fear-Self as an Addiction

We are tied to our Fear-Selves because they promise us a sense of completion. The addict fears one thing more than anything else: that he won't be able to get his next hit. In the same way, the Fear-Self is terrified of contact with the pain of the Wound. It will constantly seek new opportunities to hide the Wound with visible demonstrations of its adequacy and worth.

As with the addict, the Fear-Self's measure of success is always external. As long as we are under its thrall, we don't know how to be happy or content outside of it. The body image Fear-Self tells us that unless we are looking great and our body has just the right proportions, we will be miserable. Until the Spiritualist is enlightened, he can never be content. Without positive acknowledgement, the Pleaser must always be searching for new strokes.

At face, the Fear-Self seems right. That's because underneath the voice of the Fear-Self is the Wound, which we have sought to escape since we were young children. To the Body Person, decline of the body means the re-emergence of self-disgust and self-contempt. If the Pleaser fails to keep everyone happy and approving of her, she sees herself as an outcast. These messages emanate from the Wound that underlies the Fear-Self. We are thus attached to our Fear-Selves like an addict is attached to her addiction. The promise of happiness and safety comes with every Fear-Self, and that is the one belief in which we desperately place our faith. We sustain the Fear-Self as long as we continue to believe its promise.

The addiction is the interplay of two beliefs. Belief one: I am inadequate (the invalidation belief). Belief two: I must prove my adequacy (the false healing belief). Both are untrue, and as long as we live in the interplay of the untrue, we can never be authentic.

Any drive we possess that promises self-completion and is compulsive in nature is related to a Fear-Self. Contrary to all the Fear-Self's protestations, we are complete prior to the evolution of the Fear Self, but also prior to the formation of the Wound. Liberation from the Fear-Self calls on us to understand this dynamic clearly. We will live in persistent insecurity and fear until we see this process for what it is: a belief in a lie and our response to that belief. Until we release ourselves from this identity structure, we will live as invalidated beings ceaselessly searching for something, anything, that promises us escape from the "monster in the closet."

Ultimately, the Fear-Self is an image or pretense. It is the person we "need" to be. This image is what makes us feel "special," "worthy." We expend an incredible amount of energy pursuing this image, and in doing so, we fail to experience our authentic being. Indeed, we can't even imagine who we would be were we not a Fear-Self.

In broad terms, we can see the progression from Original Goodness to Invalidation to the compensating Fear-Selves in Figure 1. This illustration shows that Fear-Selves can be both "positive" and "negative".

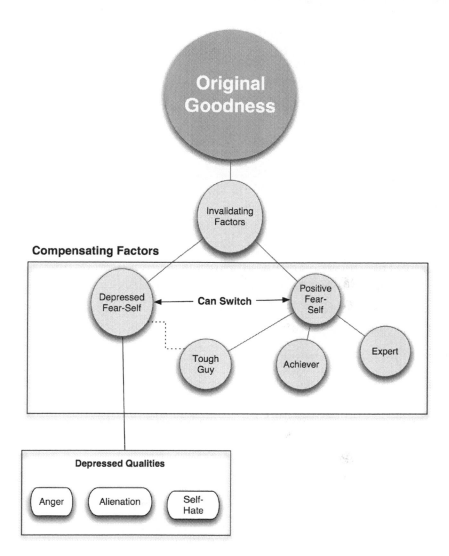

Figure 1: A Broad View of the Progression from Original Goodness to the Fear-Selves

This is not an error or fault. It is exactly the way life should play out given our origins and circumstances. Through the Wound of invalidation, we became cut off from who we are. Liberation is the pathway back.

The Fear-Self and Suffering

There are two types of suffering. Authentic suffering occurs when we lose something that we need or love. Examples include loss of a loved one, the loss of our physical well-being, loss of a job that supported our family, and loss of the earth's natural resources. The second form of suffering is fear-based, and involves contact with the Wound. It is the suffering that occurs when we feel our underlying sense of inadequacy, insufficiency, worthlessness, and incapacity to be loved. These are the sufferings of the Fear-Self.

Note that unlike Eastern philosophies such as Buddhism and Advaita, Liberation acknowledges the authenticity of suffering. Some belief systems posit that the world is ultimately an illusion. Understood this way, even grief over the loss of a child is considered unreal, a construct of the mind. Liberation declares that some misery is very real, and is part and parcel of the human condition; it is only the suffering of the Fear-Self that is illusory.

The Fear-Self as Our Body

The Fear-Self lives in our bodies as tension. The source of this tension is our identification with any Fear-Self as our true self. This belief is in constant conflict with our authentic self, which continues to live below the level of the Wound.

Often, this tension is so habitual to us that we are either unaware of it or think of it as normal.

But the constant background noise of tension is not normal. It contributes to our overall physical discomfort, undermines our ability to sleep, and makes us more prone to irritability and violence. As a very complex machine, the body will at times experience physical pain; that is normal. The discomfort one's body feels from the Fear-Self is limited to the tension that arises when we are not living from the core of our authentic being.

As the Fear-Self, we are in constant conflict with our authentic being. Our thoughts, feelings, and actions serve the Fear-Self's needs—the demands of an image—and in this way create suffering for ourselves and those around us. Physical maladies associated with this conflict include tension headaches; restlessness; shallow, upper-chest breathing; strain around the eyes and mouth; and stiffness in the neck and back. These pains represent the body's feedback mechanism, which dutifully informs us that we are not living in balance and harmony.

The more committed we are to a living as a Fear-Self, the more body tension we will experience. Often, others are more aware of our tension than we are ourselves, because we are closed-off and habituated to the effect. But while these discomforts are a source of pain, they can also be signs that help to draw us back into our authentic selves.

Summary

For most of us the Wound of our invalidation is never healed. Instead, it is accommodated. We spend our lives chasing after projected images of how we are supposed to be. We believe these identities will give us lasting comfort and strength. Belief and faith in these False-Selves is simply a continuation of our larger belief in our inadequate and insufficient natures. Once we believe in this central lie about ourselves, we become lost in the world of images and masks. Few can find their way out of this maze. The key to liberation is the willingness and capacity to see the false as false.

Many children lie to protect themselves from parental punishment and to please their parents. When the object of our lies is someone we care about, the energy we expend to maintain these falsehoods is exhausting, and our dignity is eroded by the choice to lie. When the pain of maintaining the lie becomes sufficiently great, we find the bravery to confess, and in that confession there is great beauty and relief. This is the light emanating from our Life Force. When we move from falsehood to truth, we and our world are uplifted. Breaking our ties with falseness is the forge of self-transformation. Try to remember a time when you ceased listening to the voice of cowardice and fear and "came clean" with some truth. Try to feel that same process and sensation in reference to your Fear-Selves. Seizing that opportunity is a key to our liberation.

6 - Invalidation in the Larger World

Many other sources of invalidation, extending far beyond our families of origin, help to form and nurture the Wound. School, work, religion, and social relations all require us to sacrifice our authentic voices for the sake of achieving some external end. Invalidation becomes real to us when we, consciously or unconsciously, believe and absorb the messages of the invalidating sources.

These negating entities reinforce and deepen the Wound already established in each of us when we were very young. They also feed the evolution of our protective Fear-Selves. Because the fundamental nature and quality of the Wound varies from person to person, so will our sensitivity to negating forces. Becoming alert to how we are molded by invalidation is an essential part of the process of liberation.

Because our primary identities—our desire to become a better "me"—are shaped by invalidation, a person weighed down by self-contempt can be nothing more than a thought seeking to counter the overwhelming power of the Wound. The goal of a "better" me is, therefore, entirely an artifact of our Wound. That is why all of our actions based on "hope" will fail to arouse sustainable change in us. Hope subtly adds credence to the Wound. Hope is a very tempting, but ultimately false, remedy to our desire for freedom from pain.

The goal of a "better" me is, therefore, entirely an artifact of our Wound. That is why all of our actions based on "hope" will fail to arouse sustainable change in us.

It's not that systems requiring obedience, discipline, and other conventional forms of invalidation are inherently "bad" or "evil." They are what they are. Civilization requires accommodation to institutions possessing authority and significance in our lives. The only issue that matters is whether we believe this invalidation and integrate it into our Wound. From Marine basic training to criminal activities, elements of life that might seem to be invalidating don't have to be. They only contribute to the reservoir of the Wound if they are able to attach to it. When that happens, they add credibility to our belief in our inadequacy, insufficiency, and worthlessness.

In modern society, most of us are motivated to become recognized power holders. Advancement at work, in income, and even in spiritual pursuits appeals to our desire to be and have more. A diverse range of social institutions creates productive and compliant workers by providing countless opportunities to achieve and assume roles which can attain visible outcomes. We buy into this model of social being because it feeds the needs of our Fear-Selves.

This is not a simple, straightforward process. Most organized systems require conformity, obedience, and discipline. They nurture the Wound and Fear-Selves when their structures reinforce our beliefs in our personal inadequacy, insufficiency, and worthlessness and when they encourage behavioral norms that inflate our egos. In the former case, they nurture our Wound and in the latter they sustain our Fear-Selves.

Let's look at an example of this process. Many school teachers use "gold stars" as a way to reward accomplishment. The honored students may gracefully accept the praise—these are the resilient students who are working purely from the joy of the task—or they may use this accomplishment to prop up a superior image of themselves. Students who fail to achieve special status can react with hurt. Those who are hurt are experiencing the stimulation of their already established Wound. This is why systems reliant on rewards are, for the most part, toxic. The prizes are often awarded according to subjective criteria, yet those who don't receive them can take to heart the message that they are incompetent, while those who do receive them can undergo inflation of their Fear-Selves. Either way, the system engenders disharmony in the social fabric.

Here's another example. Schools require obedience to their rules. Lateness to school or class is punished. For young children, who may have difficulty understanding the requirement for promptness, the Wound may be fed by the punishment they receive. How this message plays out in later life varies; it can teach the power of authoritarian systems, or it can turn the young person off to education altogether. Either way, the student learns that she is powerless. She must either accede to this arbitrary authority and become compliant, or express her hurt through other, less sanctioned channels. Ultimately, one way or another, she will find a way to express her power; we can be assured of that! One potential outcome is that she will strive to become the power arbiter, so that one day she can invalidate others in hopes of repairing the harm done to her.

I recently heard an example of just how far institutional invalidation has gone in the United States. In Texas, many school districts are now empowered to send pre-school-age children to special disciplinary schools if they act up in class. In America, no one is too young to suffer personal and publicly sanctioned invalidation. Our social institutions' need to establish authority is, essentially, without limit. We need to teach powerlessness to all of our young people, if we are to increase the dominance of institutions in our society.

Achieving clarity regarding the invalidation by outside forces rests on our ability to recognize that we have dealt with such situations in our own lives. But delving into *how* these structures have affected our lives is ultimately of little consequence. It is enough to know that they did and to move on from there. We can spend a lifetime thinking about the past, but such thinking does not offer a pathway to liberation. Instead, it devolves into a fascination with the Fear-Self, which thrives on therapy and self-examination. These are forms of self-inflation.

Achieving clarity regarding the invalidation by outside forces rests on our ability to recognize that we have dealt with such situations in our own lives. But delving into how these structures have affected our lives is ultimately of little consequence. We can spend a lifetime thinking about the past, but such thinking does not offer a pathway to liberation. Instead, it devolves into a fascination with the Fear-Self, which thrives on therapy and self-examination.

While none of us fully escapes the many invalidating effects of society, there are forms of social relations that are validating. We are all victims of the separation trauma and inconsistent love within our families of origin, yet there are many truly loving families. Love that is largely unconditional will validate children. Even parents who mainly apply invalidating elements in the raising of children do, on occasion, offer unconditional love. This often comes about as the result of a crisis, such as a life-threatening illness or accident, which reminds parents of the preciousness of their children.

When we love a child unconditionally, we are in direct contact with our Life Force. When we love unconditionally, we love what is, not what we prefer or need. Virtually everyone has the capacity to love unconditionally, although few have the inclination. We are wired for unconditional love, but we have been conditioned by a variety of social mechanisms to close off that part of ourselves.

While essentially all established social institutions can be invalidating, they can also serve as a source of nurturing relationships. Many of us remember a teacher who took a personal interest in us or a boss who was respectful and supportive. Often the expression "making a difference in someone's life" means providing someone a channel through which to express his or her authenticity. These special individuals make it possible for us to express our authentic selves within an organization. One of the keys to reversing invalidation is not only to listen to other people, but to accord their voices importance. Love and support that nurture our authenticity are among the most powerful agents of transformation.

Invalidation of any kind is a violent assault against our innate dignity as living beings. This applies equally to non-human systems. When a factory kills a stream with its run-off, it has attacked the dignity of the stream and everything that lives in or near it.

People of all ages suffer the damage of invalidating social institutions. a consequence of profoundly unequal power relations. In the United States we use the rhetoric of freedom and equality, but we rarely encourage true independence and self-expression.

The effects of invalidation can be seen in an individual, an organization, a culture, or a nation. The rage currently expressed against the West by Islamic peoples is a direct reflection of their disempowerment and domination by oil-hungry Western countries over the last century. They are seeking to regain a position of power and expel external agents who are meddling in their affairs and stealing their non-renewable resources. These cultures also possess their own collective Fear-Self, which motivates them to blame external forces, such as Israel or the United States, for all of their problems.

Similarly, inner-city youths who act out violently against property and people are reacting against their powerlessness. To counter their Wound-engendered belief in their utter impotence, their public personae (the Fear-Self) boil with the desire to control others through intimidation and force. Even loud swearing is a sign of this powerlessness.

When greed and power-holding become a society's *sine qua non*, as is the case in the United States, classes of people who are correspondingly poor and powerless will be created. High crime rates and social fear are a direct consequence of the wounding of these groups and communities. Street violence is born from the subtler forms of violence perpetrated on the poor: racism, classism, unfair social legislation, and indifferent politicians. Our society, our culture, and we, as individuals, live as both the invalidated and the invalidators. We live as both guard and prisoner.

Powerlessness is the fuel of every form of despotism. Tyranny, whether it comes in the form of the state (secular), religion (spiritual), or corporations, needs people to be powerless. The person identified with powerlessness wants to be subjugated and wants others to experience his pain. In its more extreme form, powerlessness is perversion. The deviance of powerlessness comes in many forms, but some of the best known are violent rape, the molestation of children by priests, sociopathic cruelty and murder, and organized genocide as it manifests in places as diverse as Sudan, Rwanda, Cambodia, and the United States.

This is the result of invalidation on a mass scale. When the deeply scarred, powerless person or group gains access to power contaminated by self-hatred, horrible events will unfold. Darfur, Treblinka, the "killing fields" of Cambodia under Pol Pot, and countless other places and eras are monuments to mass invalidation. The Wound of invalidation will always find an outlet, whether through the quiet depression of an achievement-obsessed college student or through a Hitler who needs to project his immense pain and suffering outwards.

When we are victims of invalidation, our inherent dignity is eroded. This is the process that feeds our Fear-Selves, since it is they who we rely on to counter the ever-growing pain of the Wound. Acknowledging the power of social invalidation in our lives is key to our self-understanding and, ultimately, to our awakening to our authentic selves.

7 - The Role of Gender and the Fear-Self

The role of gender within the Wound/Fear-Self dyad is complicated. While gender is not a primary theme of <u>Liberation from the Lie</u>, it does contribute to our understanding of the development of the Fear-Selves. The term "gender" is used here exclusively to mean the physical sex of a person. In a psychological sense, men and women can have varying gender elements. A woman may behave primarily like a man, and vice versa. Each of us carries both gender energies; how these energies are expressed and in what male-female proportion depends on our presenting Fear-Self and the context of a situation.

Men and women tend to express power differently from each other. Traditionally, men have tended to express power through channels that are public and explicit, while women were expected to express power in ways that were private and implicit. Either sex would leave themselves open to ridicule if they were to express power in ways associated with the opposite sex. This has become less true in recent decades, but it is still relevant because such conditioned and stereotypical identities and behaviors are well-embedded and resistant to change. Moreover, the level of social acceptance for those who diverge from gender expectations varies greatly by place, class, age, and race of both the individual and those interacting with him or her.

Women tend to adopt Fear-Selves that reflect their normative gender "power style," which is subtle and private. Therefore, typical female Fear-Selves include the Pleaser, the Body Person, the Terrified One, and the Imitator. Men, on the other hand, tend towards Fear-Selves that more publicly and overtly convey their sense of potency, such as the Tough Guy, the Achiever, and the Expert. Let's examine why this dichotomy has developed.

As civilization evolved into the vast and complex social system that characterizes our current way of life, the matriarchal societies characteristic of hunter-gatherers were usurped by the patriarchal orientation of agrarian and urban cultures. The role of women evolved from equal and decision-maker to baby-maker and nurturer. The egalitarian, non-gender-specific power structure of the hunting-gathering cultures was replaced by a male-dominant configuration whereby the most powerful male in a group made the important decisions.

This transition meant that men began to occupy the most visible social roles, while women retired to the private world of the home. Both genders faced new pressures. The visibility of men brought with it significant vulnerabilities. Any male who is unsuccessful in the public arena opens himself up to the ridicule of others and the shame he experiences as a result. Even within the hunter-gatherer context, a hunter who failed was an object of derision. For this reason, individuals whose Fear-Selves have a public focus are haunted by the fear of humiliation and shame, which evoke the pain they suffered at the formation of the Wound. A Fear-Self whose outward behavior has been "positive" can morph into a "negative" Fear-Self characterized by anger and the propensity for violence.

As it says in the Tao Te Ching:

> *'Be wary of both honor and disgrace'*
> *What does it mean,*
> *'Be wary of both honor and disgrace'?*
> *Honor is founded on disgrace*
> *and disgrace is rooted in honor*

Both should be avoided
Both blind a man to this world
That's why it says,
  'Be wary of both honor and disgrace'

When the Fear-Self fails, we experience humiliation and shame. We are drawn back to the Wound. In this way a "positive" Fear-Self morphs into a "negative" Fear-Self, characterized by depression and anger. The Fear-Self is created through the Wound and, over time, it will return to the Wound.

When the Fear-Self fails, we experience humiliation and shame. We are drawn back to the Wound. In this way a "positive" Fear-Self morphs into a "negative" Fear-Self, characterized by depression and anger. The Fear-Self is created through the Wound and, over time, it will return to the Wound.

The decline in the public stature of women resulted in their development of relatively private Fear-Selves. Not having the opportunity to achieve and possess socially important positions has meant that, for the most part, women live in closer proximity to their underlying Wound. When women began to find their validation largely through maintenance of the home and the raising of children, they became subject less to public scrutiny than to the scrutiny of their men. Because they are relatively unseen and acknowledged only by a small inner circle of family, a woman's achievements provide only a thin cover over the aching neediness of the Wound. The cost of that position has been a greater tendency toward depression and feeling psychologically and emotionally appropriated by male dominance. (Yet living in closer proximity to the Wound also allows women to live in closer proximity to their Life Force.)

Even the "female" Fear-Selves reach out for the recognition of a wider audience at times. The Pleaser, for example, gives parties and hosts other types of social affairs in order to display her domestic prowess to those outside the family. Of course, by doing so, she is also risking more public shame and humiliation if her guests perceive her efforts as less than satisfactory.

Mothers are particularly susceptible to the shame parents of either gender can feel due to failures of their children. Children who do not live up to their parents' standards and expectations often are subject to parental anger and rejection because of the underlying message about their parents' abilities (or lack thereof), which a child's failure communicates to the world at large. Conversely, the public success of a child is reflected glory for the parent. In this way, children are objectified as supporters (or underminers) of our Fear-Self in its role as parent. This is a particularly ugly way the Fear-Self expresses itself between generations.

Over the last 40 years, the delineation of gender-based Fear-Selves has become less clear. With the opportunity to move past their private Fear-Self worlds, women have entered the more public domain of the traditionally male Fear-Self. Women are, therefore, more likely to develop Fear-Selves that have previously been identified as the province of men. This shift risks the disapproval of men, as well as the humiliation and shame public failure brings in its wake. However, the women who are gender-role pioneers have been afforded some protection from these Fear-Selves, since the women attracted to gender-busting roles tend to be evolved and well-adapted individuals.

Every Fear-Self contains elements of our Life Force, and some identities are an outgrowth more of a person's authentic passion than of a need to serve the Fear-Self. For some adventurous women who thrive in conventional male roles, success can be attributed to living their lives as their authentic selves. In fields as diverse as policing and medical research, the love and passion of these women for their roles has helped them to outshine even their best male counterparts. This is especially true if the men have assumed their roles out of insecurity and a fear-based motivation to serve their Fear-Self.

When we fail to heed the call of our true love, we have chosen to live within the falsely safe confines of a Fear-Self. The more conventional a role is by gender, race, or class, the more likely it is to be occupied primarily by a Fear-Self, because when we opt for the tried and true simply out of dread of any other path, we have stepped firmly into the Fear-Self world. This is as true for the stay-at-home mother as it is for the female CEO who has broken through the corporate glass ceiling; as accurate for the man who fills a traditional male role such as soldier or scientist as it is for one who opts to spend his days as a homemaker and parent.

Thus is revealed a core principle, for men and women alike, of living a life essentially free of insecurity and fear: doing what one loves for the simple joy of doing it.

This is living the life of authentic goodness. Life calls on us to express our love and passion. Fear calls on us to protect the fragile self we falsely believe ourselves to be. We can choose to live either in the shadow of the Wound or in the bright light that burns in the heart of our authentic self.

8 - The Persistence of the Wound

Until we find our passion and make the brave choice to live it (a topic that will be covered in detail in Part Three of this book), we will live with the dominance of the Wound. Seeing the Wound does not necessarily mean liberation from it. The Wound is an intrinsic part of who we are. It does not go away with observation--nor should we want it to. But we can discover that the Wound does not need to occupy the role of primary villain in our lives. Paradoxically, it is ultimately an essential resource for us, once we clearly understand its true purpose. But until that subtle lesson is understood and experienced directly, we will continue to stumble our way through life, living primarily through one of our many Fear-Selves.

We evaluate our self-worth through the accomplishments of the Fear-Self. Our Fear-Selves are indispensable to us as long as the power of the Wound holds sway over our lives. We will continue to live out the desperate call of our invalidated selves until we wake up from the thrall of the Wound. Even when we "work" on a particular Fear-Self, we are, in effect, sustaining the influence of the Wound in our lives. The individual who "works" on a Fear-Self as a kind of self-improvement is just another Fear-Self. This observation explains the inevitable failure of self-help routines.

As long as the Wound persists, it will continue to reinvent itself into a myriad array of Fear-Selves. The self that is drawn to self-improvement is one that dreams of a better you. This is the exclusive domain of the Fear-Selves. All of their positive variants are designed to create a better you. The self-help movement is a consequence of the shadow of our Fear-Selves in American culture. It does not matter whether that Fear-Self reads a million books, or seeks liberation and understanding through sit-down therapy, or spends 20 to 120 minutes a day in meditation. In each case, it is likely that that the person doing the reading, participating in therapy, or sitting at the feet of an imagined guru is a Fear-Self. There is just no escape from the Wound. No matter what we do, we seem to live out our lives in what Thoreau called "quiet desperation."

While our needy personalities are expressed as Fear-Selves, it is important to know how the Wound is experienced as a feeling in our daily lives. The primary sensation of the Wound in our lives is lack. This can be experienced as a nervous hollowness in the center of our chests. The silent message is, "I need to do something to fill this sense of lack." It inspires a sense of separation from the world. It is directly connected with our archaic sense, from our earliest childhood, that we are missing something essential in order to be deserving of parental love. Like the background noise of the Big Bang that fills the universe, our selves are filled with the background noise of lack that stems from our own personal "big bang" of invalidation.

The primary sensation of the Wound in our lives is lack. This can be experienced as a nervous hollowness in the center of our chests. The silent message is, "I need to do something to fill this sense of lack." It inspires a sense of separation from the world. It is directly connected with our archaic sense, from our earliest childhood, that we are missing something essential in order to be deserving of parental love.

The Wound needs us to continue responding productively to its call. It is precisely our compliant response that keeps the Wound dominant in our lives. How do we respond? We respond by creating a story in which we are the main character seeking external validation. This "me" needs to attract attention.

There is one major exception to this pattern and this is the self that emanates directly from the Wound. What do you fear doing, yet must do in your life? It could be opening up a bill we are fearful of paying; it could be calling a doctor to check on a biopsy; it could be answering a phone call from someone with whom we fear speaking. This is an identity that seems neither positive nor negative; it is simply fear itself. This is a conscious self for which no adequate Fear-Self has yet evolved. Most of us possess this self, and it will always emerge in those life situations that we most greatly fear.

It is helpful getting acquainted with this self, because it provides us with a direct taste of the Wound. It is a powerful reminder of the fears we experienced in our earliest childhood. They are palpable, deeply upsetting, and impossible to avoid. They just happen.

One of the reasons so many people are drawn to self-help, therapy, and Eastern philosophy meditation practice is the desire to deal with the raw fear of this base identity. It is a kind of prime mover. As long as we are achieving, as long as we are maintaining our beauty and style, as long as others recognize our expertise and authority, there is little need for improvement. But when we come face to face with our own fundamental terror, we suddenly need help. What we think we need is a self that can quickly cope with our bottom-line dread. It is, literally, a gap in our phalanx of Fear-Selves. After years of failure to control this feeling, we might choose to medicate ourselves in response, and the American therapeutic community is only too happy to help us out. And yet this is the one problem that seems unaffected by our mighty efforts to transform it.

This is the raw material for all of our Fear-Selves, but now we are experiencing it in a form that is not covered over by a Fear-Self whose precise purpose is to shield us from this category of fear. This identity is fresh from the world of our innocent suffering so long ago.

Recall that the primary purpose of any Fear-Self is to exert power and control on its presenting environment. In this case, the environment is in control of us! Whenever we are not equipped with a readily available Fear-Self to deal with a situation, we will believe that we truly are operating from a position of inadequacy, insufficiency, and worthlessness. The situation is clearly calling the shots, and we recoil from it in fright. In desperation, we call our therapist, change our medication, seek advice in whatever form, or just sit our rebellious bodies down into some mediation posture. Or maybe we just do the vacuuming, wallowing in apprehension.

Curiously, we don't even need to be confronting a provocative situation in order to feel this base fear. Most of us, living in our imaginations, can project experiences that evoke our deepest anxieties, such as abandonment by a loved one or our inevitable death. In fact, most of us seem to need to live with this level of fear. We seem to be wired to experience the Wound in our lives over and over again.

It is possible to view this phenomenon as an opportunity for self-understanding. The reliable brilliance of everyday life provides us with many chances to wake up to our authentic selves. The first step in awakening from the trance of the Fear-Self and its underlying Wound is being willing to experience the pain that will always manifest when we are in direct contact with the Wound. Feel the profound suffering that we sustain when we live through our Fear-Selves' obsessions with empty accomplishment. The persistence of the Wound in our lives is a gift. Without it, we could only persist in living out our inner unhappiness without ever finding an opening in the wall of suffering that is maintained by it.

The call to liberation starts with experiencing the pain we avoid by living a false life based on accomplishments that are, ultimately, unfulfilling. We thereby embark on a journey that leads to understanding and liberation via our Life Force, which is always available to us when we are open to its voice. When we respond to this call, we come back to the path that inexorably leads to our authentic selves.

The Wound is always there. Underneath the layers of our Fear-Selves and our well-intended drive to escape the Wound's dark shadow, its scary mask is ever there for us to behold. What lies beneath this fearsome mask is the person we were prior to our separation from love. It is our Life Force patiently waiting for its rediscovery. It is our direct, authentic connection with life. It is wonder and spontaneity. It is free of the many fetters of belief that keep us shackled as slaves, unaware of our enslavement.

The journey to freedom begins and ends with awareness, understanding, and direct experience. It begins with our awareness of pain and the salvation that lies at its core. In preparation for our release from our enslavement to falseness, we first need to dig a little deeper into our Fear-Selves. With understanding comes liberation! We have now reached the point where we can prepare to board our own Freedom Train.

9 - Common Elements of the Fear-Self

In order to find our authentic self, we must be able to recognize our Fear-Selves. The degree to which we are able to see how they play a role in our life is the same degree to which will we be released from their thrall. However, the Fear-Self can morph into countless types. Those that are most difficult to identify are those that emerge during the process of self-liberation. The purpose of this chapter is to get a clearer sense of the elements all Fear-Selves have in common so we can more easily identify them.

Key Point: All Fear-Selves are projections from our core belief in our inadequacy, insufficiency, and worthlessness. They are what we believe will heal our Wound. This is why we are so deeply attached to them. They are maintained by our fear that we cannot be anything besides a Fear-Self.

All Fear-Selves are so well-established that they have become habits. They are like computer programs invoked automatically without thought or choice: They come to life in particular environmental situations, and we are so accustomed to their automatic manifestation that we fail to recognize their habitual emergence in daily life. The way they feel is the way we feel. The Fear-Self is as close to us as our skin.

We believe our Fear-Selves to be intrinsically who we are. Because they are so close to us, they are often hard for us to see. After all, the one doing the seeing is likely to be a Fear-Self!

We already know the primary purpose of a Fear-Self, which is to shield us from our profoundly self-negating identity (the Wound) and to provide us with a vehicle to wield power. Anything whose principal duty is to protect must have power in order to do its job. The source of that power is our belief in it. The more we believe we need to be protected, the more we will need fear-based power to achieve that purpose. A Fear-Self's vigor derives from our level of need for self-protection. The more we are identified with a Fear-Self, the more we are closed off from the spontaneous flow of life. Our belief in the need for protection blocks that flow. We invest enormous energy in protecting ourselves from a lie.

Resiliency across situations indicates a reduced need for protection and self-defense. The resilient self is concerned with life as it presents itself and not in protecting an illusory entity. True liberation occurs when there is no longer the need to defend anything. Conversely, psychological enslavement results when defense of the self is the primary organizing principle of the individual. The Fear-Self is the agent of that self-defense. As it is written in Stephen Mitchell's translation of the Tao Te Ching:

> *The master doesn't try to be powerful*
> *thus he is truly powerful.*
> *The ordinary man keeps reaching for power*
> *thus he never has enough.*

Identification of our Fear-Selves requires honest self-reflection. We must be willing to take an empirical look at how we act in the world and the motivations behind our actions. Our identity has been tied to these personality types for nearly all our lives. The key is to see how these Fear-Selves are fed by the attention they garner for us and the protection from failure they provide.

In my own case, as a highly invalidated child, my fledgling self sought a personality model that could provide me with the protection I needed from anything that could raise my Wound to consciousness. For a Fear-Self to connect, it needs to be appealing; it has to connect to something that is authentic in us. The self that is in pain needs a replacement self that is not in pain. This process can be seen in the illustration below.

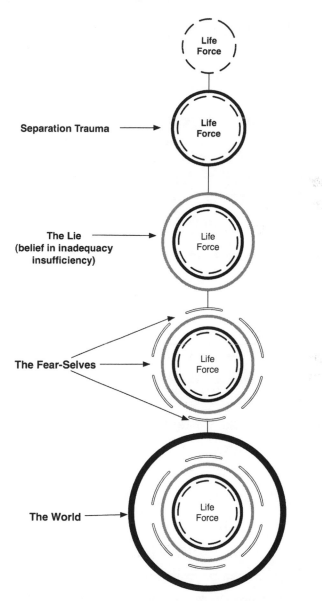

Figure 2: The Development of the Fear based Person

We cannot understand our Fear-Selves without understanding their appeal. Just like an infection or tumor that forcibly invades our body, a Fear-Self must find elements within our authentic self with which it can connect. Each Fear-Self connects with parts of us that are genuine. For this reason, it can be said that each Fear-Self has an element of our inherent Life Force. This is one reason why the process of seeing our Fear-Selves can be so challenging.

Just like an infection or tumor that forcibly invades our body, a Fear-Self must find elements within our authentic self with which it can connect. Each Fear-Self connects with parts of us that are genuine. For this reason, it can be said that each Fear-Self has an element of our inherent Life Force.

So, getting back to my story: My parents presented me with two very different models. My father was moody, often violent, somewhat anti-Semitic (although he himself was Jewish), corny, and not very urbane. My mother was more sophisticated, opinionated, had a quicker intellect, and, unlike my father, was not angry or prone to violence; instead, she was emotionally detached and distant. I also had a third model: my brother, nine years older, who was immersed in the world of classical music and far more knowledgeable about the arts and literature than either of my parents. He was also cold and emotionally detached, except when some musical work (often Mahler or Wagner) aroused his passion.

I feared my father and completely rejected his personality model. So the Fear-Self that evolved within this milieu was one that refuted my fear of being irrelevant or stupid and emulated those traits I found appealing in my mother and brother. What resulted was an urbane, highly opinionated person with strains of arrogance and a deep fear of intimacy. Love of classical music was authentic in me, as was a general interest in the arts. But emotional distance and a sense of superiority served the needs of my Fear-Self well. When anyone tried to get too close to me, I fell back on my superior knowledge and sophistication and found them ultimately unacceptable.

My Wound informed me that my authentic being was irrelevant. This meant that if anyone really liked or even loved me, there had to be something wrong with them. The more they liked me, the more vigorously I rejected them. Those who rejected me, I also rejected on account of my self-defined superior knowledge and culture. I held myself aloof.

However, this quality of aloofness failed to serve another Fear-Self I had developed, that of a rebel who found much to love in leftist politics and the downtrodden masses. As someone who identifies strongly with my Jewish heritage, the Holocaust has always strongly resonated in me, and it is part of my integral Life Force to align myself with any groups or individuals who suffer from prejudice. Also, I cultivated an urbanely ironic, yet likable, sense of humor which drew some people to me. My Fear-Selves therefore operated perfectly. I was overtly warm-hearted for people in general, but sufficiently aloof to keep them at a distance.

Even at a very young age I knew what my Fear-Selves were costing me. Because of my intelligence, artiness, sophistication, and decent looks, occasionally the very girls who I wanted to like me did—but I just couldn't allow them to get close to me. I was keenly aware of my dilemma but could do nothing about it. Intimacy was terrifying. Many nights I lay in bed utterly disgusted with myself. This element of my personality felt not only automatic, but also absolutely in control. I kept this misery a complete secret to others. It was more important to me that my public personality maintain its affable, iconoclastic nature which, ironically, attracted people to me. The downside was that the people most important to me would, eventually, grow weary of my intimacy avoidance; over time, they would drift away, and I would be left lonely and completely revolted by myself.

This is a good example of the persistence of the Fear-Self when it is key to our need for self-preservation. I was dependent on an identity despite my knowledge that it caused me intense grief and self-contempt.

We can never be completely released from our Fear-Selves. For the most part, they are here to stay. Trying to completely eliminate a Fear-Self only results in the emergence of another Fear-Self. Struggling against a Fear-Self is one of the favorite tactics of the "Better Me" Fear-Self.

However, we can lessen their grip on us considerably. The purpose of this book is not to show how we can eradicate the Fear-Selves or the Wound—we can't. It is simply to provide the opportunity to rupture the trance they induce in us in order to allow our Life Force to shine through. Those who believe that they have completely let go of their primary personality elements are only fooling themselves. They are an innate part of who we are. We will revisit this topic toward the end of the book, once the whole process of liberation has been fully described. All that is needed for this process to work is to understand how the Fear-Selves and Wound operate in our lives. When we are able to weaken their grip on us, then, and only then, will we be able to cease toiling to create a life that isn't a response to a belief in our inadequacy and insufficiency.

All Fear-Selves are compulsive. They represent a cluster of actions that we believe we must do. The Expert needs to demonstrate her expertise. The Pleaser needs to always say yes to others who "matter." The Spiritualist needs to maintain her search for enlightenment. The Tough Guy needs to show his authority. The Fear-Self would seem to suggest that our integrity, even our very existence, is on the line if we don't follow the automatic dictates of our fear-based mind. The mind has been habituated, over many years, to follow this personality pattern no matter what its cost might be to our selves and our social relations. What makes a tragic hero truly tragic is the inevitability of his predicament. So it is with our primary Fear-Selves. Our life becomes one long narrative characterized by struggle and avoidance.

Most Fear-Selves are designed to impress others and ourselves. Consider that last statement: We need to impress ourselves! Let that idea sink in, and see how it resonates with you. Why should we need to seek attention from ourselves? One of the more immediate steps we can take is ceasing the absurd attention on seeking to impress ourselves.

Fear-Selves are achievement-oriented. They seek out opportunities to show the world our worthiness. They will tell us, "I am adequate...I am lovable...I am sufficient to the demands the world places on me."

Another common role of the Fear-Self is to experience the world as inadequate and/or insufficient. The source of invalidation always begins as an external event. The trauma of childhood is that is created by the world and not ourselves. As a result, each Wound will possess an element of disdain and fear for the world, for it is the world that set in motion the experience of self-negation. It becomes necessary to develop a compulsive Fear-Self that responds to the contempt we feel for the world. This category of Fear-Self will seek ways to break the dull routine of life and find excitement. Such Fear-Selves might always be on the lookout for new relationships, new ways of making money, and new high-risk activities. Such people are highly invested in short-term, intense experiences. Yet the high-wire life is also a treadmill, which can rend the fabric of relationships and introduce forms of recreation that harm the self or the environment.

A variant of this Fear-Self is the Spiritualist. He rejects the world as it presents itself and seeks to either transcend this world or experience it differently from the way it is by his senses. The Spiritualist's profoundly invalidating belief is that the world and the self, as they are perceived by the conditioned mind, are unacceptable. The Spiritualist rejects both by seeking a new self that can experience the world in a new way. He is motivated to become enlightened, since the literature of enlightenment speaks broadly of experiencing the world differently after enlightenment. The invalidating potential contained within Eastern philosophy is almost limitless. It is necessary to understand that in nearly all cases when we seek to fix the world or ourselves, we are really trying to control our experience through a refined form of escape. This is resistance and unacceptance of life as it is. We can never experience this life until we are able to see the filters we place on it.

When the Wound contains a belief in the world's inadequacy, it will also have a primary belief in one's own inadequacy/insufficiency/unworthiness. The primary theme is consistently invalidation of the self.

The Fear-Self is always other-oriented, and even the evaluating self (myself) is treated as an other. Happiness and self-satisfaction are dependent on the capacity of other people or situations to make us happy. In contrast, authentic joy is not dependent on external people or situations. This is experienced when an act is performed simply for the joy of doing it. That is the decisive difference between the actions of a Fear-Self and those of an authentic self.

The Fear-Self is always other-oriented, and even the evaluating self (myself) is treated as an other. Happiness and self-satisfaction are dependent on the capacity of other people or situations to make us happy. In contrast, authentic joy is not dependent on external people or situations.

We can safely assume that the absence of inner balance and harmony is linked to some belief that we and/or our world ought to be different from how we perceive it to be. The world and ourselves are never enough. As a consequence, we are ceaselessly consumed by needs. Fulfillment is, inevitably, fleeting. Life becomes unsatisfactory. In this way unhappiness is tied directly to our Wound.

Because a Fear-Self's bases their success on externalities, it can never be entirely secure in its own actions. The best it can do is to temporarily allay its insecurities. Feelings of insecurity and lack always follow in the wake of a "successful" behavior/event when its effect has worn off.

The Fear-Self presents itself in either a "positive" mode, which is achievement-focused, or in a "negative" mode, which is one of depression. The positive Fear-Self seeks to impress others or one's self. It needs to prove, constantly, its worthiness. Between its "worthy" achievements, it will often feel a kind of malaise or unworthiness. It must always be looking forward to its next "hit" (another reminder of the addictive nature of the Fear-Self). It hungers for its next high, whether it comes as a heroin hit or a blissful meditation.

The negative Fear-Self, or depressed type, manifests in a way that suggests its closer proximity to the Wound. Unlike positive

Fear-Selves, it does not live for achievement; rather it seeks out opportunities to draw attention to its version of personal victimization. Its identity as "victim" is primary to it. By consolidating its life around that identity, it, in effect, steals the claim of victim hood from positive Fear-Selves which conceal their acknowledged victimization behind the thin facade of the positive Fear-Self. This is how depressed types suck energy from others. They compete for attention in subtle ways, often by appearing with the ruse of not wanting any attention. Positive Fear-Selves may therefore resent negative types because they tend to win the battle for attention. This is why it is challenging spending time with depressed types; they appear to steal a core need of the positive Fear-Self identity. Fear-Selves love the spotlight, even if it appears that they need to escape it. It is a world of drama.

Although the affect of depression suggests that the depressed type is closer to the underlying Wound than positive Fear-Selves, this actually is not the case. The depressed Fear-Self will defend its core identity just as aggressively as any other Fear-Self. The Fear-Self does the same thing for the depressed type as for the positive type: It defends and protects. Vulnerability is experienced as weakness. In the depressed type it is often expressed as, "I am so vulnerable that any attack on me is a demonstration of your cruelty." Its world is made safe and complete and miserable.

But Fear-Selves are not complete people. They are overlay personalities designed to cover over the Wound. In fact, the Fear-Selves do not pretend to be complete. If we listen to their voice carefully, we are able to hear their promise of completion sometime in the future. Because they are riddled with insecurity, they need to assure us that we will be complete eventually. One day, I will finally "make it." One day, people will admire my beauty and grace. One day, I will dominate my field. One day, I will be enlightened. We must work ever harder to fulfill the promise of the Fear-Self. This is, of course, a struggle without end. "One day" never arrives, because the Fear-Self is an artifact. It is not a being—it is a story.

Each Fear-Self tells a story about who we are. The Expert Fear-Self relates his epic journey from ignorance to brilliance. He lists the many schools he has attended and the hundreds of major works he has read. He may express the milestones of his career in a light-hearted manner, but the story is vital to the seeming reality of his Fear-Self. The Fear-Self has a compulsive need to continue its story. The Achiever presents the account of his rise through the ranks. He regales us with the many challenges he has overcome. He talks about his growing power within an organization and some of his stumbles along the way. The story has a past, present, and future. The Fear-Self appears to be a whole person, but in actuality, it's a story with us as its star.

The Trap

Try to see the Fear-Self as automatic. It takes us over with light-ning speed and is absolutely unmediated by thought. Our mind and body become it. When it takes us over, we radiate it.

It often expresses itself with anger and/or impatience. It feels pressured. It is energetic. A feeling of exasperation often accompanies it. See how you experience this in your own life. These feelings lurk just beneath the surface of our daily experience. It is so second nature to us that we assume in the moment that it is who we are. We accept persistently stressful feelings as normal. They are just a part of modern living. That's why I call it a trap. It literally traps us in its insidious and tight grip.

My daughter and I were shopping for a present for her mother's birthday at a local bookstore. She had been browsing for quite some time, asking repeatedly for my help in selecting something appropriate. We had been browsing the cards for quite some time when suddenly I felt overwhelmed with impatience. I really wanted to finish the shopping trip and get home, where I had other things to do that were important to me. This unpleasant feeling came over me without warning, and abruptly a pleasant afternoon with my daughter began to feel strained and tiresome.

I realized that this was a characteristic Fear-Self descending upon me. It was automatic, fast, compulsive, and unpleasant. It was also accompanied by self-centered thoughts, another trademark of the Fear-Self. The Fear-Self always organizes itself around a cluster of self-centered thoughts. Because its story appears compelling, it is persuasive. The story of the Fear-Self is always more important than the story of anyone else in a presenting situation.

I could feel the Fear-Self fill my mind and my body with tension and weight. I felt its anxious quality emanate from my being, and I feared that even someone standing near me might sense my aggravated thoughts as a kind of prickly force that invisibly pushes others away. This was my Authority Fear-Self. I needed to be heard and obeyed.

For better or worse, I was quite familiar with this Fear-Self. I knew it as a primal and automatic energy, which didn't reflect my heart-centered being and which obscured my enjoyment of the time, I was spending with my daughter. By catching my Fear-Self in the act, I was able to peel back its overlay and feel the natural pleasure of the being that lives underneath—my original Life Force. When you are able to do this, you will be —as I was — suddenly flooded by a kind of benevolent and laughing light. We see through the seriousness of the Fear-Self and natural humor emerges. This is the energy of liberation in action.

The Structure of a Human Being

We are born whole and complete. However, that wholeness is undermined through invalidation. The amount of negation one experiences varies among individuals, families, and cultures. But no one is spared. Earlier in this book, the point was made that hunting-gathering cultures emphasized unconditional validation far more than modern civilization, but even within contemporary culture, the amount of validation a person receives differs widely from family to family. Also, personal durability and resiliency differ between individuals from the time we are newborns.

The Wound is a porous shell covering our Life Force. On account of its porosity, we never entirely lose contact with our authentic being, but we do lose, absolutely, our identification with it! Our authenticity precedes the Wound. We are our Life Force, but we had nothing to do with creating it.

In contrast, we are co-creators of the Wound. We experience persistent invalidation, we assume responsibility for parental rejection, and we create a masterfully powerful belief in our inherently flawed nature. The entity that creates this belief is the entity that we assume to be our authentic identity. This is the decisive error. It is a judgment we make in our very early youth, and it sticks with us. As long as we believe ourselves to be this person, no amount of therapy, meditation, or self-help regimens can substantively change the way we see ourselves and others.

We experience persistent invalidation, we assume responsibility for parental rejection, and we create a masterfully powerful belief in our inherently flawed nature. The entity that creates this belief is the entity that we assume to be our authentic identity. This is the decisive error.

This explains why, when we directly experience our Life Force–not an unusual or uncommon event—we usually attribute the beauty of the experience to something outside ourselves. We will always return to our primary identity as inadequate.

The Fear-Selves that develop around the Wound are also porous. This means that they allow the inherent reality of life into the self, and they also allow for the agony and terror of the Wound to interact with life as it happens. The Fear-Self is the membrane that interacts directly with life events. It is also the recipient of the underlying turbulence of the Wound-based psyche. Below are two different ways of visualizing this structure.

The challenge of our lives is to find a way to release the light of our own Life Force into consciousness, to rediscover the person we are beneath the Wound and its galaxy of Fear-Selves. All that we can do is to understand. As our understanding grows, the porosity of the Wound will grow.

We can't make either of these things happen directly. The only thing we can do is to see how these processes have evolved in our own life; in that seeing, their power over us is released. We must take the brave step of letting go of exactly those personal identities to which we most strongly adhere. This means being willing to plunge into the unknown in the very area of life that is most intimate to us: the knowledge of our own self.

Because all Fear-Selves are porous, they are, ultimately, ineffective shields against the terror of the Wound. As long as we seek to protect ourselves from the Wound with a Fear-Self, we will not only maintain the strength and vigor of the Wound; we will do nothing more than spin our wheels. The belief that we can find happiness and sustainable contentment by working to "improve" a Fear-Self is exactly what we have been doing our whole lives with little success. It is time to get off the bandwagon of external achievement and see the process for what it is--a hopeless and desperate attempt to secure psychological safety and well-being. As long as there is an implicit identification with the Wound, any "progress" we make in this endeavor will be illusory and, at best, temporary.

When we believe that the Fear-Selves and their underlying Wound are true, we place the locus of control of our lives outside of ourselves. Living as a Fear-Self, we are always seeking more control within a world that cannot be controlled. This will always threaten to undermine our fragile sense of well-being. In fact, the need and desire to control is the source of all our suffering.

Control is solely an issue for a Fear-Self. The need to control points directly to whatever is false and seemingly vulnerable in our lives. The more we seek to control, the more we strengthen a Fear-Self. Conversely, the more we feel free to relinquish control, the more we weaken a Fear-Self. The process of liberation is one that sees all forms of control as a desperate way to demonstrate adequacy and sufficiency.

The Life Force is not concerned with control. It is content just being itself. It delights in the world as it is and freely expresses itself physically and emotionally. It lives with integral trust in itself and the world. It does not need to identify with a fear-based person who frets about an imagined future. In this way, we can step out of the shadow of the story defined by our Fear-Selves—and into the light of liberation.

10 - Subtle Elements of the Fear-Self

When we identify with a belief in our inadequacy, insufficiency or unworthiness, our lives fill with suffering and desperation. No matter how confident or self-assured we might appear, even to ourselves, these beliefs lurk just beneath the surface. They represent the vast shadow of invalidation and the failure of love in our lives. We have every right to defend ourselves from accusations suggesting our inadequacy, but if our defensiveness is compulsive, we can be quite sure that we are identified with a Fear-Self.

Let's take a look at the core terms of the Wound: inadequacy, insufficiency, and unworthiness (often the belief that we are unworthy of being loved). When we or someone else says that we are "inadequate," what exactly does that statement mean? At face, it suggests that we should be better at something than we appear to be. It suggests that we are less of a person than we or someone else has believed ourselves to be. Whether it is our own belief that we are inadequate or someone else's, a projection is being made. If we fail at something that we believe we ought to have mastered and label ourselves as inadequate, we have then projected an identity of ourselves that reifies the Wound. In either case, the mind is at work creating pain and suffering; the Wound is emerging in the wake of a Fear-Self collapse. Our projected self has "failed" at a life situation. When Fear-Selves fail, the Wound will always come to the surface in the form of psychological anguish. When that happens, many of us risk falling into the negative Fear-Self of the Depressed One as we move from one false polarity to another.

All of our Fear-Selves exist as either-or polarities. We either succeed or we fail. It's always black or white. We are either beautiful or we're ugly. We are either the Expert or an abject fool. We either have power or we are weak. This is another great way to spot a Fear-Self: Anytime the mind appears as identifying with either side of a polarity, you can bet that a Fear-Self is expressing those beliefs alongside its best buddy, the Wound.

> *Because Fear-Selves are perfectionists, they fail far more often than they succeed, which is why many of us feel bad much of the time. Despite the illusion that we embrace mostly positive Fear-Selves, most of us live either within or just on the periphery of a depressed Fear-Self.*

Because Fear-Selves are perfectionists, they fail far more often than they succeed, which is why many of us feel bad much of the time. Despite the illusion that we embrace mostly positive Fear-Selves, most of us live either within or just on the periphery of a depressed Fear-Self. In effect, we are always living in the world of "we are not enough." Firmly established in this position, we can never be fully happy and content.

When we live as victims, life is seen as unfair. We seem to be the ones who always pick the slowest moving lines at a supermarket, we have amazingly bad luck with traffic lights, our health is precarious, others make unwelcome demands on us, and our families are sources of stress and anxiety. This is a very short list of the victimizations most of us believe we experience every day. These negative experiences shape our life story. We have something to complain about to our friends and co-workers. "Poor me" is the refrain we hear from ourselves and others so much of the time.

It is an intriguing irony that people suffering from HIV or terminal cancer often talk about the beauty and vividness of life as they approach their final days. The motivation to complain has seemingly become irrelevant to these people, who instead live in wonder and reverence of the simplest things in life. They have risen above the tribulation of their lives. Yet we, who live far away from the spectre of death, fume violently over the slow driver ahead of us who is on his cell phone, forcing us to endure yet another red light. These words are not intended to make you feel guilty. That is never the purpose of this book. When we approach our own passing, as those with terminal illnesses do, we can transcend the relatively petty demands the Fear-Selves make on our lives. Such people have returned to their authentic selves and are living in the light of their Life Force.

Fear-Selves seek to use life. All things are evaluated for their benefit to the presenting Fear-Self. Wonder, intimacy, and aliveness wither whenever the prowling Fear-Self emerges with its perennial question, "What's in it for me?" The terminally ill patient is no longer concerned with that question. What matters is the natural unfolding of life itself. Obsession with the self has declined in preference to the wonder of connection with others.

Exercise 1: Experiencing life without seeking a use for it

Try spending the next several minutes without any sense of how you would use life. Cease asking life what it can do for you, and then see what feelings and experiences unfold. Turn your attention outward and just experience sound, sight, and touch without seeking to gain anything from it. Get a feel for that. Then try turning your attention inward with the same perspective. What does it feel like to perceive yourself without any sense of needing to reach a goal? Try seeing the quality of connection contained within the whole of your perception, and then contrast that with the solitary concern for one's self. What does that feel like? How does experiencing life with the purpose of using it differ from how you felt during this exercise?

Fear-Selves are the dominant form of personal identity, and they are linked to patriarchal systems. These systems organize themselves around the concept of use. Women are useful for sex, babies, and home maintenance. Nature must be used in any way possible to satisfy the needs of people and civilization. Weapons and war are used against anything that threatens production and income. Economic and political organizations are pyramidal. People on the lower levels are used to make money for those above them. People and things are divided up into the useful and the useless. Power is disproportionately concentrated among those who are served by the most used. The scraps that remain are distributed among those who serve the higher-ups. They get enough to be thankful for what they have and to assure their docility.

Fear-Selves operate in much the same way. Their payoff to the individual is enough to maintain stability. That is why so few of us are attracted to the concept of self-liberation and fewer still will take the journey to freedom. We are content enough with our enslavement. Seen from the larger perspective, our domination by fear comes cheap. We are willing to despoil the world to keep the deepening sickness of overheated civilization going. Those who are used fight the wars for their masters, who sit more or less comfortably in their plush boardrooms with the belief that all is well in the world. For them, the shaming operation of invalidation works very well ,and they enjoy expounding about how the spirit of freedom always comes at a price: the wars fought for them and obedience to the values and organizational structures they define.

Our Fear-Selves are like those masters of civilization. We too have lived in a trance, blind to our own compliance to forces that keep us exhausted and insecure. Desperately we look for lifelines to make all of this worthwhile. We dream of the next five-day vacation, the drink after work, a romantic sexual liaison. If time cannot serve our interests to bloat and excite our Fear-Selves, we complain bitterly of the monotonous grind of daily life. And so it goes, day after long day.

Exercise 2: Our Internal Monologue: Friend or Foe

Seek the Fear-Self as that master whose voice speaks in your head without end. Note the critical nature of the voice. It not only complains endlessly about the grind of daily life, but it will attack the very body/mind from which it would seem to speak. Our internal monologues speak more critically of us than would our worst enemies.

For the rest of today, listen to the voice in your head. Listen particularly to how it refers to "you." Listen to the criticisms it makes and the advice it spews out. Now pretend that the voice is not in your head, but is actually that of a friend . Imagine this friend speaking to you in exactly the same words you hear in your head. Afterwards, ask yourself how you would feel about this friend?

Now ask yourself, who controls this voice? Who chooses the words it says?

If your answer is "me," Ask yourself, is that really true? You might want to answer "me" because the tone, style, and content of the words are so familiar. But do you really consciously choose the words in your head, or do they just happen? And if you aren't choosing the words, then who is?

By now, you are probably thinking, "One of my Fear-Selves must be this voice in my head." I would agree with you. Now ask yourself, is this Fear-Self voice me? Really consider that question carefully. If you answer with a "yes," then you again are faced with the question of who puts these thoughts and sentences together in your head. If you answer with a "not me," then who or what is the source of these words?

This exercise shows that the voices in your head are not yours at all. By the time we notice them, they have already happened. These voices come from a Fear-Self, and that Fear-Self is a direct consequence of the invalidation you experienced in your early life. The voice sounds like you, speaks like you, and selects vocabulary that mirrors your own. The reason for this similarity is that the Fear-Selves evolved into language and personality at the same time that your body was evolving into language and personality. The implications of this relationship are larger than we have thus far explored, but the voice in your head should sound exactly like your own voice, because the two are, essentially, the same.

What this suggests is that your own voice, the voice you use in your daily life, is also, to a large extent, the voice of a Fear-Self. The voice of your daily life will follow the dictates of your interior monologue. Because we believe that our internal voice is our own voice, we ultimately speak as one, even if it appears that we are two people: the speaker of our internal monologue, and the responder to that monologue. Because we believe our inner voice is our own voice, we are trapped by its content.

If it is perfectly clear that the voice that rambles on and on in your own head is not your own but is the loud proclamations of a Fear-Self; if we are now armed with the realization that we have been following that voice in lockstep; what might this extraordinary realization suggest? To put it bluntly, the person we have believed ourselves to be is not who we are! From the smallest details of our memories to our largest dreams, that story is not our authentic one.

Do you choose the agonizing thoughts that course through your mind?. What are your most painful thoughts?

These are the voices that condemn us to our own self-defined failure, our bad behaviors, our laziness, stupidity, drug abuse, etc. They are thoughts of shame—in other words, they are agreements with our own invalidation!

Where do these thoughts originate? Once again, it should be clear that the most painful thoughts come from the Wound, our belief in our own innate inadequacy, insufficiency, and worthlessness.

Seeing our internal monologue as entirely Wound-based is an over-simplification. Our inner voices are also the source of essential knowledge and wisdom.

Recall that our authentic core identities, which I have called the Life Force, and the Wound are porous (as are each of our Fear-Selves). This means that the light of our Life Force will always shine onto the Wound. The porosity of our personality shells means that thoughts received from the Wound also possess elements of our original Life Force within them. This is a blessing. If we were to be utterly closed-off from our Life Force, we could never find the way back to our authentic selves.

It is this element of our inherent Life Force that gives each Fear-Self credibility. Let's say that to prove your adequacy, you become a lawyer and land a position at a big-name firm. Your fascination with analysis or love for advocacy may originate from your Life Force, but the need to use your position to convince yourself and others of your intelligence, power of personality, or just plain hard work is likely to arise from a Fear-Self. Let's say that you make a large donation to Amnesty International and want your name made public on a list of important donors. It may be integral to your Life Force to stand up for those victimized by corrupt political regimes, but your interest in publicizing your donation comes from the fear-based need to show the world how generous you are.

Now let's take a look at those critical voices that emerge in your internal dialogue. Let's say that one of those voices tells you what a terrible parent you have been. Certainly those words are forged within the Wound, but they also possess elements of your Life Force. Our conscience is often closely aligned with the Life Force.

The choice to have children places a great responsibility on us. Most of us know that the generosity of our love is a key element in quality parenting. This knowledge is a direct emanation from our Life Force. It is basic to our human wiring. Yet we know of times when we have been less than unconditionally loving. Raised in environments that favor aggressive patriarchy the seemingly "feminine" values are often perceived as weaknesses. Babies need discipline. We must learn to be strong and ignore their cries; otherwise they will grow up spoiled and needy. As parents, many of us have been deeply conflicted in this area. If we have been strict disciplinarians who only occasionally showed our children unconditional love, we may look back with regret at the harshness of tone we have used, the mean words we have spoken, and perhaps even times when we actually used physical violence. That critical voice is a plea from the Life Force to be the best parent we can be, but it has been filtered and combined with beliefs embraced by our invalidated self.

Our inner voice possesses elements of both Life Force and Wound. This is a very nuanced point. When we speak with both these elements, others may hear us as harsh and invalidating. This can easily lead to quarrels and misunderstandings. Often our intent is good, having our authentic self as its source, but our harsh mode of expression is mediated by the Wound and Fear-Self. Knowing how our voice is often filtered through our sense of inadequacy is a powerful insight into how we create unnecessary conflict in our lives. The positive intent originates with our Life Force, but how it is expressed is a consequence of being filtered through the Wound.

A call for love and integrity will always be deeply colored as it passes through the Wound. This is a subject we will revisit in more detail, but understand that positive intent, when expressed through the vehicle of criticism, is a good example of the melding of the Life Force with its overlying Wound.

Previously, we have talked about the interconnection each Fear-Self has with the Wound. A similar interconnection exists between the Life Force and the Wound. These interconnections are shown below:

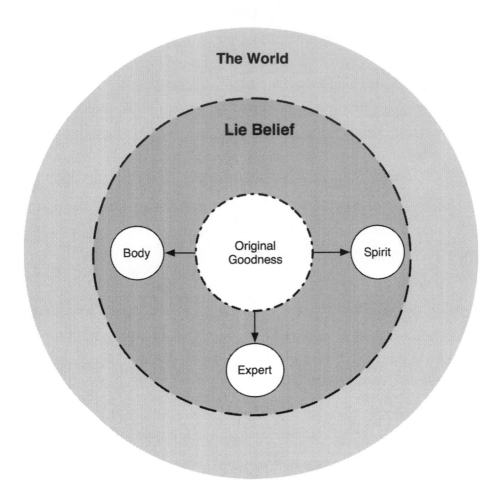

Figure 3: The Porosity of Life and the Fear-Based Person

This figure shows how the Life Force connects with both the Wound and each of the Fear-Selves. The strength and vigor of the connection varies. But we cannot invest our identity with a Fear-Self unless it possesses an element of our authentic self. The Fear-Selves represent a kind of adaptive life choice that emerges from the confluence of our Life Force and the consequence of our inevitable invalidation, the Wound.

There is still another way of understanding the Fear-Self: as our way of creating a personal story in a dangerous world. Each

Fear-Self is an attempt to project our energy out into the world and to draw energy from the world to us. But because the Fear-Self is a direct child of the Wound, it cannot be authentic or spontaneous. Each Fear-Self is, therefore, a kind of complex calculation our psyches produce to maximize our impact in the world.

As a calculation, the Fear-Self is conceptual. This is a term that will be used with greater frequency in our discussion from this point forward. A concept is a thought. For example, we have a concept for chair, but that concept cannot describe or be any actual chair we might encounter in the world. The thought of a tree is neither a tree nor does it accurately represent any real, living tree. Yet the concept of a chair or tree is necessary, because we need concepts in order to communicate.

In much the same way, a Fear-Self is built on a concept. If our underlying Wound says that we need to be beautiful to be loved and respected, then our countering Fear-Self is built around our concept of beauty. The word "beauty" is a concept. My concept of beauty is likely to be quite different from yours. But beyond our respective concepts of beauty lies the actual world, where things are as they are and not as we conceive them. Notions of beauty and its absence are foreign to the real world. Beauty is only a word, but it is, more importantly, a belief, a value judgment.

As you can start to see, concepts, instead of real life, will begin to dominate us.

Let's take a look at the Expert Fear-Self. The Expert has an idea of what constitutes an expert, then seeks to achieve that conceptual standard. Of course, different individuals' concepts of expertise vary greatly. The Expert Fear-Self will never be expert enough, because the concept of expertise will always just elude his reach; it is easy to continually imagine higher levels of expertise, or, for that matter, beauty, spiritualism, toughness, etc. The fear-based identity is always chasing a concept.

All Fear-Selves are perfectionists. The concept of a thing or quality is perfect, an ideal. No one can ever achieve ideal expertise, ideal beauty, or ideal spiritualism. As mental constructs, they will elude us forever. We can never be good enough. Failing to achieve the ideal of the "well family," we must have a family with problems. In the black and white world of the conceptual, our dreams of achievement must always fall short.

Every Fear-Self has a narrow concept of what it needs to be happy. Happiness, as a concept, is intangible. What is it for you? How many of us have invested our dream of happiness in that next vacation? We imagine ourselves sitting on a beautiful white sand beach. The sparkling waves of a turquoise sea splash not far from our feet. Our beloved is lying beside us. Now *that's* happiness. Or is it? Happiness is a raise. Or is it? Happiness is sex. Or is it? The more we try to define what will make us happy, the more ignorant we are of what true happiness is. Now we are slaves to yet another thought!

Happiness happens and unhappiness happens. Both energies are indifferent to our plans and ideas, but the more open we are to the opportunity for happiness to occur at anytime, the happier we will be. Happiness is there waiting for us to stop blinding ourselves by our own beliefs about what we require to be happy. Start relaxing and happiness will emerge where you would have least expected it. This is freedom from concepts.

Happiness is there waiting for us to stop blinding ourselves by our own beliefs about what we require to be happy. Start relaxing and happiness will emerge where you would have least expected it.

Each Fear-Self is a form of conceptual perfectionism. It is a projected ideal that we can achieve only in fleeting moments. No matter how extraordinary our achievements, the high that comes from external validation is unsustainable. As long as we pursue a concept—any concept—we create the conditions that will land us back in our own apparent inadequacy, insufficiency, and worthlessness. There simply is no escaping failure. The Fear-Self will occasionally succeed in achieving its goals, but the Wound will also succeed in achieving its unquestioned dominance.

This is the dance of the Wound with each of its Fear-Selves. The failure of the Fear-Self assures the continued and far more sustainable "success" of the Wound. Just as the Wound keeps all of our Fear-Selves alive, the Fear-Selves do their part in the bargain and keep the Wound alive and well. It is a perfect feedback loop. We know it hurts and so we seek therapy, self-help, and Nirvana. We can't do it on our own; we need external experts to tell us what to do. Of course, these people are probably living out their own Fear-Selves. They need us to affirm their own insecurities, and we, inadvertently, keep their cycle of Fear-Self and Wound going. Gurus must have followers; therapists need patients.

The power of concepts in how we see ourselves and the world is immense and is one of the primary topics for the remainder of this book. But before we move on, let's examine one of our most core concepts: safety.

Seeking to Know

When we are insecure, we are driven to control. The sense of insecurity is the Wound, and the Fear-Self becomes the designated controller. We control through force based on knowledge that we assume to be true. Both are functions of the Fear-Self. This is the life of distrust. We will seek to control to the same extent that we cannot trust. The Fear-Self settles on a sense of knowing ... something ... anything. At one moment, a man's Fear-Self might know his wife as someone he really loves; at another moment, this same Fear-Self might know his wife as someone he really doesn't love. This extreme change in "knowing" can happen in a moment. Virtually everything we believe we know is only provisional knowing. What we take to be knowing is just a judgment, and our judgments change as situations change.

What we presume to "know" is really the objectification of a desire. We want to know because we want some measure of certainty and control in our lives. Within a universe of apparent insecurity, the Fear-Self gives us security through its belief in what it knows. My father would tell me how much he loved me in between bouts of violence and outright contempt. He needed to believe that he loved me, and I needed him to be a hypocrite and an enemy. Our knowing was a source of profound ignorance and discord.

Of course, a Fear-Self cannot know anything. It only *believes* it knows people, things, feelings and thoughts. An image cannot know anything. Our knowing is, in a word, empty of authentic certainty. It is as changeable as our moods. This is not knowing, it's just the awkward gestures of the Fear-Self as it seeks to assert security in an ever-threatening world.

Exercise 3:　　Seeing Knowing as Desire

For the next hour, try seeing everything you appear to know as a manifestation of needing to control. See this world of provisional knowing as an expression of desire. Processing knowing as desire is much closer to its integral truth. When you see apparent knowing as desire, it is a lot easier to loosen the grip of false-knowing. Apply this principle to everything as it enters your sensory world: things you see/hear/touch/smell, thoughts, and feelings. When an experience takes on a sense of knowing, try seeing it as something you need to know and therefore the expression of a desire.

How does the Fear-Self establish its knowing? The answer to this question is simple; it establishes its knowing by what it believes it knows. This sentence may appear absurd on the surface, but there is a powerful insight embedded within it. Such knowledge is not knowledge. It is belief, and it is subjective.

As long as we attempt to know ourselves or know our children or know anything else, we are merely building another form of belief through the efforts of a Fear-Self. It is a complete waste of time and effort. Try detaching your interest in knowing anything. Authentic knowing happens before we attempt to seek it out. When you completely lose interest in your need to know and control, you will be free.

It cannot be said often enough: A belief in your knowing something is not, necessarily, a bad thing. As human beings communicating with other human beings, we need to have many things understood, and this understanding needs to be held in common. There is an essential role to conventional knowing. Problems arise when our knowing enters the realm of our personal identity and the way we identify others. Usually this is false-knowing.

The greatest acts of apparent evil are done in the name of knowing. The Nazis sought to exterminate world Jewry because they "knew" that Jews were "subhuman." Many people hate gays because they "know" that they are not "normal." The American pioneers massacred tens of thousands of Native Americans because they "knew" them to be "savages" who were clearly not equal to white Christians.

Africans were brought to America to be sold as slaves because they "known" to be inherently inferior. And on and on it goes.

The hatred the Nazis had for the Jews was a direct reflection of Germany's national degradation (invalidation) following World War I. The dehumanization of Native Americans and Africans was essential for European settlers to justify their seizure of land. Notice that what we call "evil" exhibits certainty in its belief system and requires massive and pervasive group invalidation.

The four primary vehicles of false-knowing are patriotism, racism, religion, and sexism. Power expressed through false-knowing is the cause of most interpersonal violence. In far too many cases, otherwise innocent people, often children, are victims of another person's false-knowing.

For the Depressed Fear-Self, knowing takes the form of certainty of one's inherent worthlessness. In this case, the energy of invalidation is extended inward.

Our hatreds are always a consequence of invalidation extended outward. Fear-Selves need to separate themselves from what they believe to be inferior or maladjusted. In this way, we create the world of separation and discord, between religions, straight and gay, white and non-white, rich and poor, etc. This is the garbage of belief. It is not a matter of respecting another's beliefs that delivers us from evil, but seeing the inherent falseness of all our own divisive beliefs.

It is in the realm of our certainty where we often need to raise our most self-searching questions. To all such beliefs, we are mindless slaves. It is time, as Krishnamurti said, to see the false as the false. Great suffering will be avoided the moment we wake up from our beliefs of separation and isolation. Hopefully that time of awakening is not too far off.

Authentic Knowing

There is a knowing that is outside the domain of any Fear-Self. This is the knowing that is immediate and requires no mediation from the mind. This realm of knowing possesses two discrete qualities. First, it is immediate and physical. When we stick a finger onto a very hot surface, we remove it instantly. We do not need to think about our response. It is perfect as it is. This is authentic knowing.

The second quality emerges only when we are free of the grip of our Wound and its Fear-Selves. It is also immediate and unmediated by the mind. It is as spontaneous as the instantaneous withdrawal of our finger from the hot surface. But this form of knowing happens outside our personal, self-centered beliefs. We experience this form of knowing when we see the transcendent smile of a child, or feel the majesty of nature when we suddenly come upon a vista of surpassing beauty. We also experience it when we share agony, as when we see images of war and the desolation and despair that thrives in its wake. This knowing is immediate and authentic.

The second quality emerges only when we are free of the grip of our Wound and its Fear-Selves. We experience this form of knowing when we see the transcendent smile of a child, or feel the majesty of nature when we suddenly come upon a vista of surpassing beauty. We also experience it when we share agony, as when we see images of war and the desolation and despair that thrives in its wake. This knowing is immediate and authentic.

These experiences are not linked to our personal preferences and desires. They are universal. We close ourselves off from these experiences when we are self-engaged and attendant to only our own anxieties. At such times, a Fear-Self is in all but total control of us. We are in the state of full self-enslavement.

When we are fully identified with the beliefs that have evolved as a consequence of our own invalidation, the cost is spiritual death. We pay this hefty cost every day, without the slightest concern for what it does to us and those with whom we live and work.

This applies to every belief that is divisive. I am a Christian/Jew/Buddhist/Muslim; I am straight (which is normal); I am gay; I am male; America is great; America sucks; I am smart; I am artistic; I am ugly/beautiful.... All of these and thousands more thoughts are beliefs, and when we identify with them, we deaden our hearts. They are all forms of knowing that create false-universes. Go back to the last exercise and apply that principle to your most personal beliefs. Try seeing the occurrence of each belief as a fulfillment of a desire. That which underlies the desire is the authentic you—your Life Force.

While all personal knowing is a belief and not a fact, beliefs are often directly linked to apparent facts. We live in a social world, and within this world there are agreements about good/bad, beautiful/ugly, and many other beliefs. If a person is perceived as generally unattractive, that person is vulnerable to accepting the belief of his or her unattractiveness as a fact. If that belief becomes dominant, it will create a force that radiates the belief to everything else in that person's life. We might need to recognize the limitations of the body, but we never need to make these social limitations the primary identity of our lives, unless a depressed Fear-Self wishes to use them to assume the powerful role of perennial victim. Only understanding can set us free. We are called upon to see how beliefs morph into facts and how those facts filter our experience of life and living.

Exercise 4: Getting Past the Conceptual

The mind operates entirely in the conceptual. It does this by transforming sensory data into a concept that it can deal with. In this exercise we will try to be both mindful of that process and resist it. We do this by first seeing how the mind visits the sensed world only for an instant and then conceptualizes it. Connect with your senses and stay there without imposing any external effort. Do not conceptualize the experience. Know that this sensed world of objects, feelings, and thoughts is all that we ever have. It is our life. We flee from it when we conceptualize it. In this way we continue living in the mind instead of in the actual world. We can apply this exercise to even the most painful emotions. When we stop conceptualizing them, in any way, they become beautiful and even fun. The mind will continue doing its thing of trying to conceptualize and categorize everything, but we will ignore that effort and just enjoy the ride for now.

Safety—The Ultimate Truth

This small sub-chapter is perhaps the most important section of this book, because it presents the core quality of the Fear-Self. Please read this part carefully, because it holds the key to self-liberation.

Recall that the process of invalidation occurs on the very cusp of our birth. Outside of families who express unconditional love, provide extraordinary mentorship, and contribute to our own inherent durability as human beings, nearly everything in our very young lives is set up to negate our intrinsic goodness. For each of us, this is an experience of pain and suffering. Its dark echo resounds in our life for the rest of our days.

The trauma of separation begins the great journey of looking for solace in a dangerous world. Our inherent trust in the bounty of life is severed, and we begin a journey that unfolds across a vast plain of insecurity. Most of our important decisions are guided by the desire to find shelter in a storm. Acting through our fears, we are inclined to do the safe thing. This can manifest as pleasing our parents or important others. Our authentic voice is lost in the drive to find security in a world that guarantees that it will never be found. We choose friends and careers that provide us with the impression that they will reduce insecurity in our lives. Because we are inherently insecure and anxiety-ridden, the thought of making an already painful and threatening situation worse is anathema.

We raise our children in much the same way. Don't question authority. Do as you're told. Be a good girl or boy. Always be neat. Always be courteous. Stop imagining. Get out of your own head and listen to your teacher. You can't do what you love; you need to do what makes sense. You need a career. Don't get involved with that guy, he's weird. Safety is conformity. Danger is following your own voice (assuming you can still hear it).

For most of us, our voice was lost a long time ago. This book is a pathway to rediscovering it, but even the whisper of personal authenticity has been lost in the din of social pressures and the trauma of invalidation.

Nearly all Fear-Selves are expressions of safety-seeking. They are assumed to be safe harbors moored in the stormy setting of life. Even somewhat iconoclastic interests, such as Buddhist meditation, are attempts to find a safe place. The crushing irony of safety-seeking is that it is the one place where we are absolutely assured that there will be no clear pathway back to our authentic selves. The move toward safety is always a move adapted to counter the terror invoked by the Wound. It is, therefore, an implicit expression of that self-same Wound. We contribute to the wall that separates the Fear-Self and the Wound by using safety as our primary pivot in decision-making.

That is not to say that we should put ourselves or anyone else in danger by making risky decisions. That is, as we have previously discussed, just another of the Fear-Selves responding to the Wound based on the belief that the world is insufficient. The point is that in response to the crushing experience of mass invalidation, our exhausted selves yearn for a safe place, and the means of securing that safe place is the Fear-Self.

The Wound says, "The world is a dangerous place." The Fear-Self says, "Do what I tell you and you'll be safe." The thought "the world is a dangerous place" is a direct expression of the inadequacy/insufficiency/worthless belief. Any place or situation that could cause me so much pain and suffering can never be safe; I can never allow myself the risk of vulnerability. In exchange for the promise of safety, we have given up our integrity as authentic beings.

Here is another perspective to consider: We tend to think of the Fear-Self as our adult selves. There is some truth in this because our adult selves are reflections of the needs and desires of the Fear-Selves. However, it is also true to say that each Fear-Self is really a childhood version of ourselves. That is why a Fear-Self when it is frustrated will act in ways that are explicitly childlike. The Fear-Self is an emanation from our youth. She is a gatekeeper that monitors our world for danger and opportunities for self-inflation in the form of attention-gathering. This energy is often referred to as the "ego. This child-you is fully invalidated and is taking the first desperate steps to adult selfhood through countering the awfulness of the Wound. When you go to your therapist, you are that child seeking safety. When you sit down to meditate, you are that child seeking a life free of the Wound's pain. When you are the Expert seeking to dominate a group discussion, you are that suffering boy or girl who was ignored as a child. When you are that beautiful person, you are that body your parents and friends deemed worthy of admiration. This is exactly why the term "Fear-Self" has been used in preference to ego. It is an expression of self that is molded by fear.

Exercise 5: Seeing the Fear-Self as You the Child

The next time you feel the pull of a Fear-Self, which should happen anytime between now and two minutes from now, imagine that the speaker in your head is really a 4- to 6-year-old version of yourself speaking precisely the same words to you. Imagine the child-you saying such things as: "I really need to get that new eyeliner," "I need to put that fool in his place," "I need to meditate an extra 10 minutes tonight to show that I'm serious about getting enlightened," "I really enjoy hanging out with this person, but I need time by myself," "I need to say yes to this person, I would hate to have them upset with me," and so on.

This voice in our heads is the Watcher. This is the entity that scans our environment, making sure that everything is okay. It is a nearly silent master Fear-Self. It is the connection that links the Wound to each of the Fear-Selves. The Watcher is the explicit manifestation of the Wound in our lives. It is the entity that ceaselessly evaluates everything that comes into our life. It is both our refuge and our burden. But because it is based on a lie, the validity of its voice is, in nearly all cases, absent. It feels legitimate because there really are dangers in life, and we naturally confuse real dangers with false dangers. But we don't need the Watcher to keep us safe from real dangers. The natural wiring of our bodies will do that for us.

The Wound and its array of Fear-Selves are inauthentic psychological modes of being. A false being needs no protection.

It is, after all, false. You can't protect a mirage. But the more psychological armor we give it, the more entrenched it will be within our self-identity.

On one of my first visits to the Diné Nation (the Navajo Nation), Philmer Bluehouse, a Peacemaker and traditional counsellor, told me this: "There are three levels of reality. First, there is the world as perceived by your senses. It is wholly real and sacred. The second level is your hopes, desires, opinions, and fears. This is your psychological being. It is wholly false, and the source of all of your pain and suffering. The third level is the ceremonial, where all elements of the first level and ourselves are experienced as one." The Watcher is that energy that invokes our hopes, desires, opinions, and fears by ceaselessly keeping on edge in its role of protector in a universe that offers little control and no consistent safety.

Please don't start thinking that you need to get rid of your Watcher. That is, yet again, another Fear-Self in action, seeking safety in an insecure world. All that is asked of us is to see this process exactly as it unfolds. At first, that seer may be the Watcher in disguise. It is a very cunning and crafty energy which can morph into a myriad of shapes and forms. We can see through its mask by sensing the energy of evaluation as it is felt within the moment of its happening. Once we can separate that energy from the immediacy of Now, we can begin experiencing the vibrancy of life just as it is. This can be a powerfully liberating moment for us. We don't try to "let go" of the Watcher; we just try to gently disengage from its gravitational pull.

Remember that every Fear-Safe needs to feel safe and to be in control. It is the purpose of the Watcher to look for anything that threatens our sense of safety and control. It also seeks opportunities where the self-inflationary needs to the Fear-Self can be expressed.

The difference between healthy evaluation and fear-based evaluation can be seen in how it manifests in our life. Healthy evaluation is a relatively modest requirement of our moment-to-moment lives. It requires little energy and has no emotional charge to it. Fear-based evaluation is much more intense. It attracts all of our attention, it is severe, it is inattentive to detail, it is lightning quick, and it is based on primal beliefs.

The Watcher separates us from the natural flow of life. It is a wall we erect for our own protection. It is isolating. The Watcher projects danger where there is none. The Fear-Self may say that there is danger, but it is life, and the Life Force says that you are always safe, because the psychological being you believe yourself to be and which the Watcher assiduously guards is a fiction.

This process must be seen in order to be understood. It is never a matter of mastering your shyness, for example, and then setting out on a life where you assault everyone you encounter! The self that contains the polarity defined by shyness and physical aggression is false. It is not a matter of warring with one's personality, although it might appear that this is exactly what this chapter recommends. It is not. We will explore the issue of personality later in this book. You will always have a personality, and no matter how liberated you become, your personality probably will not change all that much. The only thing that will change will be the locus of your self-identity.

Ultimately, the devastating irony of any Fear-Self is that it promises us release from the Wound, when it is actually a cloaked expression of our belief in it. The Fear-Self is the Wound in a compelling disguise.

Section 2:

The Life of the Fear-Self

11 - The Fear-Self in Time

The Fear-Self is embodied in conceptual time. What does it mean to be embodied in conceptual time? It means that each Fear-Self has a history through which it builds a future. The Fear-Self is a story that unfolds in time. This story is a creation of the mind, a stream of thoughts generated to support the reality of the dominant Fear-Self.

A Brief Digression on the Mind

The mind is an extraordinary mechanism. Its capacity to learn and store information is remarkable. Its power is so pervasive and wondrous that there should be no wonder that we assume it to be our very identity.

The mind learns, and through this learning knows things. It also responds to things that enter its zone of attention. It even responds to things it doesn't know, because one of its most brilliant attributes is its limitless capacity to create patterns and linkages between objects. It is a powerful data organizer, and it uses these data to create a universe of patterns based on its experience and knowledge. It is a thing maker. It creates its universe through the mechanism of thought.

But here's the kicker: No object in the universe is a thought. We may have thoughts about something, but those thoughts can never be the thing itself.

No object in the universe is a thought. We may have thoughts about something, but those thoughts can never be the thing itself.

The mind understands things by responding to them and, sometimes, by thinking about them, in ways that are so fast that the process eludes conscious attention.

But the mind assumes more than it knows. Raise your arm. Do you really know how you did that? Does it really matter how you did it? We can all do it; frankly, no one really knows how it is done. A scientist could describe the process of neurons stimulating muscle tissue and all the rest, but that is only a description that leads to countless other questions. You have the thought, "I will raise my arm," and you do it. But where did the thought "I will raise my arm" come from?

Try picking up a rock (a process that itself remains a mystery) and ask yourself: Outside of the label of "rock," which is just an arbitrary sound, can you say that you know this object in your hand? What, exactly, is this thing I call a rock? Can you truly say you know it? An honest answer can only be "no."

So what *do* we know? What *can* we know? Based on this very brief discussion, it appears that we know very little, and that even what we are most confident that we know is probably a belief masquerading as a truth. Where does that leave us?

Our minds organize life and experience by manipulating concepts about objects. In the truest sense of the word, the mind is wholly conceptual. It thinks it knows things through thoughts, but that's just thinking (ha!). We seem to be left with a potential poem whose title might something like this: "A Rock is Not a Rock is Not a Rock."

The mind is a conjuror of knowledge, but ultimately all things, even rocks, are mysterious. If we cannot truly know a rock, how can we say with any confidence that we know ourselves? What would it be like to rouse ourselves from the deep veil of false knowing?

Now back to the topic of this chapter, the Fear-Self and time.

Just as a story needs to unfold in time, so The Fear-Self must unfold in time. Let's trace the story of the Fear-Self from its beginning.

The Life Force thrives outside of our notions about time. To thrive outside of time means that it has no observable beginning or end. It just *is*, in the joy, boredom, or sadness of itself. It does not need to have a concept of time because it does not need anything *per se* to give it a story. But once we identify with the Wound, our life as a story unfolding in time begins.

The Diné (Navajo) believe that a human being's life begins when the baby first laughs. That occasion, aptly called "Baby's First Laugh," is the celebration of a person's birth as a human being. From the Diné perspective, it is the capacity to laugh that most distinguishes human beings from the other animals of the world.

The Diné (Navajo) believe that a human being's life begins when the baby first laughs. That occasion, aptly called "Baby's First Laugh," is the celebration of a person's birth as a human being. From the Diné perspective, it is the capacity to laugh that most distinguishes human beings from the other animals of the world.

We are not Diné. We are modern Americans, a people fraught with stress and full of needs of all kinds. Our true birth begins when we first identify with our self-contempt contained in the non-verbalized Wound.

With laughter, the Diné baby enters the clan and tribe. With our identification with the Wound, we enter our lives as individuals enmeshed within our aloneness and isolation. The starkly different gateways posited by the Diné and modern American cultures reflect the key differences we have drawn between the hunter/gatherer and civilized approaches to human life. The Diné emphasize the power of connection, while Americans emphasize the primacy of the isolated individual pitted against an often hostile world. One is oriented toward balance and support, the other to need and achievement. The seeming failure of the American Indians to adapt to the modern way of life reflects this world-view schism. (The dominant culture has demanded that they abandon their focus on group and connection and embark on the path of the individual, where group affiliation and connection are quaint, if irrelevant, cultural norms.)

Once our identification is firmly seated in the darkness and fear of the Wound, our life of struggle begins. The first task of our fragile and vulnerable selves is to counter the oppressive weight of the Wound; thus begins our first fitful attempts to become a person who is adequate and worthy. Our story may begin with how we sought to earn the love of our parents. If that ploy pays off, it may become the primary story of our lives. We can then move past the need to please our parents and move on to striving to please peers, lovers, spouses, bosses, and perhaps even our own children. Seeking to prove our lovability can become who we are in this life. If our attempt to please our parents meets with something less than clear success, we may struggle with this losing battle for a lifetime—or , perhaps, we may chose to reject *them* as unworthy of our love, and seek to create selves capable of earning our own satisfaction and/or the approval of others.... And on and on it goes.

Over a surprisingly short amount of time, the story of the fledgling Fear-Self becomes our own story. It is the epic of who we believe ourselves to be. However, our own stories are often not of our devising. In many cases, our stories are those projected onto us by significant others. Our stories become appendages to their own stories.

My father was a furniture salesman. At one time he probably wanted to be a professional athlete of some kind. As a young person who enjoyed playing baseball, I demonstrated modest talents which stimulated my father's lost dream of himself. He saw in me the potential to become a pro baseball player. If you could see me now, you would have some idea of how funny and ridiculous that was, but he went to the considerable trouble of hiring a baseball talent scout to observe me play. After some time, they had a very serious meeting behind closed doors about me and how I played baseball. I listened behind the door with great fear and anxiety; my father was a very strong man who often expressed himself in physical and scary ways, and the meeting worried me greatly. Their discussion ended with the burly, blond scout leaving our house in a bit of a hurry. My father called me in, and I could tell by the tone of his voice that he was angry. I opened the door with trepidation and walked uncertainly into our wood-paneled den. My father asked me if I could guess what the scout said. I can't remember my reply, but I do remember my father saying, with his voice rising rapidly in growing fury and disgust, that while I did possess some talent for the game, I didn't have enough desire to win—I really didn't have what it takes to be a winner. My father's rage and disappointment could be contained no longer, and he punished me severely for my "attitude problem."

I failed my father's dream of himself and thereby enabled him to experience the pain and confusion of his own Wound while I took the heat for it. This is a scenario that is played out in countless homes. For me, the thought of living one of my father's dreams filled me with horror, if not repulsion, but many young people do seek to complete their parents' dreams, if only to earn their love and respect. It's a plan that cannot work. No matter how much payoff we receive, we have dishonored our own authentic selves, and the consequence is always self-desolation. It's a favored theme of many novels and movies because it is something to which most of us can intimately relate.

The Fear-Self can be seen not only as something that unfolds within time in the form of a personal story, but it can also pass from one person to another. It is not uncommon that when a parent, particularly a father, has a highly remunerative or prestigious job, the children are pressured to follow in his footsteps. Although this is not always an example of Fear-Selves passing through the generations, it can be.

Powerful teachers, like Eckhart Tolle, tell us of the power of living fully in the "now." We are led to see that now is all that exists. This insight is obvious to the mind, but it is invariably over looked. The reason we cannot live in the now is because a Fear-Self can only live in the conceptual past or future. Its happiness hinges on good things that will happen some time in the foreseeable future.

This is why the only meaning "now" has for a Fear-Self is, "What's in it for me?" The Fear-Self's primary focus is the hope that things break in its favor. If its hopes and goals are not achieved, the Fear-Self experiences insecurity and depression. In other words, it returns to its Wound of inadequacy, worthlessness, and insufficiency. Its elusive fulfillment must always occur in the future; thus it can never be fulfilled.

Because the Fear-Self cannot live in the now, it focuses on the time and experience that follows now. It needs always to be moving on to the next thing. The mind races ahead of the now, seeking fulfillment in the next moment. On the micro level, this is the way all Fear-Selves operate. The mind keeps the story of the Fear-Self moving forward by giving its attention to whatever is next. Not only can it not live in the now, it is, in effect, ceaselessly fleeing the now. This is exactly why "trying" to live in the now is impossible. The mind will work tirelessly to tug us away from the now and get us moving on to the next "important" thing. Its central need ceaselessly dangles itself in the future, just out of reach.

How we relentlessly focus our needs in some future time is a subtle process and may take some very alert observation to notice. Our movement away from the living now is deeply habituated. To get into the now—and whatever unfolds afterward—Is not a matter of effort. What it does require is to see the Fear-Self in action through its ceaseless movement away from anything that fails to meet its needs and hopes. It is in that self-centered dynamic form that the Fear-Self finds life. Remember, it is tirelessly seeking completion that can only occur in the future. It is always moving forward. It finds the now boring, already used up. There is nothing in the now to know, to accumulate, to use, to impress, to achieve. To the Fear-Self, the now and the vibrant immediacy of life unfolding is already history.

If the Fear-Self exists only within a time that is aligned to its needs, this time can only exist in an imaginary future. The Fear-Self can be clearly seen as a wholly imaginary construct. It is, literally, full of sound and fury, signifying nothing that is real. The life of the Fear-Self is a belief. It is what we believe ourselves to be. Ultimately, it is only a thought, just like everything else created in the mind.

The constructs of the mind are beliefs. Recall: If we can't truly know a rock, how are we to know ourselves?

Living the life of the Fear-Self, we are cut off from the immediacy of life. It is a flight from life itself.

In the psychological life of our imagined selves, we are constantly referencing the next moment. We need to plan our days and the practical elements of our life.

If we are ever to live in the now, we must be able to sever our identification with our primary Fear-Selves. This is not a matter of releasing our goals, but of seeing them in light of our understanding of this process in its entirety. Using effort to pull ourselves into the now, for example, is the goal of a Fear-Self who believes that living in the now will fulfill a Fear-Self need. We must release the self-contempt that keeps the game of the Fear-Self in place. This is the meaning of Liberation.

Recall that every Fear-Self projects completion at some future time when we will have achieved what the Fear-Self believes it needs to achieve. Completion and lasting contentment always reside just past that next bend in the road. We will finally find ourselves in that terrific new job, that new house, that new relationship, that Buddhist retreat, that next book, that new marathon milestone, that facelift. Has that ever worked for you? The only way out is to leave by the same way you entered; it means to go back to the root of your being and see through the thick veil of the Wound and all of the Fear-Selves it has spawned. When you do that, a whole new you will be born.

Completion and lasting contentment always reside just past that next bend in the road. We will finally find ourselves in that terrific new job, that new house, that new relationship, that Buddhist retreat, that next book, that new marathon milestone, that facelift. Has that ever worked for you? The only way out is to leave by the same way you entered; it means to go back to the root of your being and see through the thick veil of the Wound and all of the Fear-Selves it has spawned.

What is Meant by Living in the Now?

Liberation takes a different position from other books that focus on the "power of now." It simply is not possible for the wounded self to live in the now. As it is perceived, the now has already happened. It is, in effect, dead. The Fear-Self has already decided that it is of no use and will resist the now by moving forward from it. It is addicted to its needs, hopes, and projections. The now cannot satisfy these. Even in the best of circumstances, when the Fear-Self is in its full glory of achievement, in a short time the excitement will have passed and it will inexorably be moving on to the next high.

In Liberation, the now is the energy of life as it surges forward. Where the Fear-Self asks "what's in it for me," the liberated perspective is just to be open to life, however it presents itself. It is even open to the ego's self-centered proclivities. It is open to whatever happens and sees how the next moment unfolds, essentially without any need for engagement with an ego (even as the ego is observed). Life pushes and forces us into the next moment. This is the vigor of life. To deny this energy is to deny life. We are liberated to experience the whole range of life, whether it be a sexual orgasm, doing the laundry, or the moment of our death.

Where the Fear-Self sees itself as an isolated being in a largely indifferent and hostile world, the liberated self enjoys being aligned with the unfolding of the world. There is even joy when we are clearly not aligned with the unfolding of the world. This is what is meant by now in Liberation from the Lie.

Exercise 6: Living Life as It Truly Is

This is an exercise you can do for the rest of your life. It possesses the key to living life free of the Fear-Self and the Wound.

Center your awareness lightly on what is happening now, and then observe how the next moment arises. Continue doing this until you have a very clear idea of how actual life unfolds.

You should notice that life, contrary to all of our planning, contrary to all of our insecurities, contrary to all of the imperious dreams of the Fear-Self, happens with total indifference to all of our conceptual thinking! This is life free of any conceptual thought. This is living life without fighting it.

Because we are so closely identified with our thoughts, we really don't notice how life unfolds in the now and the next moment. Notice, with as much clarity as you can muster, just how different actual life is from what you think it is. You should also notice that life contains your thinking process, but your thinking process often has very little to do with actual life.

This is it! This is life.

Exercise 7:   Relaxing into the Now and Seeing Through Thought

It is now time to stop believing in the incessant, needy ranting of the Fear-Self. To stop believing in the Fear-Self, you also need to stop believing in the Wound that gives it life. That means you stop believing in your innate inadequacy, insufficiency, and worthlessness. To stop believing in the Wound means you allow your Life Force to shine. You begin relaxing into the ever-present now and see the beauty of presence begin to glimmer through the haze of Wound-based feeling. Thought will want to co-opt the experience of the now; don't try to silence that thought. Just see it and stop buying into its story. Do this time and again, and before you know it, the cacophony of endless thinking will begin to grow quiet, and the full radiance of our Life Force will have been rediscovered.

Timing and the Fear-Self

Each Fear-Self has its own distinct speed. Some Fear-Selves need to be quick. These types will be easily irritated by the slowness of others. This Fear-Self is more common in large cities. This insight opens up yet another element of Fear-Selves—that they have geographic qualities. Areas that require faster and more agile forms of thinking, such as New York City, will produce more Fear-Self people with those qualities. They will also draw such people to them. Other types of Fear-Selves need to be slower and appear more at peace with themselves. This type of Fear-Self will be uncomfortable with the fast types and will criticize them as people who can't sit still, who always need to be on the go even if it appears that they aren't getting anywhere. Fear-Selves need to feel superior to alternative types of Fear-Selves, and this superiority is often experienced in the dimension of time. Spiritual types will often appear slow because slow is a quality that Fear-Selves associate with spirituality. A temporal dimension, however, does not reference the Life Force.

We can notice the speed of our own Fear-Selves by observing how compulsive our actions are in the field of time. This is not to suggest that those who are quick ought to be slow, or that those who are slow need to do things faster. The point here is to see the compulsive quality of our orientation toward acting within time. Most Fear-Selves are quick because of the compulsive nature of their achievement need. The exception to this category is the depressed Fear-Self, which is often sluggish or unwilling to move at all.

The speed of the authentic self is appropriate to the requirements of life as it presents itself. The Life Force is fluid. If the presenting flow of life calls on us to move quickly, the authentic self moves speedily without effort. However, for the most part, the call of life would appear to be slow compared to the average pace of modern life. The call for speed is exceptional. Ultimately, the Life Force has no inherent association with time. Its deepest expression is stillness, which we experience when life takes us unaware and we enter a timeless dimension.

With this knowledge, we can now compare our own inner clock with the apparent nature of the now. The inability to flow with the now is a sure sign of a Fear-Self in pressured action. Remember that, for the most part, thought finds the now not only extraordinarily elusive, but also downright boring.

By rejecting the now, the Fear-Self rejects life.

The only value the Fear-Self gives to thought is its use as a stepping stone to the next exciting thing. Only those elements of life that serve its explicit needs are valued. The massive assault on the environment where animals, plants, and whole habitats are crushed before the onslaught of "progress" is a visual representation of this process in the physical world. Most environments, animals, and plants are not useful to the needs of people. In fact, they are usually obstacles to those needs. They are therefore destroyed in service of the dominant agenda of human beings. As each person has his or her own distinct Fear-Selves, the industrialized world has its own dominant Fear-Self. It too seeks achievement to cover its own implicit self-contempt on a mass scale. Just as we strangle the life of our Life Force, such actions strangle the life of the planet itself.

The Fear-Self is a sub-belief of the Wound. When we are living within the polarity of those beliefs, we are living within the land of thought. We believe this is reality, but it is not. It is reality projected by a very well-entrenched belief system. It feels true because it is so close to us and so deeply habituated. Earlier in this book, we compared investing our identity in falsehood with the deception that can result from information processed by our visual sense. The Earth appears flat, but it is anything but flat. It appears that the sun and the stars revolve around the Earth, when the exact opposite is true. So it is with our Wound and our Fear-Selves. They look and feel real, but they are, ultimately, false.

If the Fear-Self is false, does that also mean that our notion of how time ought to flow is also false? Knowing that the next moment never arrives, is it not also equally valid to say that the previous moment never happened? As we can project a future, we can also project a past—but is a projection real? By definition it is not. The past, even the very last moment, is itself a projection recollected through our subjective memory. Its existence is an essential part of the story of the Fear-Self. From the perspective of a Fear-Self, that is the "use" of the past. After all, the way you experienced the last moment is entirely different from how anyone else experienced that same moment. It appears to have existed, but in truth, the moment itself is subjective and self-referencing.

Exercise 8:   Exercise: Imagining the Last Moment

Try playing around with this idea. Even though it probably contradicts your most fundamental beliefs about the world, pretend that the last moment is as unreal as the next moment. Then ask yourself how that changes your experience.

This exercise should feel like a kind of rebirth. You are living entirely in the now. Does it feel strange? Does it feel a little unsafe? Do you feel that you are less guarded? Do you feel more alive? Can you feel more alertness in your body?

For me, when I first did this exercise, I felt buoyed by a force that felt like life itself. Dropping the illusion of the persisting reality of the past moment made me feel instantly more alive. Suddenly the now felt filled with life and potential. The life force seemed to pulse powerfully into the now.

Now try this variant of the exercise: Imagine that the past moment also does not exist for anything in the fields of your senses. Looking out of my window where I'm writing this book, I can see one dominant tree, a group of smaller trees, and a brick house somewhat further away. Seeing these objects as if they themselves don't possess a past moment gives them an aliveness I could not sense before. How we respond to exercises like these is individual, but for me this is a powerful approach to reinvigorating relationships that have grown tired as they play out in the projection of thought and the self-centeredness of the Fear-Self. When we "remove" the last moment from a sensed object, its vitality in the now becomes greatly elevated. It might take some time, but if you don't get this feeling from this exercise, consider coming back to it after you've finished Liberation. It should work for you then.

The Fear-Self pines for a future that never arrives. On the other side of the time polarity, it is weighed down by its belief in the last moment. Feeling the weight of the past like an anchor dragged across a sea bottom, it needs the eternal promise of the next moment and the vast future that extends beyond it to pull itself out of the muck of the past. This is how it moves through time. We live for hoped-for excitement, while the weight of the past keeps dragging us down.

Consider this: If the past is only a projection of the Fear-Self, does that not also mean that the Wound is also, in its entirety, untrue and unreal? If you can see the truth of that statement, you are wholly liberated from the accumulated weight of the past. There is no past, and there is no Wound. We are utterly free in the now, the only place where the whole of the universe unfolds in its vastness.

The Life Force does not experience the weight or promise of the Fear-Self. It is alive and radiant in the now, fully indifferent to our personal stories. The Life Force lives outside of time.

The energies of the Wound and our dominant Fear-Selves probably never disappear entirely. Moreover, their total disappearance may not be a good thing. We will explore this issue throughout much of the rest of this book, but suffice it to say that our goal has never been to be in conflict with these energies. Our goal has always been to understand them. The concept of having goals is one primarily embraced by our Fear-Selves. They thrive in an environment where this understanding is absent. Ultimately, we shall see that our journey does not take us to the place where the Wound and its Fear-Selves are necessarily vanquished, but to a place where they are transformed. As they are transformed, so are we.

Exercise 9: Fighting With Time

The mind, nearly always, is in the process of wanting time to move faster. It is saying, "Enough with now, let's get on to the next thing." This is conflict. Our whole sense of self is embodied within this conflict. When we are in conflict with time, we live in the superficial level of the mind. Watch how the mind fights with time; then, as you see this process in your own life, release it and see what happens. Feel the depth of life when you stop fighting with time.

That which fights time is the conditioned, superficial self. It is precisely the part of us that is unavailable to liberation. It is precisely the part of us that is habitual, known, monotonous, and predictable. But there is another part of us that is aligned with time, that is entirely new, unpredictable, liberated. For some of us, the whole secret to liberation can be found within this exercise.

Liberation is life. Separation is the self.

12 - Three Fear-Selves Up Close

In this chapter we will more closely examine three different types of Fear-Selves: the Achiever, the Body Person, and the Depressed One. The purpose is not to imply that achievement, focus on the body, or depression are, in any way, wrong. There is achievement that is compulsive and fear-induced, and there is achievement that reflects one's authentic passion, for example. What separates the motivations and actions of a Fear-Self from those that are authentic is their root source: the insufficiency, inadequacy, and unworthiness of the Wound. Sometimes it can be difficult to experience that difference. One of the key purposes of this chapter is to make that distinction clear.

The Achiever

All Fear-Selves are out to prove something, and in no Fear-Self is that need more apparent than in the Achiever. The Achiever's actions seek to demonstrate his adequacy to himself and the world. Unlike the person who achieves as an outgrowth of his authentic passion, the Fear-Self Achiever's primary motivation is to prove to himself and others that he is special. The passionate achiever does what he does for the joy of the doing. He is not motivated by the need to impress himself or others.

The great American composer Charles Ives wrote music throughout his late youth and middle adulthood which powerfully challenged the traditional and conventional notions of serious musical composition in the early 20th century. His music was ignored by not only the public but by other musicians throughout his life. Imagine a man writing some of the most complex and magnificent music ever composed in the United States, yet never having even one of his works performed. He could hear them only in his head or if he himself played them on the piano. Recognition of his genius occurred only very late in Ives' life when Leonard Bernstein and the New York Philharmonic performed his Second Symphony in 1952. The rather crusty Ives declined Bernstein's personal invitation to attend the premiere, but it is said that he listened, in secret, to its broadcast on a radio.

The French artist Georges-Pierre Seurat is acclaimed as one of the greatest of Impressionist artists. His masterpiece, "Sunday Afternoon on the Island of Le Grande Jatte," is one of the crowning jewels in the Art Institute of Chicago's outstanding collection. Not only was Seurat rejected by the most esteemed art authorities of his era, the Paris Salon, but he was unable to sell a single work his entire life. His love of painting transcended his need for recognition. He painted out of love and clearly had no need to impress anyone. While it must have been very painful for Seurat not to receive monetary or popular recognition for his creations, he nevertheless followed his authentic passion and vision.

The contemporary German-Czech writer Franz Kafka is today considered one of the towering figures of 20th-century literature. His depiction of nightmarish modern bureaucracy and the alienation of the individual has had a profound impact on not only the arts, but also on how we perceive and experience modern life. Yet during his life he published only a very small number of writings in very modest venues. For all intents and purposes, his writing was entirely ignored by the established literary world even at a time when such avant-garde composition was rather commonplace in the European literary scene. He wrote for the love of writing and his own passion for understanding human relations within the family and society. Kafka was also keenly aware of the toxic repercussions of invalidation and was motivated to write as a direct consequence of his own wounding. His writing was a passionate response to his recognition of this immense challenge to our lives.

Because the Achiever's primary goal is Fear-Self inflation, he will choose a path where such inflation is likely. Ives, Seurat, and Kafka were not concerned with public accolade. Each loved their art first. Issues of public recognition appear to have been, while not irrelevant, secondary for them.

Because the Achiever's primary goal is Fear-Self inflation, he will choose a path where such inflation is likely. Ives, Seurat, and Kafka were not concerned with public accolade. Each loved their art first. Issues of public recognition appear to have been, while not irrelevant, secondary for them.

Earlier in this book, we broached the idea that the Life Force and the Fear-Selves have elements in common. A doctor who has chosen the field of medicine primarily for its financial rewards has a motivation that is, primarily, fear-induced. However, that same person may also have a strong interest in science and healing. This is what makes the distinction between motivation by fear and motivation by love sometimes difficult to discern. Often there are elements of both, particularly with the Achiever type.

Both the Fear-Self and authentic passion possess elements of need. At face, both appear compulsive, a quality which we have, thus far, associated exclusively with the actions of a Fear-Self. It is suggested that the fundamental difference between authentic passion and a Fear-Self is that in the former, actions are taken for their own sake, while in the latter, they are taken for external reasons—namely, to dispel fears of inadequacy or worthlessness. The creative actions of our authentic passion may call for struggle and hard work, but these we gladly do for the love and joy they bring. In the case of the Fear-Self, there is little joy or love. There is compulsive action to prove one's worthiness.

The Body Person

The Body Person demonstrates his worth and potency through the appearance and vitality of the body. The expression of power through physical strength is a quality that is found more often in men, while women tend to gain power by using their appearance to control or influence people. While the Achiever can hope to die with his achievements as lasting examples of his worthiness, the Body Person is all but guaranteed to die with his body old, worn down, and hardly beautiful in a way that is conventionally defined by society. The Body Person is a tragic type, if only because failure is unavoidably built into the very vehicle he has chosen to manifest his achievement.

Of course, the Body Person knows this and thus resists the onslaught of time. He adapts by adjusting his basis for comparison to people close to his own age, or he lives within an illusion of youth to which he must desperately cling. Clinging to illusions is what Fear-Selves do, which makes the Body Person a good example of this flaw which is an intrinsic part of the Fear-Self.

Without beauty or strength, the Body Person must revert to his own Wound. In this condition he is without power. He has become as vulnerable as a child, and this is the one place he needs to avoid at all costs. His body is his shield against experiencing the Wound.

Unlike many Achievers, whose accomplishments can be known only by a select group of people (those who know the Achiever personally), the accomplishments of the Body Person are, essentially, public. Their success is therefore open for all to review, particularly those who place value on appearance. They must endure the glare of external evaluation and live within its universe of insecurity. As age takes its inevitable toll, the Body Person must either collapse into an alternative Fear-Self, redouble his efforts to stay "youthful," or just surrender to the ravages of age.

At the same time, however, aging presents the Body Person with a golden opportunity. Many Fear-Selves live their whole lives without ever having the incentive to rediscover their original Life Force, but thanks to the inexorable demise of the body, the Body Person is inevitably confronted with reality—just look in the mirror! This opens up the potential for making a breakthrough in his resistance to his underlying Wound. Yet few choose to come face to face with their Wound. Most Body People continue the struggle simply by adjusting their standards of comparison. They might at some point find the capacity to laugh at their vain pursuit, but without understanding, that is unlikely.

Most modern people live sedentary lives sitting behind desks and peering into the glow of a computer (I am no exception). Even most Body People live sedentary lives, which is why they need to spend so much time at a gym, or under a surgeon's knife. In contrast, hunting-gathering people lived lives that were physical. As nomads they hunted for much of their food and carried their homes on their backs. Yet, if we compare the body of a hunter-gatherer with a modern Body Person in his prime, they are very different. The hunter-gatherer is not overtly muscular and even a little flabby in the mid-section (particularly those in their 40s and older); the Body Person is massively muscled. There is, ideally, not a sign of fat on him.

The hunter-gatherer is naturally fit and ready for intense action. The Body Person is unnatural, the product of exercise irrelevant to the high-energy physical activity a human being would expect if living in the wild and enhanced by pharmaceuticals and other artificial supplements. He dreams to be like an ancient Greek statue, frozen in time and perfect.

The voice of the Fear-Self tells to run just a little harder, exert just a little more pressure, and we'll get to the Promised Land. The Wound drives the self towards the carrot, and we can never entirely rest. There is always that next hurdle, that next challenge. This is the life of dis-ease.

Because all Fear-Selves crave and promise completion, their benchmark is perfection. The flip side of perfection is insecurity. The Fear-Self must always maximize the distance between it and its underlying Wound, while ceaselessly striving to be more. The "completion" carrot dangles before us, just beyond our reach. The voice of the Fear-Self tells to run just a little harder, exert just a little more pressure, and we'll get to the Promised Land. The Wound drives the self towards the carrot, and we can never entirely rest. There is always that next hurdle, that next challenge. This is the life of dis-ease.

The Body Person appears to struggle against an implacable foe—time itself. But that statement is not entirely correct, because only the Fear-Self lives within the domain of time. The real foe of the Body Person is his own body!

Just as there are Achievers whose motivations and accomplishments grow out of authentic passion, there are individuals whose lives revolve around their bodies purely out of sheer love of physicality. The stories of men and women who lived their joy through their physical bodies and with other bodies are innumerable. Love of sport and joy in competition are expressions of our authentic being. The key difference between the fear-based Body Person and those who lives a physical life based on passion is that the latter care very little about winning or losing; love of the game is what matters. The sensuality of movement, of muscles, of the body is expressed eloquently by Walt Whitman in his extraordinary <u>Leaves of Grass</u>.

Those who love movement often take to the hills, streams, and mountains to commune with nature. Such journeys require not only endurance and strength, but agility and specialized training. The mountain climber who boasts of "conquering" a high peak in the Andes or Himalayas is another Body Person emphasizing achievement, while the person who just loves the climb, the mystery, the touch of the extreme elements is liberated of the need to prove anything—although that can be fun, too!

The Depressed One

While it is true to say that all Fear-Selves are victims, since they are a response to their primal invalidation, the Depressed Fear-Self is the only one that claims the victim role as its primary identity. Other Fear-Selves will claim victim status when the core need of the Fear-Self is not realized. But in contrast to the Depressed One, other Fear-Selves mostly direct their attention to forms of accomplishment that promote opportunities for personal inflation.

The Depressed One, among all Fear-Selves, lives closest to the underlying Wound. They will neither deny nor embrace their self-contempt. Instead, they experience self-contempt as an inescapable prison. The underlying theme of depression is quiet anger at both one's self and one's narrowly defined world. Attempts to escape this world are likely to fail, because the Depressed One's dominant identity is entirely contained within its depressed Fear-Self.

The porosity of the Depressed One's Fear-Self—its proximity to the pain of the underlying Wound—can be seen as both a blessing and a curse. It is our distance from the Wound that keeps it vigorous, which is why the more we identify with a Fear-Self, the more hidden the Wound will be. Unlike types such as the Achiever or the Body Person, the Depressed One lives in the dark shadow of her own invalidation experience. In that zone, she is in pain. The compulsive "doing" that characterizes most Fear-Selves is all but absent in the Depressed One, who is often more comfortable not doing anything. This identity is a potential blessing because the Depressed One is in a better position to come to terms with her Wound.

The Depressed One, however, is unlikely to move toward sustainable well-being as she sheds her depressed Fear-Self skin. Instead, she is apt to move in the direction of developing a new, more positive Fear-Self. The purpose of therapy, meditation, and self-help is to develop better coping strategies. So morphing into a more positive Fear-Self becomes the primary function of the Depressed One. But this is unlikely to deliver sustainable well-being, since the deeper source of insecurity and fear—the Wound—is rarely confronted.

This is unfortunate in the case of the Depressed One because, in theory, her identity lies closer to its source of liberation. Later in this book, we will see that the most cathartic approach to severing one's identity with a Fear-Self is through one's grief portal. The Depressed One has a built-in advantage over other Fear-Selves since her identity lies closer to the source of the authentic self and its Life Force. But, sadly, the pain and suffering of the Depressed One acts more often as a catalyst to move away from the Wound by sheltering itself in unchallenging talk therapy or psychotropic medication.

Ironically, even the Depressed One seeks inflation. She does this through actions designed to attract attention to her victim identity. She uses her sadness as a way to proclaim specialness; she views her sadness as unique compared with the sadness of others. She desperately craves attention, risking even negative attention. The admonishment of others to just leave her alone in her misery is a potent form of attention-getting.

Many depressed types are attracted to solitary pursuits, including the arts and sciences. Success in these endeavors can provide the Depressed One with a transition into an Achiever or Expert Fear-Self type. Yet even when success is achieved, attachment to the underlying depressed Fear-Self tends to maintain its dominance. When other Fear-Selves collapse into depression when they fail in their Fear-Self needs, this is experienced as a temporary holding zone. The fallback for the Depressed One represents a return to the dominant and primary state. Relapse is therefore somewhat less catastrophic for them since it is perceived as normative.

The Depressed One's creative life can represent true passion. Some of the greatest achievements in the arts and sciences have been created by people who were otherwise depressed and introverted. Because the Depressed One lives closest to his Wound, this also means that he lives closest to his Life Force.

The Depressed One's creative life can represent true passion. Some of the greatest achievements in the arts and sciences have been created by people who were otherwise depressed and introverted. Because the Depressed One lives closest to his Wound, this also means that he lives closest to his Life Force.

At the same time, we cannot deny that in some circumstances, sadness and even depression can be authentic responses to negative life experiences. Depression is often unjustly criticized. In a society where only the "bright" side of the personality coin is perceived as normative, the experience of melancholy and depression can, and often is, itself a form of invalidation. However, some of the greatest artistic achievements have come from people who were able to ignore society's view of "normal." The sad emotions perhaps reveal more about the contemporary human condition than others, and the painters, composers, artists, and poets who have found a home in these darker places have paradoxically produced some of the most life-affirming art in whole catalogue of passionate achievement.

Sadness is, more importantly, a part of life. Seeking to transcend tragic moments in our lives is a pure expression of Fear-Self. This pathetic version posits a superego belief that "I should not be affected by human events." There are stories from the Zen tradition where students watch as the Master weeps at the funeral of a young person. When they challenge him, he responds with some surprise, saying simply, "I am sad for this person. My hearts breaks for him." This is just life as it is, and living life as it is, whether happy, bored, confused, or sad, is all part of the authentic life of the liberated person.

Summary

Taking the long view, we can see how Fear-Selves are well-adapted to modern civilization. While the hunter-gatherer is wired to get along with his group and within his environment, modern life demands continual production, and the Fear-Self spurs people to achieve. Considerations of balance, quality of life, and living in harmony with plants and animals are all secondary to the need to produce.

The life of the Fear-Self is, fundamentally, life out of balance. It is always restless, never content. Because it can never find contentment within itself, every Fear-Self looks outwards for the magic ring, that one and only thing that will bring it completion. Since the magic ring is only an illusion, this dream keeps us endlessly racing on our treadmill of achievement, including the unreachable goal of self-improvement. The self needs no improvement. It needs only the understanding that will enable it to see through the veil of the Fear-Selves and their interplay with the Wound. The <u>Tao Te Ching</u> (Chapter 24) says this perfectly:

> *On his tiptoes a man is not steady*
> *Taking long strides he cannot keep pace*
>
> *To the self-serving, nothing shines forth*
> *To the self-promoting, nothing is distinguished*
> *To the self-appointing, nothing bears fruit*
> *To the self-righteous, nothing endures.*
>
> *From the viewpoint of Tao, this self-indulgence*
> *is like rotting food and painful growths on*
> *the body—*
> *Things that all creatures despise*
> *So why hold onto them?*
> *When walking the path of Tao*
> *this is the very stuff*
> *that must be uprooted, thrown out,*
> *and left behind.*

13 -The Fear-Self in Relationships

Thus far we have talked about the Fear-Self as an individual unattached to other people and outside of relationship. In this chapter we move beyond the individual and explore the actions of the Wound and Fear-Self in relationships. Not only does the theory of the Wound and its Fear-Selves explain much about our individual lives, but it also makes an important contribution to our understanding of ourselves in relationships.

First, let's recap a little. The enduring power of a Fear-Self is the sense of security it promises us. We believe the Fear-Self is our channel to proving our worth and adequacy. The Fear-Self is designed to increase the distance between the Wound and our presumed sense of self. We have seen that the Fear-Self inevitably fails in this endeavor. Its actions will do just the opposite—it will, over time, bring us in direct contact with the Wound.

Nevertheless, we persist on viewing the Fear-Self as our best and only hope. A "good day" is when we are engaged in activities that fulfill the needs of the Fear-Self. The Imitator gets lots of advice, the Expert has a platform from which he is able to hold court, the Body Person has a great workout, the Tough Guy has opportunities to enforce his authority, the Spiritualist has a peaceful meditation. A "bad day" occurs when a Fear-Self is blocked. Such experiences are painful because they open up small holes in our otherwise confident Fear-Selves, and we experience our Wound. A person who is easily frustrated has a relatively weak Fear-Self that collapses easily into its Wound through minor irritations.

Just as we would like all of our days to be "good days," we would like all of our relationships to be "good" relationships. Relationships are viewed as "good" when they protect us from our Wound. They become "great" when they help us achieve the needs of a Fear-Self.

The world is a place of ceaseless change, but Fear-Selves see the world as static. The Fear-Self experiences its world as a set of objects whose value is established by its capacity to inflate the Fear-Self. See if this is not true in your own experience.

We end up judging our world in stark, black-and-white terms. This person is "good," and that person is "bad." The mind of the senses and of the body is fabulously complex, but the mind of judgment seems, in comparison, remarkably simple and naive. We could say that it's simple-minded.

Governed by a Fear-Self, we seek out people who appreciate not our true selves, but the selves we need to be. We search for another Fear-Self to complement us. The Achiever is happiest with a companion who is impressed by her achievements and vision. A Body Person wants his companion to find enjoyment in his fitness and beauty. This type of love and attachment celebrates their mutual Fear-Selves, and they may indeed live happily ever after.

Governed by a Fear-Self, we seek out people who appreciate not our true selves, but the selves we need to be. We search for another Fear-Self to complement us.

Our affections go to those who validate our Fear-Selves. Without this element, few relationships could get off the ground. The relationship is made even stronger when our Fear-Self validator increases our ability to avoid contact with our Wound. When we assert that our companion is in our corner, it means that she keeps us safe from our fears of inadequacy and worthlessness.

One of the most direct paths to experiencing our Wound is to be outside of an intimate relationship. When we are lonely, we come face to face with our Wound. Alone we are unprotected and vulnerable. When we are alone we are, in effect, replicating the conditions of our very distant childhood at the time of our decisive invalidation. Being completely alone, without seeking safety through distraction, is one of the most powerful ways of getting in touch with our Wound and that is why it is the condition we most fiercely guard against happening in our lives. Fear of aloneness is the driving force in motivating us to find a relationship with another. Alone we are in touch with our pathos. We will do almost anything to avoid that.

Precisely in this way, our relationships keep us locked in our Fear-Self identities.

Two people who share the same Fear-Self type are likely to have difficulty establishing or maintaining a successful relationship. For example, two Experts may devolve into a competition of who knows the most. The loser of that competition will, of course, face his greatest fear—his failure as an Expert, his own innate inadequacy. Recall that Fear-Selves are perfectionists: I must be the best Expert or I am an abject failure. The double Expert relationship can only work if their areas of expertise do not overlap. But even then the relationship is probably doomed because the Expert Fear-Self needs a receptive and deferential audience, and that is not likely to be found in another competitive Expert (recall that we are talking about Fear-Self expertise rather than genuine expertise, which is a function of joy and love; compatibility and love can surely flourish between two genuine experts).

The fear-based roles in relationships vary by gender. Because the conventional female Fear-Self tends to organize around private validation, she demands appreciation from her intimate partner, not from the world at large. She believes she deserves this appreciation in return for her sacrifice for family and home; the victim is owed her due. This demand is the flip side of the stereotypical male Fear-Self who seeks public accolade for his achievements/authority/expertise. His female companion is simply expected to express how impressed she is with his grandiosity.

People play these roles with little heart but lots of desperation. Guilt is a common byproduct of failing to validate the fear-based achievements of our partner. Because providing constant admiration depletes our individual energies (since it is often not of the heart), it can and generally will bleed the energy out of a relationship. When partners are profoundly identified with their conventional gender roles, the relationship may survive on the basis of shared guilt and the pressure of required reciprocity. Such relationships are reduced to mutual cheerleading societies. They are a ceremony witnessed by significant others, but are otherwise dead and often sexless. This is a common characteristic of traditional patriarchal family structures.

Failing to reproduce our conventional gender Fear-Selves can also be a recipe for relationship disaster. For many men, women who are motivated to achieve outside of the home are seen as abdicating their home-based responsibilities. They are threatening. Similarly, some women see men who are "feminized," who are not motivated to achieve in the conventional public way, as failures. These women need a grandiose male to give value to their victimized status (a Wound echo). The power of conventional gender roles continues to shape the emotional life of many relationships.

Failing to reproduce our conventional gender Fear-Selves can also be a recipe for relationship disaster. For many men, women who are motivated to achieve outside of the home are seen as abdicating their home-based responsibilities. They are threatening. Similarly, some women see men who are "feminized," who are not motivated to achieve in the conventional public way, as failures. These women need a grandiose male to give value to their victimized status

In times of crisis, which in this context is defined as an occasion when one partner makes contact with his Wound, the other partner will provide support by helping him distance himself from the apparent source of his suffering. By doing so, the dominant Fear-Self is validated. This is what "good" partners do. Of course, this is cheerleading masquerading as love, which is expressed by providing protection from the other's Wound.

Relationships become stressed and often collapse when one partner fails to adequately validate the other's Fear-Self. All Fear-Selves experience crises. There are big crises and small crises and everything in between. One of the primary roles of the partner is to validate the essence of the Fear-Self during a crisis of any proportion. The partner rescues the other by helping him to avoid experiencing the full power of his Wound. In the absence of such validation, direct exposure to the Wound occurs, and the aggrieved partner blames the other's lack of support for his emotional suffering.

Blame is the most favored interpersonal ploy of a Fear-Self. We shift focus away from our Wound by blaming another for our pain. If we blame another for our suffering, we don't have to take responsibility for our own pain. Because all Fear-Selves are perfectionists, we blame others for failing to be perfect. Blame is the purest action blinding us from our Wound.

When relationships collapse, we revert back to our childhood condition of psychological terror and paralysis and our search for a Fear-Self that will save us from the suffering. As children, we redoubled our efforts to please our parents. As adults, we look for a new partner to reassure us of our worth and value. We become attached to our partners when they play the role of Fear-Self lifesaver.

> *When relationships collapse, we revert back to our childhood condition of psychological terror and paralysis and our search for a Fear-Self that will save us from the suffering.*

Our need for saviors extends far beyond our closest intimates. They may include relatives, neighbors, friends, co-workers, and, of course, God. God is the ultimate rescuer. If all else fails, the responsibility for our well-being falls to Him/Her/Whatever. There is also a veritable mountain of self-help, like chanting mantras, imagining a "better now," believing that "everything happens for a reason," etc., all of which can also play the role of rescuer in times when we draw close to the belief in our innate unworthiness. We could even suggest that this is the basis for organized religion, therapy, meditation, and a slew of self-help books. Even this book could be construed as part of this dubious family of lifesavers (I have only myself to blame!).

This happens in most "successful" relationships: The partners reinforce each other's post-invalidated Fear-Selves. The relationships begin to decline when the energy for that validation languishes or is inconsistently provided. Every Fear-Self, even the Depressed

One, wants an appreciative audience. The conventional relationship provides for just such an audience. This means that we fall in love with an image with which our Fear-Self "fits." We "fit" with another when we are able to provide mutual validation needs. This creates a workable, albeit slippery, slope.

The validating needs of a Fear-Self vary depending on its level of neediness. Again, I urge you to remember that no one is a pure Fear-Self. Every shell is porous. Moreover, each of us has resilient/durable qualities that require no explicit external validation. But at times of personal crisis, it is exactly our resilience/durability that tends to collapse. Even the most resilient types will fall back into their relatively mild Wounds during crises. On the other end of the spectrum, extreme Fear-Selves require constant external validation. If an extreme Fear-Self (let's call that type E-Fear-Self) gets involved with a mild Fear-Self (which we will call an M-Fear-Self), the demands on the M-Fear-Self will be considerable. Over time, these demands are likely to undermine the strength of his love and commitment. It is a simple cost/benefit ratio. The relationship will then enter crisis mode and move toward collapse. Each person will then reorganize with their own hardened Fear-Selves and go their separate ways.

Recall that each Fear-Self is an illusory journey toward illusory completion. Because it is achievement-oriented, it will tend to go after accomplishments that contribute most to its essential inflation. So a restive Fear-Self will grow tired of a relationship that fails to maximize his relational achievement potential. This is truer of men because, in general, men need and seek public accolade more than women. As a man moves up the achievement ladder, he may develop the need for a partner who more appropriately complements his elevated status. He may then decline to continue validating his current partner with the ulterior motive of weakening the relationship and giving him the opportunity to land a "better" (better matched to his newly elevated status) partner.

The mirror image of this pattern involves the man who under-performs in the public forum. Most women have achievement standards that they apply to their male partners. When the man fails to achieve up to standard, she begins to validate his Wound, poisoning the relationship and contributing to its dissolution.

Many of us want to believe that the "Kingdom of God" is within us, but we simply don't know how to find our own beauty in a way that is clear, natural, and immediate. So we seek it externally, with the primary external vehicle being our closest relationships

---

One of the overarching qualities of the Fear-Self is its fundamental self-centeredness. Each Fear-Self is supported by a belief system that asserts its own isolation in a dangerous world. Most Fear-Selves (except for the Loner) experience aloneness as agony. They crave validation from the external world. Many of us want to believe that the "Kingdom of God" is within us, but we simply don't know how to find our own beauty in a way that is clear, natural, and immediate. So we seek it externally, with the primary external vehicle being our closest relationships. Yet for many of us, these intimate relationships do not provide validation for our Life Force, but nurture our Fear-Self. In fact, the only way these relationships can truly thrive is through mutual Fear-Self validation. This is false love.

A Fear-Self can only deal with another Fear-Self. The importance of this observation cannot be overstated. When we believe another to be her Fear-Self, we cannot see her authentic self. This means that in our world, we are dealing only with the confluence of Fear-Selves. This is why many of us are easily insulted; we take the stress and fear of others, which are always expressions of their Fear-Selves, personally. This is the cause of most interpersonal misunderstandings, disputes, and even wars between nations.

For the person firmly rooted in the fertile soil of her Life Force, the high drama of another's Fear-Self is never taken seriously. Having seen her own Fear-Self in dramatic action, she recognizes that the Fear-Self is often stressed, seeking attention, wanting to impress, and ever desiring to demonstrate its power. The Guru who pontificates, the Expert who holds court, the Pleaser who attends to every detail, the Loner who shies away from contact, the Tough Guy who must be obeyed—she knows that these are all masks hiding a frightened and vulnerable human being. When we identify with our masks, which we do most of the time, we are not ourselves. We are fakes—dangerous fakes.

Responding to Comments from Others

In everyday life, just as we relentlessly judge others, we too are judged. What a drag (both ways)!

When someone in our life judges us negatively, it excites our Fear-Self and our Wound simultaneously. Let's say someone criticizes the way you look: "You're looking kind of tired today. Is there a problem?" If the Fear-Self is stimulated, we will believe the remark to be either an unwarranted attack or proof that we are wearing our inadequacy in a public way. The Wound might speak to us: "I am worn out and I'm looking pretty crappy. Oh, God—my life is a wreck."

Comments made by others represent fantastic opportunities for seeing the interplay between the Fear-Self and the Wound. This is the kind of understanding that can lead to our liberation, if we are ruthlessly honest with our self-observations.

Our Life Force does not take such comments seriously. From the perspective of the Life Force, the statement is interesting, fun, or irrelevant. *Pretending* that such statements are interesting, fun, or irrelevant is exclusively the realm of the Fear-Self. A transcendent response either happens or it doesn't—there is no middle ground. The Life Force cannot be faked.

But there is another way around this conundrum. We can observe the person who has made the comment and our reactions to him. If we are able to see him in his entirety, from a place that is unaffected by him, that place represents a portal to our Life Force. The key to this understanding is observing the presenting event and its full array of responses, including the "fake spiritual" response of phony transcendence.

The same holds true for the petty, ego-based judgments we make of others. As long as there is a self who believes these judgments, we are living from the perspective of a Fear-Self. There is nothing wrong with disliking someone for the harm he causes, as long as we remember that we are observing his Fear-Self in action. Your judgment may also be the result of not understanding another's actions. We can choose to recognize that we don't always know other people's motivations and simply be patient with presenting situations,no matter how challenging and confusing they may appear.

Starting now, you could start seeing the desperate stress, drama, and power-seeking of others (as well as yourself) as nothing but the habituated actions of frightened people who are trying to protect themselves from pain and suffering.

Enemies: The Glue of Relationships

While mutual validation works to support thinly veiled "love" relationships, the same process occurs with those we condemn within a couple or group context. We need enemies, and it's even more satisfying to have enemies in common. The bond of shared enemies is among the strongest between people, organizations, and countries. Having an enemy provides exhilaration and validation. Experiencing the charge of a common enemy is a perfect reflection of the Fear-Self, which thrives in an environment of shared negativity. If taken seriously, it's a dark and self-diminishing pleasure; if played with a light heart, it's great fun.

Seeking vengeance or wishing to correct those we condemn gives meaning and excitement to our lives. Intimates need to feel similarly with regard to those they dislike and deem inferior. The perfect objects of contempt are individuals and groups that either fail to validate our Fear-Self types or stand for values that impugn them.

Janet and Tom are a spiritual and meditative couple who live in Vermont. They both attend their local Quaker Meeting on Sundays, when they connect with their community. Neither has touched a meat product for years, and they plant and cultivate much of the food they eat. Because they are strict pacifists, they will not openly condemn others who engage in conflict or wage war, no matter how they justify their position.

One weekend, two very old friends visit from New York. Debra and Richard are Jewish and have liberal political beliefs. While they are not vegetarians, they admire that life choice and sometimes wish they could do the same.

After dinner, their conversation turns to the turmoil between the Palestinians and Israel. Janet and Tom, with apparent emotion, remark about the terrible despair experienced by the Palestinian people. Debra and Richard agree, but not with quite the same empathy evinced by Janet and Tom. Janet notes how unfortunate it is that Israel uses high-tech weaponry against the "defenseless" Palestinians. Suddenly Debra rises to the defense of Israel, saying, "But Janet, can you imagine living in a place where, when you get on a bus or go to a market, you don't know if you'll be blown up by a suicide bomber? It's very easy for us to condemn Israel here from the comfort of our safe lives in the U.S." Tom defends his wife (validates her) by saying, "When you don't have a military, maybe a suicide bomb is the only way you can defend yourself from the aggressions of Israel. Not that I condone such violence. I don't—it's horrible—but that is the consequence of Israel's own regional imperialism." Richard then validates *his* wife by saying, "Hey Tom, if you knew anything about the history of Israeli/Palestinian relations, I don't think you'd be making such uninformed comments. Many times the Israelis have attempted to settle this conflict and have also been willing to sacrifice their land and resources to people who actually wish for the total destruction of the state of Israel, with the vain hope of ending this conflict." Tom then says, sanctimoniously, "I won't sit back and allow you to defend violence perpetrated by the powerful against the weak and vulnerable." And so it goes, becoming more acrimonious, until Debra and Mark feel they must excuse themselves not only from the table but from the visit, and head back to New York where they can take refuge from what they believe are the naive and arrogant beliefs of ignorant, if well-meaning, pacifists.

Note in this conversation how both sides' views contain elements of the integral Life Force, but that goodness is compromised by their Fear-Selves. Both sides believe, with passion, that they are right, and partners are pressured to validate their partners. But it is their mutual Fear-Selves that block thoughtful receptivity to the other side's position. Janet and Tom need to defend their identification with pacifism, while Debra and Mark have an element of the "Tough Guy" Fear-Self, believing that pacifism is weak-kneed, idealistic, and ultimately just plain naive when dealing with violence without perceived moral limits. Before leaving that evening, Richard, now visibly angry, says to Janet and Tom, "So I guess if a group of Jews during World War II had been lucky enough to get hold of some machine guns, it would have been wrong of them to kill off several dozen Nazis. How blind does a person need to be to see that pacifism in situations like that, and like with the Palestinians, is just plain stupid? And, by the way, for a pacifist, you sure are eager to support the violence from Palestinians." Tom shakes his head indicating his pity for the unrefined brutality of his guests: "Richard, I think you're just too invested with your identification with your fellow Jews. I can understand that, given the history, but that doesn't mean I agree with it." Debra and Richard are now openly contemptuous of their old friends, despising what they believe is smug arrogance. The two couples are fully divided and secure in their respective rightness and superiority. Their mutual Fear-Selves have won the day.

We divide our world into Fear-Selves with whom we are compatible and those we regard with contempt. In between there are those to whom we are indifferent. But it is the character of our own Fear-Selves that dictates the terms.

Healing asks us to come much closer to our Wound. So when we are in situations that compel us to come into contact with our Wound, we need to begin seeing these moments as opportunities for self-awareness. These situations stimulate our Fear-Selves to take over before we have an opportunity to understand ourselves better. The quick emergence of an energetic Fear-Self is exactly what blocks us from self-understanding. That is the moment when we need to start paying attention to how we are creating our lives. The vast majority of unpleasant and painful crises in life are interactions between Fear-Selves and any event or situation that draws us into the thorny world of the Wound. The Fear-Self will always need and crave validation.

When you begin breaking the connection with your Fear-Selves, you will hear the child's voice in your head urging you to stop being a fool and start doing what the Fear-Self tells you to do. It is that voice we all need to start hearing, but stop heeding. Life is full of challenges, but they need not fill us with rage, frustration, or hopelessness. Those states only come to life through the collapse of a Fear-Self into its Wound. It's as simple as that. For the very same reason, we are continually living in a state of insecurity as the mind ceaselessly surveys our world, looking for situations that threaten the stability of our presenting Fear-Self. Based on this scanning of the imagination, we build fortresses of self-protection. Our fears are the bedrock of our separation and isolation. Homes and relationships become safe havens in an unpleasant and threatening world.

When you begin breaking the connection with your Fear-Selves, you will hear the child's voice in your head urging you to stop being a fool and start doing what the Fear-Self tells you to do. It is that voice we all need to start hearing, but stop heeding.

The Fear-Self is, ultimately, alone in the world. It uses relationships to bolster and secure its standing. Because it can only know itself, it compares itself with others based on its own self-assessment. It will be jealous or bitter with similar Fear-Selves that are more "successful." The Body Person will feel awful about himself when he sees Body People who are more beautiful and fit, despite the vast amount of effort he has invested in himself. The Expert feels like a fool and charlatan when he is around people who demonstrate greater expertise in his field. The high Achiever feels like a failure when he reads about people whose achievements dwarf his own. The Spiritualist falls into despair when she reads about the many enlightenment "breakthroughs" experienced by those who have meditated and practiced less. The Pleaser sees others who are better liked and appreciated, and this fills her with self-contempt and even hopelessness. And on and on it goes. Things tend to happen quickly for the Fear-Self, and the fall from grace can and will happen in an instant.

As we age, our time begins to run out. The Fear-Self begins to see the handwriting on the wall and confronts its destiny of ultimately failing to accomplish what it had dreamed for itself. The Fear-Self, in nearly all cases, eventually folds back into its Wound and can only reminisce about past successes. This is the bittersweet legacy of old age and sentimentality. With age, our intensity declines, and we may find some peace from the compulsion to impress ourselves and others, and a certain measure of contentment may finally characterize our lives. However, in many cases, we transfer the insecurities with which we struggled to younger family members. As older people, we worry about their failure to achieve sufficiently so that they will be spared the pain and humiliation of failing the projected demands of their Fear-Self and the projected expectations of society at large.

The Issue of Jealousy

Jealousy is not a Fear-Type. It is, instead, an emotion that directly connects us to our Wound. Any Fear-Self is capable of experiencing jealousy.

Jealousy occurs in two contexts: one, when someone we want to control, possess, and be revered by moves away from us; and two, when another whose ability we evaluate as less than our own achieves greater success in our mutual field. In either context, we, as the Fear-Self, are losing something we believe we possessed or should possess. This represents a kind of transitional holding point where the person is experiencing the failure of his Fear-Self type, but not the full collapse into the Wound.

The Fear-Self needs to control and impress. When it fails in either regard, it will fold into the catastrophe of its Wound. When we are jealous, our status as a successful Fear-Self has ceased, but we haven't entirely fallen into the abyss of our Wound. We experience instead the pain of both domains—the diminished Fear-Self and the rising realization of our inadequacy, insufficiency, and worthlessness.

The experience of jealousy is a gift, since it gives us a remarkably clear view of how we go about hating ourselves and wishing harm on others to whom we are close.

If we are able to understand and see the experience of jealousy as the interplay of the Wound and the Fear-Self, we have taken the first step toward reducing its power to make us miserable. The experience of jealousy is a gift, since it gives us a remarkably clear view of how we go about hating ourselves and wishing harm on others to whom we are close. Fully identified with our Fear-Self, we hate the person who has diminished us. Fully identified with the Wound, we hate ourselves.

The Fear-Self: Concluding Thoughts

As the basic components of the body are blood and bones, the basic component of the mind is thought. Thought manifests in three discrete ways. First, thought is practical. It knows how to do things. It is essential to use thought in planning. Thought is also creative. It can respond to the demands of the moment by being nurturing, considerate, strong, and loving. The third category of thought is rooted in our invalidation. This is fear-based thought, and, for most of us, our primary self-identification. This thought is automatic. It is based on the belief that we are lacking and that we need to fill this lack with accomplishment, withdrawal, inappropriate rage, fear-based beliefs, and, in the absence of accomplishment, hope and religion.

The key issue is one of psychological identification. As long as we are identified with the experience of lack, we will operate from a position of insecurity and fear. This is the fast-moving trap of the thought-based Fear-Self. Remember that all psychological thought is conceptual. It is not real. The thought of a tree is not the tree. The thought of you is not you. The thought of happiness and liberation is not happiness and liberation.

The Fear-Self is the energetic rushing-in of thought. It is the compulsive sense of what we need to do, often at stressful times. The Fear-Self is a lot more vigorous when we are stressed. It fills our mind with thoughts that are not only self-contemptuous, but often angry with others and the whole world. The energy of the Fear-Self touches all of our senses and fills our body with tension. We don't experience life; we only experience the Fear-Self. The world liberated from the

Fear-Self is a place of fantastic beauty and wonder. The you, liberated from the Fear-Self, is also a place of beauty and wonder.

In the final section of <u>Liberation from the Lie</u>, we will explore this world and find the entranceway to it. And, as Franz Kafka said in "Before the Law", this entranceway has been made only for you.

14 - A Case Study of the Wound and Fear-Self

This chapter details the process of identifying a Fear-Self and its Wound and the ensuing transformation. Please don't read this as a prescription to follow in your own life. The goal is not imitation, but understanding and insight. This process must grow out of the context of your own life. Individuals may have very similar maps of self-exploration and discovery, but the journey is always personal and unique.

Don't read this as a prescription to follow in your own life. The goal is not imitation, but understanding and insight. This process must grow out of the context of your own life. Individuals may have very similar maps of self-exploration and discovery, but the journey is always personal and unique.

I have always had problems with intimacy. For various reasons, women have often been attracted to me. These women appear to enjoy my sense of humor, my involvement in the arts, my enthusiasm, and even my very occasional manliness. I enjoy sports, have a gregarious personality and have enough rough edges to keep things interesting. I was married for 17 years and have had several long-term relationships.

Yet, once I settle into a relationship, I begin to experience a kind of persistent, free-floating anxiety. My thinking is often a little paranoid. I interpret indifferent facial expressions as vaguely accusatory. I often wonder nervously what the other person is thinking, and

I tend to believe that they are thinking critical thoughts about me, and that the criticism is probably justified.

I am always suspecting that my anxiety and fear of physical intimacy is undermining the health of the relationship. Sexually, I become remote and disinterested. I know that maintaining distance is something I do to protect myself, yet, like so many actions of the Fear-Self, this is only an attempt to fend off anxiety. Sometimes I feel dead sexually. This always makes me feel ashamed and defensive. I feel like a relationship loser.

I also tend to rationalize these behaviors as a function of my Jewish upbringing, saying this is typical behavior for intellectual, Eastern European Jews who are often quite uncomfortable with nudity and pretty much anything physical. I use my ethnicity as a kind of protection and refuge.

At night, when I get into bed, I feel the pressure to be intimate. This ultimately causes me to flee relationships. I am uncomfortable and feel no sexuality. These feelings are confusing because there are so many ways to interpret them. I might think that my current partner is not right for me, or that I am just not the type to be in a committed relationship, or that there is something more seriously wrong about me—that maybe I should be on some kind of mood stabilizing medication. I have sometimes wondered if I should live completely alone and apart from the world, if only to avoid this anxiety and fear.

The Fear-Self is entirely self-involved. Everything that happens, from my partner's serious facial expressions, which I interpret as irritation with me, to my free-floating angst, is about *me*. The always active Fear-Self ceaselessly scans its environment, selectively picking up information to support its paranoid view of the situation.

The Fear-Self is entirely self-involved. Everything that happens, from my partner's serious facial expressions, which I interpret as irritation with me, to my free-floating angst, is about me.

There are two ways I typically respond to this kind of anxiety. I may start talking about some fairly serious topic, which will allow me some time to explore and even pontificate just a bit. I'm hoping, inwardly, that enough time will pass that sex will become unlikely and I will be relieved of the pressure to perform. Eventually, the woman will become bored or just too tired to respond, and I can feel some gratification that I was able to weather another anxious encounter. My second strategy uses humor to deflect potential interest in intimacy. Often this humor is in the context of watching a television show late at night like Jon Stewart or Stephen Colbert. TV becomes yet another distraction from intimacy and, at face, this would appear normal and even appropriate. And then there are times when I feel less pressured, and at those times I can be intimate and romantic.

Similar anxieties occur at work. I become inexplicably nervous around the boss. I have persistent fantasies of getting fired, winding up broke and homeless. I suspect that my nervousness is something that a boss can detect, and if for no other reason than that, they would be happy to get rid of me. The grandiose Fear-Self is, in fact, nervous and vulnerable. The Fear-Self and the Wound become one problematic identity stumbling through life's challenging situations.

On the other hand, I'm often a know-it-all. I seem to have everything figured out. I know why people act the way they do, I know politics, I know economics, I pretty much know everything. I sometimes aggressively express my opinions, and I often assume that everything can be understood as an objective reality. When challenged, I deflect my critics by claiming that I am well aware that everything is subjective and that I'm merely voicing my opinions. Of course, the Expert Fear-Self doesn't believe this—but it sounds good, and helps to make me more likable. Some people see me as smug, opinionated authoritarian with a wry sense of self-effacing humor. I've also noticed that some people get nervous around me. I am so self-assured in this way that I turn some people off. I am easily capable of looking down at these people as weak and spineless. Why should they be so sensitive to my opinion-mongering? The Fear-Self loves to project its Wound outwardly.

This is an extremely revealing point. Invariably the thing we really can't stand about other people is our own Wound manifesting in them. And because we love to disown our own Wound, we eagerly project it outwards onto others.

This is an extremely revealing point. Invariably the thing we really can't stand about other people is our own Wound manifesting in them. And because we love to disown our own Wound, we eagerly project it outwards onto others. This insight points the way to a powerful form of healing. Anytime you project your Wound onto another, see that person as yourself. The person you really can't stand on account of specific character traits is actually the disavowed you. He is the you that you cover up with all of your Fear-Selves. That person you hate is the critical voice in your own head that directs your life! Isn't that incredible?

Let's continue with my story.

So, on the one hand, I'm nervous, paranoid, fearful, and terrified of authorities and on the other hand, I *am* the authority.

This represents a common dichotomy. The fearful, easily intimidated person assumes the personage of the Expert who regales people with his self-certainty and fearlessness in the face of authority. This is the interplay of the Wound and a Fear-Self playing their roles in my personal and intimate life. Behind every Expert is a fearful, tenuous child; behind everyone seeking enlightenment is a sad, hopeless child; behind every Achiever is a defeated and shamed little boy or girl. This process of self-discovery may last a lifetime.

One night while lying in bed with my companion, wishing to escape from intimacy, I had a brilliant flash of violence and fear. It was an echo of a distant memory.

I was raised by a father with a violent and abusive temper who was prone to explode. I have many frightening memories about him. One time when I was about 9 years old, sitting around the kitchen table, he asked me if I had brushed my teeth. I answered yes, although I was lying. He must have suspected something, because he quickly got up from the table and walked upstairs to my bathroom where he felt the dry bristles of my toothbrush. He shouted for me to come upstairs, which I did dutifully but terrified at the possible violence that could erupt at any moment. He called me into the bathroom. It was clear when he was intensely angry—his lower jaw would stick out and I could see the veins in his forehead pulse.

Stuttering with rage, he asked me to explain why the toothbrush was dry. I can't remember how I responded, but I do remember running toward my bedroom with my father chasing me. I knew that he intended to beat me. My father was an accomplished amateur boxer and was obsessed with weightlifting. To a small, very thin 9-year-old, he was unspeakably terrifying and powerful. He chased me wildly around the room. A lamp fell and smashed on the floor. He picked it up and used it as a weapon, striking me with it on my back. I remember falling onto my bed and my father slapping me hard around the face, shouting, "Lying is worse than murder!"

This is just one example among many. Each day I ranged from mild but persistent anxiety and fear to extreme terror of his unpredictable outbursts. Even when I was 16, he struck me once so hard in my ribs that I asked to be taken to the emergency room to see if any bones were cracked. The cause of that attack? I had purchased a record album although I had been told not to.

The flash I had while lying in bed as an adult was a sharp echo of this violence, seen as a kind of photo-like vision. But it was more than that. In that flash I could clearly see that the intellectual and swaggering, self-confident versions of me were a Fear-Self compensating for the terrified and vulnerable me. In this case, my Wound was not rooted in a separation trauma, but in the potential for violence in my family of origin. To counter my fear and insecurity, I developed a kind of funny but grandiose character who loved to hold court on all things cultural and political. This was not an "in your face" obnoxious and loud character. It was, instead, a more subtle and often self-effacing person. This urbane self compensated for my terrified self. It was not an obvious Fear-Self.

I knew that this flash of insight was on the money, because I could feel an immediate sense of relief in my body. This relief came in the form of being able to breathe more easily. It was like a load was lifted from me. I could see the whole pattern of the Wound and Fear-Self and how closely invested I was in it. This is the healing power that is made possible through understanding.

But having this kind of epiphany is just the beginning. Our innate tendency is to go back to who we were prior to the flash. It's not easy to see or resist this return to the familiar, because it feels so natural. I knew that if I wanted to integrate this moment into self-awareness, a different response was called for. I needed to engage it and really get a feel for it. I needed to be keenly aware of how easy it is to drift back to the comfortable place that we think of as our self. I needed to allow its transformative power to unfold. For healing to endure, we must dive deeply into and live the understanding.

If I resisted the impulse to return to the familiar me, a new kind of energy could be felt. This is a more subtle sense of ourselves than the energetic feel of the Fear-Self, with its stories, plans, and insecurities. This new energy is not overtly dramatic. Rather it is soft and expansive, not sharp and seeking to impose itself on its world.

This new energy was not a part of the dyad of terror and swagger, the polarities of my Wound and Fear-Self. It was entirely different and not explicitly knowable. It had no role to play or role that could be known! This provided an insight of immense power and significance.

Liberated from the trance of the Wound/Fear-Self dyad, I have become better able to integrate intimacy in my life. This is the outcome of seeing the false as false. When fear happens, I don't need to compulsively occupy a false self; instead, I can be open with my partner and deal with the anxiety within a connected relationship. This is living with the direct immediacy of life, not taking flight into a being defended by the habitual armor of the Fear-Self. This is an example of how the transformative process of self-liberation happens in real life. We feel the pull of habit, see where it is taking us, and then move forward, with a willingness to be vulnerable and alive to the unknown.

When fear happens, I don't need to compulsively occupy a false self; instead, I can be open with my partner and deal with the anxiety within a connected relationship. This is living with the direct immediacy of life, not taking flight into a being defended by the habitual armor of the Fear-Self.

Our transformation cannot be sustained unless we really allow ourselves to submerge our soul into the energy of the insight on the level of feeling.

It is the moment itself without any prescribed task. It is directly connected to the freshness and immediacy of life presenting itself, free of any agenda. It is open to the moment. This openness cannot be faked or emulated; it can only emerge naturally when we lose our defenses and feel, viscerally, the interplay of our Wound and its complementary Fear-Self.

Each Fear-Self has a role it has played a million times. It is a known entity. It has a past and a projected future. It has its own form of reasoning and living. If you ever feel like life has a monotonous quality and you would like it to feel new and fresh, then it is important to point out that this cannot happen when life is lived through a Fear-Self. It already knows itself and its world. It's always revisiting old territory.

This new energy feels completely different. Because it has no set role, it can only live in the now. It is fresh and without any need for self-correction or personal inflation or diminution.

Even within this new undefined energy, I can feel various roles knocking at the door, desiring entry. The familiar characters of my own self-styled play are always hungry for more time on the stage. They have the attractiveness of familiarity. They are so very comfortable.

Notice that I didn't "work on" becoming aware or achieving some new, more resilient self. The transforming energy happened entirely on its own. It was allowed to happen because I stood back and watched the Wound and Fear-Self as they did their predictable dance, whose steps they know perfectly. It also happened because I was attentive to the process, which needs space and time to emerge. We also need to resist the urge to resume the role of our conventional self if we are to explore and experience the potential of being born anew.

The cost of this new self is the price of not knowing. It doesn't know what will happen next, and it doesn't really care. It feels deeper than the Fear-Self—slower, less dramatic, without a past or a future. It seems to be the core of awareness living in the moment without a set role.

From the vantage point of this awareness, the brutality of my youth was an essential phase of my life journey. Despite all the pain, it was necessary.

From the vantage point of this awareness, the brutality of my youth was an essential phase of my life journey. Despite all the pain, it was necessary. I was only a victim from the perspective of the Fear-Self. The same applies to my father's role as tyrant. This was an essential step in my own self-liberation. The need for blame and victimizing becomes unnecessary and even just plain wrong. I could just as well thank my father for his violence and terror-making.

The new self is just an openness that is part of the changing web of connections. If a disturbance emerges, when things start happening fast, it's very likely that some old Fear-Self will march in and take over our sense of self. That's just a part of life. But our vantage point is now changed. This sense of energy is now available to us. We have gotten a feel for its presence, which is really our presence.

Also, when we now assume a fear-based role, it is done in the light of consciousness. We are no longer slaves to these compensating selves. We can play the roles for fun or for work; after all, these are roles we know very well. They have the power to undermine our security and reinvest us with their fears and promise of future fulfilment—but only when we buy into them as our true identities.

Be warned, however, that some of these roles, those that are most closely tied to the scariest and rawest elements of the Wound, will have a tendency to stay with us. Our habitual identity with them can loosen only when we are able to externalize them. The process of bringing them to light can and probably will last a lifetime. Once you start the process of self-release, meaning that we are able to bring these roles to light in a visceral way, and once we are able to inhabit that part of us that has no prescribed role, we will have made the decisive movement to self-liberation. We have hiked to the summit and are now on the path that is more relaxed and less compulsive.

For the sake of clarity, let's review the process described in this chapter. First, I noticed how my insecurity made me suffer. It undermined my capacity to be intimate; it kept me fearful of others. I opened myself to the feeling, and then a flash of insight occurred where I could see how it was connected to a childhood fear of my violent father. I could see how I compensated for this terror by creating a rather self-confident, grandiose, yet affable personality. The linkage between the Wound and its compensating Fear-Self was established. By just allowing it to happen, I could feel a new sense of energy fill the void that was created when my identification with the fearful/grandiose me was externalized. I resisted withdrawing into a comfortable and known identity.

Note the underlying *benefit* of psychological fear. Without this fear, without this suffering, we can never find our way out of the prison of the Fear-Selves and the Wound. The only reliable passageway into the place of transformation is suffering and grief. All healing begins with pain. Seen this way, healing through the resolution of the Wound is, indeed, painful. It compels us to delve into our most frightening personal nightmares. The power of our transformation is directly proportional to the amount of "dark" energy that inhabits our life.

Upon reading this, please don't intentionally foment grief and suffering. They must come in their own way and time. Don't worry—their arrival is guaranteed. They are reliable guests. Be ready for them and use their presence as opportunities for self-discovery. Remember, we don't want to react to them. We don't want to suppress them. We don't want to oppose them. These are the actions of a Fear-Self masquerading as your best friend, which it is not. Our interest is only in understanding and staying still. Feel the energy. Listen to the voices as if listening to a sound of nature. Feel the new you who resists the temptation to flee into the familiar embrace of another Fear-Self.

Be aware, however, that the ego is brilliant at co-opting any accomplishment. If this breakthrough possesses any quality of a "you" finally "doing" it, or any sense of self-mastery, then you can be certain that you are still operating from the position of the ego, which can now assume a more refined role for the Fear-Self. This is a common course. Any change can quickly morph into a new role that you need to assume—which means you are still compensating for some insufficiency within the Wound.

The question is, always: Is the purpose of this role to prove my adequacy, sufficiency, or worth?

For example, after my own insight: If I felt that I needed to be sensitive and open to intimacy, rather than maintain my urbane, intellectual swagger, I would just be creating another role for myself. I would evolve from a place of compulsive unconsciousness, to one of being an evolved fake.

Another essential point that bears repeating: All things exist exclusively in relationships. Nothing is independent of relationships. This fact is particularly important when dealing with Fear-Selves and liberating ourselves from their trance. It is one thing to believe that you are free of a particular Fear-Self outside of the context in which it tends to emerge. The test of our liberation occurs exclusively within relationships. This does not just mean relationships with other people, but your relationship with anything that compels the emergence of a compulsive self.

This new energy is not a role or a costume you can possess. It is part of the fabric of the now. It is not an accomplishment in the conventional sense of the word. The Fear-Self always acts in service of its fears and its hopes. The actions of the authentic self manifests either as doing what it must do, i.e., maintaining a job or a family; or doing for the fun/play/love/passion of it. Here is the key distinction: The life of imprisonment is one of drudgery, and the dominant attitude is one that is pressured and compulsive. The life of liberation is lived for the sake of the pleasure of the one living it.

15 - The Nexus

This chapter presents the Liberation Theory as two dynamic elements. One, the level of invalidation varies among people, from those who are minimally invalidated to those who are profoundly invalidated. Second, as the level of invalidation increases, the tendency to flip from compulsive aspiration to depression increases. The interaction of these two dimensions is called the Nexus.

Visualized in graphic form, Axis 1 represents the level of invalidation; Axis 2 represents the level of psychological balance. These axes relate inversely: As the level of invalidation is elevated, the capacity to respond to life challenges is reduced proportionately.

The examples in this chapter are intentionally simplified. Real life is considerably more nuanced and variable than what is described here. The goal is to lay out the pure theory of Liberation as clearly as possible.

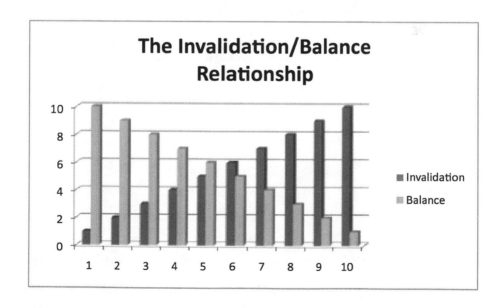

The Invalidation Continuum

Everyone experiences invalidation early in life, but the level and impact of the invalidation experience varies from one individual to another (as well as among collections of individuals, such as organizations, religions, and countries). In general, the more traumatic and repeated the invalidation experience, the greater the personal identification with inadequacy, insufficiency, and worthlessness. Conversely, invalidation experiences with more minimal trauma and fewer repetitions result in proportionately less identification with those self-negating qualities.

The vigor with which we attach to a dominant Fear-Self consequently varies from one individual to another. The greater the initial invalidation, the greater the identity with a dominant Fear-Self and the more terrifying the underlying Wound.

The more we are identified with a Fear-Self, the more isolated our life experience becomes. The less we are identified with a Fear-Self (and the corresponding decrease in terror provoked by the underlying Wound), the more connected our experience with life can be. This is the continuum of isolation/connection.

In extreme form, the totally invalidated person is a sociopath. The minimally invalidated person is resilient, durable, sensitive to the needs of others, and light-hearted.

Let's take a look at how this plays out in real life. A college student who hopes to be a physician runs into rough academic territory, performing poorly and receiving less than mediocre grades. A minimally invalidated individual would deal with this reversal in a way that was pragmatic and resourceful. He might feel considerable disappointment with himself, but he would not descend into a maelstrom of endless self-pity and relentless depression. He would reorganize his goals and get on with life, doing whatever is needed to improve his performance without excessive absorption in his travail. In contrast, a severely invalidated individual would become overwhelmed by the emotional power of the situation. He would fully identify with his Wound-based self, indulging in endless discussion of his victim status ("poor me"), withdrawing from life, and possibly even throwing violent tantrums.

The Identification Polarity

With invalidation, we need to identify with a Fear-Self. The purpose of a Fear-Self is to demonstrate adequacy, worth, and sufficiency. The negative side of the Fear-Self is its projection of inadequacy, worthlessness, and insufficiency onto the world . The Fear-Self is both validator of the self and invalidator of others. It can also reverse this polarity, validating others and invalidating self, particularly in times of crisis.

Using the same example of the aspiring doctor, let's examine the identification polarity in everyday life. Let's say that the aspiring doctor is an Achiever. He pictures himself as a successful surgeon, living the "good life" with a beautiful and adoring wife, a couple of great-looking kids, living in a beautiful downtown loft with all the bells and whistles. He will really impress his parents and show the world how successful he is. His co-workers will really admire his expertise. His competence and success will attract wonderful people into his life.

When his grades fall short of qualifying him for medical school, he is devastated. Around him are students who do have the grades to get into the medical schools he assumed he would be attending. As a consequence of this crisis, he invalidates himself and identifies with his Wound: "I'm a failure. I'm not smart enough. I didn't work hard enough. I'm a loser." Then he validates others: "They are smarter than

I am. They worked while I was out partying. They just have what it takes to succeed." Internally, the Achiever has migrated from a positive Fear-Self to his Wound. Externally, his colleagues have ascended to become his positive Fear-Self.

As a consequence of our invalidation, we are stuck in two complementary positions. One, we seek to please others and thereby replicate the position of our very young self struggling to gain the love from our parents. Two, we replicate the invalidating energies of our parents onto others (often our own children), which acts to sustain our belief in the validity of our own Wound. We live the whole of our life this way, and by so doing, we maintain the suffering and insecurity that began with our original life trauma.

This is the polarity of the Fear-Self in action. It is life out of balance. The invalidated self is prone to rapid identity reversals, from the hopeful to the disconsolate. Fear-Selves collapse abruptly when life undermines their compulsive aspirations. In contrast, the minimally invalidated person is more adaptive and has the emotional resources to address times of conflict with more resilience.

The purpose of <u>Liberation</u> is to awaken the reader to this insight.

Patterns of invalidation are replicated in our organizations, institutions, religions, and nations. In extreme form, when they need to express their underlying pain, these institutions are divisive and dangerous. They prove their power and success by invalidating others who do not share their beliefs.

Because of their drive for power, extremely invalidated forms tend to become recognized and dominant. Also, many similarly invalidated people identify with their beliefs and world views. At times of crisis, the differences between groups (and individuals) are accentu-ated, and the result is conflict, destruction, and war. This is the world of total disconnection, where the individual survival of the dominant Fear-Self is at stake—and it will do anything to assure its survival.

It is the individual and group avoidance of contact with the Wound that explains conflict and war. At times of relative harmony, conflict assumes less divisive forms.

Our individual and collective well-being calls on us to awaken from the belief in our inadequacy, insufficiency, and worthlessness. We must rediscover our authentic being prior to its infantile trauma.

Summary Table

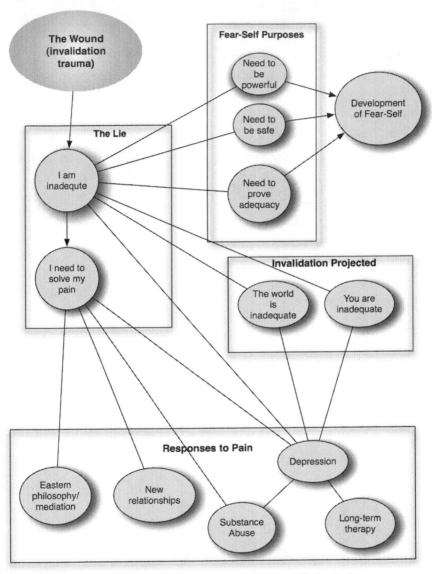

Figure 4: The Many Outcomes of Invalidation

Section 3:

Liberation—The Way Out

16 - Honoring the Fear-Self

From a certain point on, there is no more turning back.
That is the point that must be reached.

~ Franz Kafka

It may sound ironic, given all that you've read up to this point, but until we appreciate our Fear-Selves, we can never be free of their grip. We must come to enjoy exactly how we present ourselves in the world. We are capable of doing this when we fully understand the source of the Fear-Self. It is in our deepest vulnerabilities that we discover what it is to be a human being. We suffer as long as we resist our Fear-Selves! When we appreciate a Fear-Self, we are free of the trance of false identification. This does not mean that we now have permission to indulge their excesses. Exactly the reverse happens when we fully accept them without making any effort to change them—they lose their compulsive and fearful qualities, and we become transformed.

It is in our deepest vulnerabilities that we discover what
it is to be a human being.

If you are beginning to see your own Fear-Selves in action, you may be assuming that the message of <u>Liberation from the Lie</u> is that the Fear-Selves are a problem that needs to be solved by their extinction. Nothing could be further from the truth.

Every Fear-Self is connected, directly, to that part of us that is unloved or not loved enough. It is the representation of our fledgling attempts to show our worth to the world. (The Loner is an exception; she continues to respond to the pain of failed intimacy and has not reached the threshold of needing or wanting to shine in a public world.) We can hear the voice of the Fear-Self as the compensating voice of the hurt child. It does not see the world in all its complexities, but as a dangerous place where our identity and very existence are threatened. It is a voice that cries out for self-protection. Its guardianship over us is one of the key reasons we identify with it so deeply. This voice has been our companion since early childhood. Its duration and familiarity have convinced us that its beliefs, fears, opinions, hopes, and desires are our own. But it is not a whole person; it is actually a collection of conflicting concepts, ideas, and beliefs designed to promote our worth to others and ourselves, as well as shield us from the pain and chaos of the Wound.

As a life strategy, the Fear-Self represents the absence of love. Unlike nearly all self-help therapy and Eastern philosophy, liberation is not about creating a better you; rather, it's about learning to appreciate each and every Fear-Self as it emerges into consciousness. We provide the love to our unconscious selves that we failed to receive as little children. This love is different from other types of love because its energy comes from allowing, and in that allowing results our delight in what emerges.

When the automatic is made conscious, everything is transformed. We are automatic when we are unconscious. By bringing the Fear-Selves into consciousness, we are able to find our own beauty and signature within their nature. We can finally accept who we truly are. What was compulsive and insecure becomes our Life Force. We really are our own healer.

By bringing the Fear-Selves into consciousness, we are able to find our own beauty and signature within their nature. We can finally accept who we truly are. What

was compulsive and insecure becomes our Life Force.
We really are our own healer.

When we reject a Fear-Self, we are replicating the Wound in our life. When people can accept and rejoice in their distinctive Fear-Selves, they are simultaneously bringing love and healing to their Wound. When this happens, civilization itself can be transformed.

The unconscious Fear-Self inspires us to ways of life that are highly self-focused. This includes such solitary pursuits as striving to become personally enlightened. When we become conscious of the Fear-Self, our connections with other people and the world become our central orientation. Our focus migrates from "me" to "us."

The Wound and all of its Fear-Selves are the direct consequence of a world view that perceives children as entering the world flawed. We live our lives as artifacts of this world view thanks to coerced discipline and punishment delivered when we were very young. The hunter/gatherer also lived in her culture, but her culture served to fortify her links with her authentic self.

Before we can experience enduring liberation, we need to know who we are not. That has been the whole point of Parts One and Two of this book. We are not who we want to be; yet who we want to be, we already are. Sound confusing? It won't be at all confusing in time.

We honor each and every Fear-Self because it is a direct sign of who we are not and who we will never be! The Fear-Self always projects a "better" you and a "better" future. Belief in a "better" you and a "better" future requires that you always be discontent with who you are and what your world presents. The key is to see this projection as a persistent flight from one's authentic self and from one's personal

Wound. When we cease the flight by loving and rejoicing in our Fear-Selves, everything changes.

We get acquainted with every Fear-Self, first, through understanding and alert awareness. All it requires is a little practice. Remember that our only purpose is to notice and allow whatever wants to be to be. Take a look outside. We take it for granted that whatever is there is there. We allow it without a second thought. We need to have exactly that same attitude with every manifestation of a Fear-Self, but with awareness. Now, look outside again. Do you personally identify yourself with what you see? The answer ought to be, of course not. Adopt the same point of view with every manifestation of your Fear-Selves.

Let's summarize how we can identify a Fear-Self in action. A Fear-Self is:

- a personal identification with any action that is done compulsively;
- a personal identification with any action designed to impress ourselves;
- a personal identification with any action design to impress others;
- a personal action done for the sake of self-inflation;
- a personal action done for the sake of self-deflation;
- a personal action that is angrily defensive for the sake of protecting an image;
- a personal action that is angrily attacking for the sake of protecting an image;

- an internal voice that is critical of others in order to connote one's superiority;

- an internal voice that is critical of one's self in order to connote one's failure to be perfect;

- an internal voice that is self-invalidating;

- any belief in perfectionism;

- a need to use force to compel another to meet your expectations of what is right;

- a compulsive need to draw attention to one's self.

The key to understanding a Fear-Self is its quality of compulsiveness. It feels automatic, and we are caught in its grip without our awareness of it. The Fear-Self is cloaked in our belief that *it* is who we are. In this way, we live our life blind. Because it is inherently compulsive, it will often have a strained aspect to it, as if it is something that we would prefer not to do but must do nonetheless. It gets its power and authority from habit and familiarity.

> *By bringing the Fear-Selves into consciousness, we are able to find our own beauty and signature within their nature. We can finally accept who we truly are. What was compulsive and insecure becomes our Life Force. We really are our own healer.*

We have developed these false actions of personal identification over many years. They are, absolutely, actions of habit. Their purpose is to shield us from a greater level of suffering than what we are experiencing in the moment of their emergence. This greater level of suffering is contact with the Wound. They promise greater personal security and life with less fear, but deliver exactly the opposite.

By honoring the Fear-Self, we sever our personal identification with it. Anything operating within the light of awareness has been nudged outside of our personal blindness. So when you feel the compulsion to authoritatively hold court, to meditate "harder" to hasten your enlightenment, to work out an extra 30 minutes to build up those abs, when you feel lousy because you just don't measure up to what you or others think you should be, just watch the whole show as it unfolds. Feel the energy of the Fear-Self. Don't try to stop it. Our purpose is not to kill the Fear-Selves—that would be the action of another, more cunning Fear-Self. Our only purpose is to loosen our identification with these sub-personalities. Also—and this is a subtle point—try not to identify with the person watching the drama of your Fear-Self. That, too, can very quickly morph into a new and far more elusive Fear-Self.

Allow me to provide a simple, everyday example of this process. This afternoon I was entering an interstate highway. As I entered the entrance ramp, there was one car ahead of mine. From my perspective, the driver was moving much too slowly and was hesitating, exactly when he should have been speeding up to enter the flow of traffic safely. Instantly a Fear-Self took over and pronounced the driver ahead of me to be "an asshole." Making matters worse, he was on his cell phone, which only made me more contemptuous of him. I was really quite pissed off with this jerk and would have liked to have the power to swerve around him, but my car is not nearly powerful enough to do that. This was, of course, my Tough Guy Fear-Self, who is a know-it-all and is superior to all other drivers. He tends to always be in a rush and finds most other drivers stupid and timid. This is *me!* As soon as I noticed the pattern, I could really laugh at myself. Here I was projecting my own inadequacy onto the other driver, while my Fear-Self claimed all of the knowledge, power, and expertise in the situation. He was angry and really couldn't stand this other driver. The moment I honored the angry being and observed my vastly inflated personality structure in action, I could laugh and even continue the show. The key is not to stop the energy, but to notice it in its entirety. The Wound played its part in the projection and the Fear-Self played its role as the swaggering Tough Guy. Unconscious of the identification, I was just another pissed-off jerk. Aware of the identification, I could laugh at my own self-made drama. We know we have hit awareness "pay dirt" when we transfer our emotional quality from serious to humorous. Fear-Selves simply cannot laugh at themselves. They can laugh at others frolicking in their superiority, but they can't find summon up a belly laugh about themselves. Only an authentic self can feel the deliciousness of liberating, spontaneous laughter.

Key Point: The Quality of our Attention

Anytime we "work" on an anxiety-making issue ("work" meaning any attempt to correct ourselves or do away with painful anxiety), we are, in effect, agreeing with the voice of our Wound. Our need to work on these issues enables them to define our real self. Yet they are not us. They are the interplay of the Wound with a Fear-Self. They are an illusion, a ghost, a phantasm. Part of the fake drama of self-improvement is our working on our problems. We become actors on the stage of our childhood imagination. Even the act of watching the show can give them more reality than they deserve. From the mind's point of view, the goal of "working" on our suffering is to create a better-adapted Fear-Self!

At this point in our journey, observation is the best strategy we have. It is far more powerful to be a spectator than an entranced participant. When we participate without awareness, we are blind to our role; we actively support not only our own disempowerment, but also spin our wheels by continuing to run from our Wound.

Know now and forever that identification with a Fear-Self is a fake. It is a product of our sensitive and vulnerable ideation of a person no older than 6 or 7. Make the decision now to stop any attempt to do away with these issues. They are not you. They are the updated memories of trauma profoundly and innocently misinterpreted by a severely hurt young person. When you "work" on them, you are maintaining your identification with them.

The Fear-Self is absolutely invisible when we are wrapped up in its theatrics. It is only when we become a part of the audience that can we appreciate the humor of the show. The actor is never himself. The Fear-Self is the actor, and the Wound writes the script. The best humor emerges from pain.

In every moment there is a place of quiet and trust. We might try, from this point forward, to apply our attention to that place instead of "working" on the painful theatrical performance going on inside our head. Such dramas, as they are expressed, are our response to a projected crisis; they are visual representations of our internal dialogues. They are the fears of a child. To honor the Fear-Self, we honor the innocent trials and tribulations of our much younger selves. To resist them is to dishonor that younger self.

In every moment there is a place of quiet and trust. We might try, from this point forward, to apply our attention to that place instead of "working" on the painful theatrical performance going on inside our head.

As we honor our Fear-Selves, and thus our own childhood, we are also advised to honor the Fear-Selves of others, but not in a way that lends them credibility. We simply acknowledge that when we notice the manifestation of a Fear-Self in another, we honor and understand that person's vulnerable youthful self. If we allow ourselves to get drawn into their drama, we disempower the other, as well as ourselves. The response of understanding is one of compassion. We neither resist others nor further their belief in their self-destructive machinations.

Feel very free to laugh at your own script, but be very careful at laughing at the scripts of others. That can be arrogant and hurtful.

The Fear-Self is an essential signpost pointing to our own inevitable liberation. When we disengage ourselves from the ongoing high drama of the Fear-Self, we have taken a major step toward our liberation. We have profoundly modified the self-identity rooted in our childhood. The Achiever, the Expert, the Body Person, the Spiritualist, in their compulsive, driven conditions, are no longer essential to our self-identity. Our need for external validation of any compulsive, fear-based need begins to fall by the wayside. Our addiction to fear and insecurity has now begun to collapse into empty space. How does that feel?

Know that in the heart of every Fear-Self lives the knowledge that one day it must die. Like all artificial roles, it ultimately becomes tired of its own act. Many fade away as we enter old age, but others just grow tired of their own empty and mirthless bravado. In a way, we can see ourselves as facilitators of the demise of each and every Fear-Self.

17 - Honoring the Wound: The Way to True Compassion

For many of us, one of our greatest fears is to be alone, because when we are alone we confront the hollowness that gnaws at our very being. Alone, we are restless souls.

The Fear-Self is an escape from our aloneness. Yet our identification with the person doing the escaping is the portal into unhappiness and insecurity.

This is the illusion of escape. It is the foundation of all our addictions. Alone with only ourselves, we are, it seems ... like nothing. And nothing is an unpleasant state of being.

Where does that sense of unpleasantness come from? What if that unpleasantness is nothing less than the palpable echo of our childhood trauma? By experiencing our rejected selves now, we re-experience the pain of our primal rejection.

Where does that sense of unpleasantness when we are alone come from? What if that unpleasantness is nothing less than the palpable echo of our childhood trauma? By experiencing our rejected selves now, we re-experience the pain of our primal rejection.

By seeking to escape that unpleasantness through the Fear-Self, we repeat for the umpteenth time a strategy that has not worked for us in any enduring way. But when we reject ourselves, we assume the role of the grown-up who judged us as unsatisfactory so long ago. When we identify with those who felt contempt for our inner selves, we fully close the circle and become the parents from whom we craved unconditional love but feared at the same time.

Cleverly, the Wound has turned us inside out, and we become, in fact, the only authentic rejecters of ourselves!

Many efforts designed to improve ourselves serve simply to affirm the Wound. In seeking to improve, to be better, to be more, we agree with all of our invalidators that we aren't good enough just as we are. It is as simple and as complex as that. We nurture our own Wound in the endless quest to be different from who we truly are.

Prior to liberation, we are alone, interacting with other solitary objects. After liberation, we are directly connected to every energy that emerges in our life context. Our connections cross the dimensions of space and the backward- and forward-arching arrows of time.

When we seek escape from our Wound, we unwittingly sustain our aloneness. But when we understand, in the depths of our being, that everyone is wounded, we begin to realize our fundamental connection with everyone else. We are no longer special in our victimization.

When we seek escape from our Wound, we unwittingly sustain our aloneness. But when we understand, in the depths of our being, that everyone is wounded, we begin to realize our fundamental connection with everyone else.

We awaken to our intimate connection with our fellow human beings through the shared experience of invalidation. No one is spared the luxury of growing up in our modern culture without suffering. That is Rule #1. We all have suffered, and we all have created images and masks designed to show the world how well we are. For many of us, the whole of our lives has been dedicated to the purpose of appearing happy. Sometimes the job is done so well that we begin to really believe it, and we truly merge with our array of Fear-Selves. We become so invested in our clever adaptations that we lose touch with our authentic beings. This is why Fear-Selves so fiercely defend themselves: There is so much at stake.

We connect with all of our brothers and sisters through the great veil of tears that is the child experiencing her own, individual Wound when it formed so long ago. The soul-crushing traumas we have all endured are the very essence of our connection through our shared victimization. It is nothing less than the universal Wound that unites us.

With this understanding, we can never again truly resent another. We now know, through our own experience, that every other person has also suffered and continues to suffer the consequences of their invalidation and Wound. They may differ in intensity and style, but we all have this core experience. No one is spared.

With understanding, we can never again truly resent another. We now know, through our own experience, that every other person has also suffered and continues to suffer the consequences of their invalidation and Wound. They may differ in intensity and style, but we all have this core experience. No one is spared.

We evolve beyond our own narrow needs, fears, and compulsions as a consequence of this understanding. It is what ties us all together. The uniting shadow of the Wound dwarfs the shallower divisions of class, race, sexual preference, culture, and age. It underlies them all.

By honoring our collective grief and suffering, we become wise and compassionate. No longer are we solitary victims of our personal woe, but we are bound together as one, sharing the same tribulations and challenges. We can also acknowledge that the added weight of such cruel conditions as poverty and cultural dispossession act only to deepen our individual wounds.

The way of compassion does not mean that you *must* become more sensitive and responsive to the suffering of others. This is often the conventional understanding of the term "compassion." This definition creates a "rule," and rules that seek to control behavior are the stuff of authority and Fear-Selves. Rather, "compassion" means understanding that we all suffer, and that suffering is the source of intimate connection. It awakens our hearts from their self-centered slumber to know that any time a person suffers the shame and pain of invalidation, we understand their pain and are open and tender to what all of us have experienced. We replace our rage, rejection, and indifference with tolerance. We erase our smug superiority by reaching out and touching the other with the touch of equals at the level of heart. Our divisions are healed through care forged through understanding.

The Wound is, therefore, our gateway to universal understanding. That which shines brightest is often found on the flip side of brilliance. When we invest our identification in the Wound, with its reference to our innate inadequacy, we are blind to the gem that lies on its other side.

As we transform, we migrate from our individualistic identification with the Fear-Selves and merge with the collective identity represented by the Wound. The Fear-Self is the most direct signpost to who we are *not*. We see that our personal suffering, embodied by the Wound, becomes the portal to our mutual unity as human beings as we struggle to awaken to our Life Force. In this way, what has been dark becomes light.

18 - Getting Past Lack

Our approach to understanding the Wound and the Fear-Selves has thus far been primarily analytical. However, the beliefs and thoughts that undergird the Wound and Fear-Selves always have an emotional component. This emotion—the feeling of *lack*—is anxious, insecure, and compulsive. The primary purpose of every Fear-Self is to assuage these feelings. But, as we have seen, the Fear-Self actually sustains them.

The feeling of lack is the "mother" of our dreaded emotional experiences. It is a physical/bodily sensation. We experience it as a kind of inner hollowness or emptiness. We try to fill this lack with some kind of "doing": We shop, start projects, dream about new relationships, practice a religion, join groups, have children, and whatever else we think can fill this hollow core. The one thing we very rarely consider is doing *nothing*. We could indulge in talk therapy for years (which is, of course, another common response to lack) and never have the slightest impact on this feeling. We could meditate for a lifetime without reducing the power of lack in our lives. Until we are willing to be open to this feeling, we will continue to organize our lives to avoid it.

We are fortunate that the experience of lack is both common and frequent, because if we are to get a grip on it, we will need to interact with it in a way that does not create a new Fear-Self. The first step is to become mindful of what we have been doing in the past. Obviously, whatever we have been doing hasn't worked. The next time the feeling emerges, don't turn on the TV, make an unnecessary phone call, start a project that can wait, meditate, or schedule a therapy appointment. Instead, observe the feeling without getting attached to any sort of consequence or getting overly involved with the sensation.

Lack is established with the infantile trauma that gave birth to our Wound. It is the pre-verbal manifestation of our original and most decisive invalidation. When the Wound tells us we are inadequate, we experience the feeling of lack. This is the Wound as a physical sensation.

Lack is established with the infantile trauma that gave birth to our Wound. It is the pre-verbal manifestation of our original and most decisive invalidation. When the Wound tells us we are inadequate, we experience the feeling of lack. This is the Wound as a physical sensation. That's why everything we do to fill this hollow sensation is the act of a Fear-Self in its role as false healer. It is a strategy that must fail. It can only sustain the power of the underlying Wound and maintain the dominance of Fear-Selves in our lives.

Exercise 10:   Observing the Lack Experience

When we watch and fully experience the sensation of lack, our purpose is to explore it in a productive way. This is a brilliant approach to self-healing, because it displays the whole dynamic of the Wound and its corresponding Fear-Self. First we feel lack—we feel the tension that surrounds it, we feel the compulsive sensations that emerge from it, and we feel the desperate need to "do" something to reduce its weight on us. When we feel lack, we ought to connect the sensation with our knowledge of the Wound. We might say something like, "This is how I felt when I was first negated by those whose love I needed most." This feeling is the very distant echo of a much younger you. This is the pain of your invalidation, and this is also the pain you have inflicted on others when you have intentionally or unintentionally invalidated them—particularly those you claim you love.

So we watch the feeling without seeking any outcome. We are not getting involved in the drama it wants to create. We just watch without allowing any impression on the spirit that is doing the watching. I would also suggest that you not focus too much attention on the feeling, because that would be a form of intentional doing that would have an implicit interest in affecting the feeling. We do not want to "do" anything that would influence the lack experience. That is exactly what Fear-Selves do, and the very last thing we want is to cultivate yet another Fear-Self as a result of this exercise. We just let the lack experience be whatever it wants to be.

In allowing it to be whatever it wants to be, we cut off its source of power in our lives! Its power is manifested by getting us to do something to affect it. That "something" that intervenes is a Fear-Self. This is the enslaved, unliberated self. But the self that allows, the self that acts not to conduct itself as a slave, is our authentic self. Try to get a feeling of that uninvolved, observing being; really get a feeling for that. That is your true self! That is the part of you that never changes under any circumstance. That is the core you that has never been affected by age. It is also that part of you that is capable of possessing a much wider identification with the world around you.

We liberate ourselves from the power of lack by ceasing to play the game of resistance. We will always lose power and authenticity when we resist. By doing what is

non-intuitive—by doing nothing—we honor the lack
experience by allowing it to be whatever it chooses.

The path to self-liberation must pass through the portal of the Wound, and we do this on the level of feeling by simply allowing the experience of lack, whether it is mild or intense, to pass through our awareness.

Reacting to lack is the entrance to our deadened self. Any attempt we make to affect this experience is self-deadening.

When this lesson is understood fully, we begin to understand that *we* are our only effective healer. Teachings like this are only pointers to your true power and wisdom. When we put a full stop on reactions to the lack experience, we rediscover the feeling of our authentic self. We move from identifying with the feeling of lack to living the mystery of our true nature. When we can live with lack without reacting to it, a new sense of self naturally emerges. It is the self of self-responsibility, as opposed to the self that was merely reactive. We stop seeking to fill our inner emptiness and assume the ineffable quality of our authentic being.

On the other side of lack is our true, vibrant self. When you stop reacting to lack, you can feel your life come sweeping back to you. You will feel your passion no matter what conditions are occurring in your life.

The irony of experiencing your authentic passion is that, in many cases, this passion emerges in an energetic form that connects with everything else in our universe. We are no longer solitary, acting against the flow of experience. This is an awesome experience of realignment. We regain our inherent balance when we honor the lack experience and feel what manifests on the other side of it.

This does not mean that we will never again experience the lack sensation. We will, but now we will understand it as simply a feeling of habit and invalidation. We also discover a portal to our primal selves at the moment of our isolation and invalidation. Instead of fleeing toward some unfulfilling, temporary validation, we allow a new life perspective to emerge in the moment. This is not another role, a new "you." It is another *moment*. If you think of this as the birth of a new "you," then you are just creating a new, more refined Fear-Self. That is the action of self-improvement. It is not the act of liberation. Our purpose is not to create a new "you," but to connect the authentic you to the vibrancy of the ongoing moments of life. The authentic you is ineffable and untouchable. It is pre-thought. It is the "isness" that existed before any Fear-Selves arrived to steal the scene.

19 - Finding Our Passion

When living under the thrall of a dominant Fear-Self, our life choices are governed by a belief in our inadequacy. This is living the life of the Lie. Our life becomes dedicated to avoiding the underlying Wound. It is compulsive action. It has the appearance of being necessary and essential, but it does not reflect the dreams embodied within our soul.

The Fear-Self's mandate is avoidance, and it drives us to continually think of ways to steer clear of what we fear. In contrast, passion is what we are drawn to with no need for thought. Our passion certainly nurtures thought, but it is not defined by it. Where the Fear-Self seeks to protect, passion seeks to express. Where the Fear-Self separates, passion unites. Where the Fear-Self will always need more power, passion is content with the power it naturally possesses. Where the Fear-Self acts from a place of deficiency, passion flows from fullness. Where the Fear-Self lives in a universe of distrust, passion trusts itself.

Some of us are already connected to our authentic passions, but many of us have lost touch with our personal dreams. To live your passion, you will need to regain contact with those dreams.

Exercise 11:   The Diné Approach to Finding Your Passion

This exercise is designed for people who have lost touch with their passion. If you already know what excites your imagination and you are living that dream, feel free to skip this exercise.

Beginning in the mid-1990s, I had the privilege of working with traditional Diné (Navajo) counselors in their Peace-

making Division. This initiative was designed to revive indigenous approaches to conflict resolution. The traditional medicine people of the Diné believe that invalidation is the primary cause for violence and depression. My work with them was the seed for this book. This description of Peacemaking is not, necessarily, representative of the practice. This example is greatly simplified.

While most Peacemaking deals with problems between people, it is also used with individuals who are struggling with life issues. Many people went to Peacemaking because they had gotten into trouble, but others went because they were just not happy with life. While the terminology of the Fear-Self and Wound is not used by the Diné, as we proceed, you will see interesting world view parallels.

Imagine that you are in the room where the Peacemaking is taking place. It is a simple office, with inexpensive furniture, papers strewn about, and Indian pictures and sports memorabilia scattered around. Imagine that you are a young man entering the office.

The Peacemaker asks you what is happening in your life. In every case, I observed, people were unhappy. They were not doing what they wanted to do. In most cases, their relationships with family members were filled with conflict and pain, violence and acrimony. Many suffered from substance abuse. You pour out your litany of troubles.

As if blind to the specific presenting problems you have described, the Peacemaker asks you if you are living the life *you dreamed you would be living at this point in your life. "No," you reply, annoyed that the Peacemaker apparently has not listened to the list of serious issues you face. And then the Peacemaker says, "The problems you are experiencing in your life are a result of choices you have made. Isn't this true?" In this case, you've been arrested for selling crack cocaine. "Isn't this the life you have <u>chosen</u>?" the Peacemaker asks. This is not the question you are expecting.*

(From the perspective of the Fear-Self, our life is not a consequence of our choice, but from the perspective of the Peacemaker, this is precisely the case!)

You answer that what you are "doing" in your life is not your choice, but something that you need to do. This is just how life is happening; you're the victim of bad luck. The Peacemaker then asks, "But you chose this life, didn't you? Isn't this the life you have chosen?" His tone has no quality of judgment or irony.

(The Fear-Self does what it believes it has to do. It is not comfortable with the notion that it has actively chosen the life it is currently living. It feels like it is driven to do what it does.)

Each time you hear this question, you become pensive. Sometimes you resist, saying, "But I didn't choose this." The Peacemaker replies, "But you must have chosen this; otherwise you wouldn't be selling cocaine to your own people. Isn't that true?"

You become noticeably sad and inward. You are awakening to the truth of your life. You can see that you have, in fact, been the person who is making the key choices in your life. With a quality of profound, almost breathless sadness, you admit, "Yes, I guess that I have made these choices." The whole disaster of your life is now becoming apparent. You see exactly how your own conscious choices have made this life possible.

(Living as the Fear-Self, our life choices are usually unconscious. The Peacemaking process brings our life choices to immediate, living awareness.)

The Peacemaker then looks directly into your eyes and says, "So this is the life you have chosen for yourself. That is a good thing, because this life is your journey."

"Yes ... yes, this is the life I have chosen. But what do you mean, it is a 'good thing'?" you say in disbelief. "How can it be good that I'm selling cocaine to my own people?"

The Peacemaker repeats, "It is a good thing, because your life can never have been different from what it is. You are doing exactly what is right for you. This is the journey you had to take."

(The Fear-Self believes that life is not right—it is wrong, and because it is wrong, it is also dangerous. It is the purpose of the Fear-Self to improve our chances against life's threat. But the Peacemaker tells us that life is perfect exactly as it is, no matter how painful or crazy it might appear.)

When you hear the traditional counselor say that the life you are living is exactly right just as it is, you are baffled: "Peacemaker, what do you mean?"

"What I mean is that this is exactly how things are. You can say that this is the way the spirit of life (the Great Spirit) is. You were meant to live your life exactly as you have lived it. After all, it is this life that has brought you here with me. The choices you have made in your life are exactly those choices you needed to make. There is no error at all. You must know that you are a sacred being, and everything you do is perfect and sacred."

(Diné understanding is, in this way, no different from the perspectives expressed in Buddhism and other Eastern spiritual traditions. Life is perfect exactly the way it presents itself. In Diné cosmology, all acts, no matter how seemingly cruel and destructive, emerge from the same sacred space as everything else in the universe. It is all part of an ongoing process of creation and destruction that moves everlastingly from balance/harmony to imbalance/disharmony in a circular movement, which is never at rest. Yet there are things we can do to restore or maintain balance/harmony.)

The Peacemaker then asks, "Is this the life you want to be living?"

Like so many others before you, you respond with a melancholy, "No, this is not the life I want to live."

Then the Peacemaker asks a profound question—a question that seeks to arouse catharsis. He puts his arm on your shoulder, comes close and looks directly at you. "Go back to when you were young, maybe just 10 years old. Go back to that time and ask that person if he had a dream for himself."

You look up toward the ceiling and say, "Yes, I had a dream for myself." The Peacemaker asks, "What was that dream?" And then you speak of the dream that your 10-year-old self possessed. It was about having a family where there was love between parents and children, where there was hope, where they could pull through life supporting one another, where they could build a life together. It is a dream of connection in this world where you currently have none. You realize that you are now speaking through your tears..

The Peacemaker asks, "Are you living that dream now?" You whisper sadly, "No, I am not living my dream."

The Peacemaker asks, "What has happened to your dream? Where is that dream now?"

You answer, "My dream is dead." You might just as easily have said, "My dream is lost," or simply "I don't know." Your intense grief is fueled by the stark contrast between the ruin of your life as it is now, and the dream you once had so long ago.

The Peacemaker then says something else unexpected: "I feel your sadness as well. I know what it is like to see dreams die. I know what it is like to feel lost in this world. I want you to know that I wish you the very best with your life."

Suddenl your mood changes from self-engaged sadness to surprise and irritation. "What do you mean that you wish me the very best with my life? I came to you for help, and after spilling my guts to you, the best you can come up with is 'Best of luck with your life'? What is that supposed to mean?"

"It means exactly that," says the Peacemaker. "I cannot help you. If I could, I would, but I can't"

"What do you mean you can't?" you shout angrily. "Aren't you a healer? Isn't it obvious that I need help? I need to be healed! If you can do nothing to help me, then I don't know what I'm doing here. This whole thing was a big mistake. You're a fake like the others."

"If I could help you I would," says the Peacemaker, "but I knew at the outset that I would not be able to help you in the way you would like me to."

(Another Fear-Self has reared its ugly head. From the perspective of this Fear-Self, an opportunity for self-improvement via connection with the traditional healer has hung tantalizingly close, but now appears to have been snatched out of reach. This Fear-Self knows that he cannot heal or help himself—he needs external help. He is not adequate to the task of healing himself. This is the voice of the Wound speaking through the Fear-Self.)

In response to your desperate anger, the Peacemaker says, "Where do you need to find your own healing?"

You snap back, "It should be pretty obvious by now that I am not capable of making good choices. I need help, and you are not giving it to me."

"So what should you do?" asks the Peacemaker.

"I don't know. I came here to find some answers."

"Is that why you're here?" asks the Peacemaker. "What answers would you like to find?"

"I don't know—isn't that obviouss?" you say emphatically. "Why am I here?"

"Why are you here? That is a very good question, isn't it?" the Peacemaker replies. "I do not have any answers. Only you have those answers. Any answer to any question you might have cannot come from me, but only from you. There is a healer in this room, but that person is not the one speaking."

"Are you saying that I am a healer?" you scoff. "If that were true, then why am I here? I have totally fucked up my life. I am not a healer. You are supposed to be the healer."

"You are the only healer in this room, and that is the truth", the Peacemaker affirms again.

You are now both resentful and despondent. You do not believe the Peacemaker. When it appears that you have hit rock bottom, the Peacemaker hands you a sheet of paper with two columns. One column is a list of healing practices that are Native American, such as sweat lodge, singing, dancing, and working with a traditional counselor; the other lists practices that are Western, including job training, substance abuse counseling, therapy, going back to school, etc. The Peacemaker asks you to take the list home, read it carefully and discuss it with no one. He asks you to circle each item that speaks to your heart and not necessarily your head, to return the list to the Peacemaker the next day. He has given you a little nudge that encourages you to become your own healer and to move the power of your life from external, compulsive living to choices you have made from the heart.

Why were you asked to use your heart rather than your head? Traditional Dinè counselors assert that the heart is closer to our authentic being than our thinking mind is. Don't take this belief too literally—they would also assert the vital importance of the mind in problem-solving. The deeper meaning relates to our moods and immediate life circumstances: A heart-centered identity is more constant and less affected by mood or whim.

This long exercise shows a process of self-discovery that is primarily self-directed. To find your passion, you need to be alone with yourself. Go back to when you were young, before you felt compelled to satisfy adult responsibilities, and seek to recall those things that excited your spirit. What caused your heart to soar? If you were to die tomorrow, how would you want to be remembered? What would you have regretted never doing? What is your love?

Most of us, of course, have adult responsibilities which include raising a family and making a living, but you also need to make discovering your dream a priority, if only to reconnect with your abandoned self. Your dream belongs only to you. Seek it out. Make sure that it is not just another Fear-Self that wants to impress others or yourself—that is fake and inauthentic. Your dream must be something that will bring you joy. It is not something that others want from you, but what you want for yourself.

Seeking your dream should be pretty simple, and not too time-consuming. It can take the form of spending more time with yourself, perhaps taking walks in nature. It could be taking a course that excites your imagination and maybe starts you off on a new career. It could be starting to listen to what other members of your family have to say. It could be anything. The key is to just start doing what moves your heart. Most of us will need to continue supporting our family. But if that has become an expression of a Fear-Self, it may be time to reassess your work choice and plan to do something that more closely aligns with your heart.

The key is to find your heart's voice. Ask yourself, are you living your dream? To discover your dream, you might want to go back to the dreams of your 10-year-old self. What did that person dream, what did she want? Be warned that a Fear-Self can masquerade as a dream. The authentic heart is not interested in bossing others around. It does not need or depend on external validation. It is just there for you as you. If you don't start nurturing it, before you know it your life will have passed you by, and you will have lived in a way that mirrors the sources of invalidation that gave birth to your Wound. We sustain our own invalidation as long as we don't respect the voice that comes from our heart.

One more word of advice: Please try to avoid more self-understanding. That is just another Fear-Self sneaking in through the back door. Take the plunge into your own unique heart, listen to its voice, and then start exploring what you love. Leave understanding aside for now and focus on what you want.

Key Point: The Wound and Projection

The Wound will always project your inadequacy into your immediate future. This insight has pertinence to the challenge of finding your passion. Fear-Selves live in the future (or past). They always carry core elements of the Wound in their thought/feeling world. Therefore, as we reflect on living our dream, don't be surprised if a Fear-Self does its duty and tells you that you are not adequate to live your dream. Watch that process in your own life. It is nefarious. There will always be a Fear-Self on hand, telling you what you can't or shouldn't do. It will come up will all sorts of reasons. You need to attend to your family; you're a loser; you need to be more practical; you're too old; you must take care of more pressing matters before attending to your selfishness, etc. Know that this is just the voice of the Wound speaking through its Fear-Self mouthpiece. Listen to it with a light heart and continue picturing yourself living in alignment with your heart.

To show you some elements of this process that might not be apparent, let me share with you some of the things I have found that bring me joy.

My older brother loves classical music. Well before my 5th birthday, he played for me music by Bach, Mozart, Brahms, and Wagner. No one had to coax me into loving what I heard. I loved it from the very start and I love it to this day. By the age of 7 my tastes had started to take their own course; I also liked some rock & roll, particularly Motown, the Beatles, and other pop groups. But even though my brother pressured me a little to like the same classics as he, I tended not to like opera as much and enjoyed composers such as Brahms, Vaughan-Williams, and Aaron Copland who were not among my brother's favorites.

I also have always loved baseball and football, especially my home teams of the Philadelphia Phillies and Eagles. (With their perennial losing records, I don't even know why I root for them, but I do.) I love every element of these sports and feel kind of let down when I miss a game.

I adore nature in all its forms. Hearing the sounds of birds in the morning fills me with joy. Taking hikes, climbing the Adirondacks or Green Mountains of Vermont, is a great pleasure for me. I particularly love the desolate high plains of middle America. Wandering the troubled grasslands of Western Oklahoma, Kansas, Nebraska, and South Dakota, the land seems to sing to me. I certainly hear its voice.

One of my greatest passions is justice. It is hard to describe how saddened and upset I have been about the current war in Iraq. Our government seems to have been the front office for an oil cartel that has used our young men and women as its own personal mercenaries. A government that serves the rich and well-off is not a government of the people. I am outraged by our government's imperial aspirations and its callous disregard for the nation's well-being. I also despair over the agonizing troubles of the Iraqi people who must deal with the turbulence we have unleashed in that part of the world.

I am free to live and love my passions. They require no external validation; I don't love classical music to impress anyone. They are simply true for me.

The Issue of Outrage

Many teachings that are inspired by Eastern philosophy advocate a way of life that is detached from the "marketplace." They see taking a stand in the political life of a community or country as an expression of dualism, and thus a clear indication of the absence of "enlightenment." From the perspective of liberation, this point of view is not only naïve, it is wrong.

Part of liberation is the healthy freeing of one's anger from control by an invalidating superego. Far too often, teachers of Eastern philosophy and feel-good self-help suggest or say outright that the emotion of anger is soul-killing poison. Philosophies such as Buddhism emphasize peace of mind, as if emotions possess a hierarchy. In contrast, liberation demands responsibility. Our integrity as human beings depends on our ability to be responsive to our world. There is simply no other way to account for the well-being of our lives, our community, our country, and our world.

Part of liberation is the healthy freeing of one's anger from control by an invalidating superego. Far too often, teachers of Eastern philosophy and feel-good self-help suggest or say outright that the emotion of anger is soul-killing poison.

The world is perfect exactly as it is because it cannot be otherwise. But, paradoxically, this does not mean that there is not a role for people to play in its improvement. If history teaches us anything, it teaches the need to take action in the face of injustice. And because the forces of injustice are very often powerful and explicitly unfair, to take action against them requires a sense of outrage. Such outrage is, itself, an expression of love—love for our fellow human beings, for the animals and plants, and for the whole of our world. That is the sacred dimension of life. When we feel authentic outrage, we are energized to take the plunge into the well-being of our world. Sitting on the sidelines, filled with fear, straining to quell our anger, is the opposite of liberation. Liberation is not about being "content" or living up to an image that is above the din and fray of everyday life. It is about being passionate, strong, and resilient in the midst of struggle.

Ultimately, liberation is about connection. The greater our liberation, the more we are connected to the living web of this remarkable planet. We are no longer alone acting against life and the world. Our identification has moved from that of the small, calculating Fear-Self to the vastness of life itself. Our dignity is the dignity of life. That is why the ethos of responsibility is so much a part of our liberation. The extent to which we are shut off from our innate connections with life is the same extent to which we will fail in our responsibility to life.

When there is injustice, anger is a perfectly appropriate response. Anger is like any other emotion; it can be expressed in a way that is sensitive to context or it can be self-centered and dangerous. Anger is part of the palate of passion. Only the Fear-Self of the Pleaser/Do-Gooder is afraid of anger. The appropriate expression of anger is often an essential expression of one's authentic self. When it is contextual and reflects the heart's passion, it is also mindful of the needs and rights of others. Expressed in such conditions, it can be among the most powerful and necessary expressions of one's self.

Looking back on the history of the Holocaust (and other genocidal episodes), it is a great regret that the world tolerated Hitler and his obviously insane hatred of Jews, Romani, and gays. Heartfelt outrage could have saved the world millions of lives. Personally, I am stunned by how flagrantly modern civilization trashes the environment. When I see a massive SUV, I think of the needless Iraqi war, of the wasting of the planet's resources, and of the destruction of natural habitat. We live on the very zenith of the capitalist iceberg. Know that when you shop at a place like Wal-Mart, where many of the employees are so underpaid that they are simultaneously on public assistance, many of the products you are buying are produced in sweatshop environments, where workers make pennies, work like slaves, and produce industrial waste so great that the waters of the Yangtze River are too contaminated to be used by industry. There are countless issues that ought to provoke outrage if we truly love our fellow human beings and love this extraordinary planet.

Anger in the service of a Fear-Self is dangerous, compulsive, and self-centered. Frequently it seeks to harm another. This is, of course, a sign of our enslavement. Such anger always has invalidation and shame in its heart. But when anger serves the community, the well being of the environment, or any other domain that connects us to goodness, it is justified and often essential.

Liberation is a world without explicit rules. Anger isn't labeled as bad, and self-control as good. Instead, everything is a matter of context. Liberation is liberation from rules that fail to connect us with the context of our lives. Liberation asserts connection over separation, and responsibility over blame.

The Issue of Selfishness

How can one be selfish and stop being self-centered at the same time?

Authentic selfishness emerges from the heart and recognizes its fundamental connections to others and the world. Fear-based selfishness serves the purpose of avoiding contact with the Wound by pursuing self-inflation.

Let's say that your dream is to travel more, and the place you would really like to see is China. But your wife, who also is eager to take a trip, isn't interested in going there; she would prefer a more relaxing beach vacation. So you think, "I just read this Liberation book, which says that I should live my dream—and my dream is go to China." It seems as though you're in a dilemma—what do you do?

I would suggest that if your dream is directly counter to the interests of those with whom you are closest, consider taking a careful look at that dream. Make sure that it is not a Fear-Self wanting to show its power by asserting its dominance. If your primary Fear-Self is a Pleaser who is always doing what others want in order to gain and secure their affections, upon reading a book like this one, a new, emboldened Fear-Self might assume the stage and use the desire for new experiences as a way to express the self that has lived in the shadow of the Pleaser for so long. This is only exchanging one Fear-Self—the Pleaser—for its opposite—the Tough Guy. Only you can determine whether that is what's happening.

It has been my experience that the voice of the heart has, at its center, the soft glow of love and connection. It is a transcendence of the small self. It does not seek the approval of others yet no longer sees itself as an isolated operator in a dangerous world. The desire for travel to China may come directly from your heart, but I would ask you to be mindful of the remarkable resourcefulness of the Fear-Selves. They come in myriad forms.

It has been my experience that the voice of the heart has, at its center, the soft glow of love and connection. It is a transcendence of the small self. It does not seek the approval of others yet no longer sees itself as an isolated operator in a dangerous world.

Living your dream is a right that you are obliged to claim, but be mindful of all your connections. A dream that is hurtful to others or is indifferent to their voices is probably a Fear-Self desire.

Key Point: Resilience

As we move from the world of the Fear-Selves to the world of liberation, the rigidity of self-identification greatly relaxes. Where a Fear-Self is tight and rigid, a liberated self is resilient and fluid. This does not mean that a liberated self always accommodates. It means that a liberated self acts from a position of connection with the whole of life as it is unfolding in the now. Where a Fear-Self is ceaselessly past/future-oriented, the power of the liberated self is expressed within the presenting context of life. Self-assertion, when it occurs, happens without the meddling confusions of the calculating ego. Assertion happens without reference to self-inflationary needs.

You will need to share your dreams with your intimates. If there is conflict, you are obliged to listen to their voices. They may be operating from a Fear-Self position, but authentic selves can understand and appreciate that. It is not your task to be their healer. We all live in a social environment dominated by Fear-Selves. Facing this world with humility and understanding is the everyday task of a liberated person.

The Requirement of Work

For many of us, the demands of raising and supporting a family may make it seem that we simply do not have the time to live our dreams. It seems that people are busier than ever, and it is not hard to understand that when all the necessary chores are done, many prefer to just veg out in front of the television. This is perfectly understandable.

The challenge of liberation is primarily the challenge of understanding the interplay between our Wound and our many Fear-Selves. The soil of liberation needs to be tilled before it can bear fruit. Emergence into liberation is never a consequence of direct effort. Effort is force, and force is the tool of a Fear-Self. When we truly understand that process, we naturally become liberated and gain access to our Life Force no matter how we are pulled by work and family responsibilities. When we see through the Wound and the Fear-Selves, our source of guidance moves away from anxious thoughts to the calmer and more centered region of the heart. What previously seemed important and necessary can become irrelevant after liberation, and what seemed irrelevant when living under the veils of the Fear-Self can become the center of our lives.

Again, the life of liberation is distinct from fear-based life in that it is, essentially, devoid of calculation. If you inadvertently put a finger onto something hot, you recoil instantly without needing to think about it. That is a metaphor for the liberated life. It is not thought-dependent, but is a wholly natural and effortless response to life as it presents itself.

When we do what we don't want to do, we are resistant. An underlay of anger colors our actions. A Fear-Self is often furious at having to do things that act against its preferences. We become sick and tired of doing the dishes, tending to the endless needs of our children, walking the dog, whatever. But from the perspective of liberation, all those activities express our connection with life and our responsibility to our own lives. They can be performed in a way that expresses love and fun. Washing dishes no longer takes us away from what we might prefer to do, but represents just one small act through which we express our devotion to our family. It can become an activity that we share or with which we takes turns. Routine chores often call on us to be more creative in how we manage our lives. Doing tasks with a light heart and a sense of connection can never be faked. It either happens or it doesn't. You will know the difference.

Also, when we see through the falseness of our Fear-Selves, we are able to see how we have encouraged Fear-Self development in our children. We can see vividly how our fear of failure has placed enormous pressures on them. We can liberate ourselves from the belief that they have to be on three sports teams, sing in the school chorus, get good grades, and a million other things; we can see the painful insanity of the driven life. We nurture depression when we are always running to keep up with the Joneses.

A Diné healer once told me that knowledge of the esoteric must always come first. This is a profound insight. Before all of our quotidian activities, before all of our meaningless planning, we need to find our own place of resilience and equanimity. Our obsession with achievement is all about dealing with the limitless insecurity of the Fear-Selves. It is sound and fury, signifying nothing. The time to stop the craziness is now. When we give up on the false, we allow the opportunity for the real to surface in our lives. Through that channel we can live our dreams and discover our passions.

The Pitfalls of Passion

The pitfalls of embracing one's passion has been alluded to several times in this chapter, but it deserves a more direct discussion.

Indulging one's passion may feel good, but in doing so, we run the risk of establishing a new dominant identity. Let's say that your passion is architecture. You throw yourself into the joy of creation. You have devoted a great deal of energy and time to this goal, and your joy is your professional life as an architect. By embracing this passion, you have also forged your primary identity.

But when life impedes on that joy—perhaps due to the demands of parenting or because of a career setback, you will experience resistance and suffering. The extent to which you find yourself in your passion and dedicate yourself to it is the same extent to which you will experience pain and conflict if your passion is denied.

Anytime we marry a role, we divorce ourselves from the rest of life. The deeper our commitment, the more pervasive the conflicts in the rest of our life.

This is something each of us needs to understand anytime we indulge our passion: There is always a cost.

The point is not to ignore your passion, but to understand its down side. If you are unwilling to compromise your passion, then the cost of being part of a family may be too high and you might be better off remaining on your own. These are the choices we must make, consciously or unconsciously. Every choice we make creates a universe of consequences.

No matter what else you do with your life, your dreams, whether attended to or ignored, will always cast the longest shadow. What does this mean? It means that if you honor your heart and the desires it expresses in its soft voice, then you will not die with the terrible regret that you never lived your authentic self. If you fail to attend to that voice, you will live with the hollowness that is the signature of living an inauthentic life. Your heart will either fill your life with grace or, by ignoring it, fill your life with sorrow. The choice is yours.

20 - The End of Self-Identified Projection

The Fear-Self is projection. The vitality of its projection varies from the intense and profoundly unstable to the extremely subtle, where it is all but invisible.

We cannot see how life really is unless we are able to see how we project our psychology onto life. Operating from the perspective of projection, we are ceaselessly reactive. Our sensed world is divided up into discrete categories of what serves our purpose (a very small percentage of what is actually sensed) and what does not serve our purpose (everything else). When we are dominated by projection, we are not open to authentic life. Instead, life is only what we experience through the filter of a Fear-Self.

Projection pulls us away from the now. Living in projection, we are sensitive only to the ceaseless press of a Fear-Self: "I must do this"; "I must do that"; "I must find things wrong"; "I must locate potential dangers." The now, where everything actually happens, is overlooked. We know ourselves and our world only through projection.

Underneath all projections is the Wound. Projection organizes experience into crude categories of good and bad. Because it is predicated on an iron-hard belief in our own inadequacy, the purpose of projection is to discover opportunities to counter this belief. It is, in fact, projection that creates Fear-Selves and Fear-Selves that maintain the projection that gave them birth.

Let's see how this operates. A Pleaser fears rejection (her Wound belief that she is worthless). Through projection, she categorizes people into those who help to counter this painful belief and those who do not. The latter group she hates because they threaten to bring attention to her Wound. She works tirelessly to produce opportunities to maintain and improve her standing in the "approved" community of "good" people and thus sustain distance from her Wound.

When we see through the Wound and the Fear-Selves, the power of our projection diminishes greatly. As it declines, our own authentic power fills the space. The Pleaser can finally take a rest from dividing people into friends and foes and living in terror of failing at her next public exhibition. What a relief that must be!

When the Body Person sees through his Wound and dominant Fear-Self, he can still be active and fit, but he is no longer haunted by his inevitable physical decline or other fears related to his appearance. He is free to be himself. For the first time he can have a good laugh at himself, and those around him can breathe a whole lot easier when his compulsive projections have relaxed their dark grip

The Loner can begin to re-engage with the raw vitality of life and stop being a slave to her fears. She can recognize and honor the power of her Wound, yet take steps to connect with people. At first, she might be tentative and guarded, but she no longer needs to flee. She may preserve her preference for aloneness, but now this preference is informed by understanding and compassion. It is no longer compulsive and desperate.

The relentless Achiever can stop and ask herself, do I really want to be doing all of this? Is this really me? What sacrifice am I making for my self-interested accomplishments? If I'm telling myself that I must do these things for the sake of my family, am I certain that is true? When the Achiever sees through her projections, she can finally take a long, languorous breath and start regaining her balance. Indeed, she might find that she truly loves what she is doing, but she is no longer driven by fear of failure or by compulsion. People around her can feel her transformation. Suddenly she is warm and vulnerable and capable of deeply connecting with others in her life. Even her dog greets her with more excitement when she returns home after a "not as long" day at the office.

Living life through our projections assures us that our insecurities will be maintained. This is a world of danger, where our survival as a worthy being is always in doubt. In direct contrast with the world of the hunter-gatherer, in the world of projections, trust, if it manifests at all, is a very fragile and tenuous commodity. The mind needs to constantly survey its small world for enemies and threats to its flimsy security. For many of us, this is the only way we know how to live.

Projection is like a fog that surrounds us with its distorted perspective on the world and life. It is the price we pay for our purported psychological protection. The consequence is a life lived with fear. It is toxic not only to ourselves but to everyone else in our life.

Projection is a ceaseless flight from projected fear. As it turns out, passing through our fear—a fear that we now can see to be an insubstantial phantom—is the only journey worth taking.

Key Point: Resistance to Projection

Projection is part of the interplay of the Wound and the Fear-Selves. It is never advisable to resist it or seek to stop it. Instead, we honor projection by understanding it as a sign of our Life Force. Seeing projection without getting involved in its voice or even allocating too much of our attention to it is the secret to seeing through it. A feeling of relaxation will naturally emerge as its grip on your identity is loosened.

Finding the Place of No Harm

Every Fear-Self is created to provide safety to a wounded image of one's self. Thought ceaselessly spins stories of danger, and thus the Fear-Self is sustained throughout our lives.

A young child needs love and care. That is the full expression of their being. But when he is invalidated, a new element of being is created—the unwanted self. Of course, the unwanted self morphs into our more mature sense of inadequacy and insufficiency. The unwanted self is the Wound in the form of the injured personality.

As long as a baby or young child is received for its innate beingness, which is expressed as through unconditional love, support, and care, the "unwanted self" is not formed.

All of our Fear-Selves are adapted to counter identification with the unwanted self and make ourselves safe from harm. Yet here is the irony: We can only be harmed by something with which we identify. Our images of ourselves as an Achiever, a Tough Guy, a Pleaser, an Expert, a Body Person, a Spiritualist can and will be damaged. An image is always tenuous, not fully certain of itself, and often brittle. It is a belief set out into the world, and it will suffer all the wear and tear that the physical universe inflicts.

We can only be harmed by something with which we identify. Our images of ourselves as an Achiever, a Tough Guy, a Pleaser, an Expert, a Body Person, a Spiritualist can and will be damaged. An image is always tenuous, not fully certain of itself, and often brittle.

No matter how great the hurt, no matter how great the tribulation, there is always a part of us remains untouched. That is our authentic being. It needs no image. In fact, if we try to attach an image onto it, it is not possible! Our authentic self is not an image. Yet we seem to "know" only our images of ourselves and others. All Fear-Selves, no matter how refined they might be, are ultimately images.

The final knowing of one's self is not a knowing at all. We can only trick ourselves into "knowing" something outside of our authentic being. Our authentic self can never be known. It can only be, no matter what else we do or is done to us in our lives.

That is why our authentic selves can never be harmed. We are absolutely 100% safe when all our false images are allowed to disperse and our authentic selves can finally live in the light of day.

When that happens, we are nothing and everything at the same moment, for no dividing line can be drawn between the authentic self and anything the mind labels as "other."

Anything you are defensive about is an image! Observing your defenses is a great way to discover your false self-images. Nearly all of us are defensive about our bodies, our feelings, and our thoughts. They are, therefore, not our authentic selves. They are fake. The instant we identify with any image, thought, or feeling, we indulge in the fantasy of the falsely known self. We are not our bodies; we are not our thoughts; we are not our feelings. But while the body, thought, and feeling are not who you are, they are a part of you! It is a paradox.

The intensity of our defensiveness is also a mark of how identified we are with a particular image. That image is a marker of our dominant Fear-Self. Conversely, we most intensely engage with those invalidators who remind us of our original invalidators, especially our parents. If we are still seeking approval, we will find merit in their invalidation. If we are still hurting from our invalidation (and most of us are), we will very deeply resent them. These intense feelings sustain our identification with the Fear-Self. We are most ready to take offense with those we need most. Children need their parents, and often it is the parents who receive back the lovelessness they displayed many years ago.

The liberated person is all but indifferent from any form of attack on her image. She has discovered her true self and identifies with no image. This is the only place of sustainable and tangible safety. She is always safe and secure.

21 - Giving Up on Knowing

When we say we "know" something, we can mean many different things. We "know" something because we have seen it: "I know there is a tree in my back yard." We "know" something because we have done it: "I know how a computer works, because I put one together." We "know" something because we believe it to be true: "I know I'm a good mother—look how happy my children are!"

Most people would agree that the form of knowing based on belief is not true knowing—it's really just wanting something to be a certain way. But even the forms of knowing based on observation or experience are problematic, for if we base our knowing exclusively on what is sensed, we can run into many difficulties. Based on sight, for example, the Earth appears flat when it is anything but. Based on sight, the sun and stars revolve around the Earth, when the truth is exactly the opposite. In fact, we are deceived by our mind and our senses all of the time.

We might say that we know from experience. But just as we are deceived by our senses, we are also often deceived by our memories. How many of us believe that we really love someone, then something happens—an affair, a change in circumstance, and we fall *out* of love. What we believe we know is as much a consequence of context as it is of memory. It is neither stable nor reliable.

If we are completely honest with ourselves, we come to realize that we cannot truly know anything. This is a remarkable insight. We assume we know so much, but when we examine our knowing, all of it can be undermined by reasonable doubt. We have no idea what we will be thinking five minutes from now and we probably don't know what we were thinking five minutes ago. If I were to pluck something as seemingly simple as a blade of grass and asked you if you understood this blade of grass, how might you respond? Beyond describing it, we really cannot say what that blade of grass is.

So what can we know?

We can know only one thing; we are. *What* we are may be a mystery, but we can say with full confidence that we are. From this perspective, we can say life cannot be known, it can only be lived.

When we speak of "knowledge" in Liberation, we are speaking of psychological knowledge, which refers to our personal collection of beliefs.

Try to recall the last time you felt really happy and relaxed. Did you feel a pressing need to understand *why* you were happy? Did you feel a strong urge to analyze the situation? Once the happy and relaxed mood passed you may have felt those needs, but it is very unlikely that you felt that way in the happy and relaxed moment.

When we talk about the things we "don't know," we can divide them into the things we don't care about knowing and those we want to know.

We tend to feel the need to know something when we are not as happy and relaxed as we would like to be. There is an underlying belief that if we had more knowledge, we could discover the way to always be happy and relaxed.

Life does not work this way. Accumulating knowledge designed to control our feelings and thoughts is a total waste of time and energy. Knowledge about happiness does not lead to happiness.

We might ask ourselves, what part of us seeks to control life through knowing? In unison we could all reply: "A Fear-Self!" And we would all receive gold stars. When we are happy and relaxed, we are not motivated to control. At those times, life is great exactly as it is without any need for us to control anything.

In a psychological sense, the compulsion to know is directly linked to our desire to control. This is the work of a Fear-Self, who is motivated to control life as a way to avoid contact with the Wound. The Fear-Self tells us that if we knew something about a problem we could control it. This might work in practical instances such as fixing a broken appliance, or cooking a complicated recipe, or programming a computer, but it doesn't work in the more intangible areas of life, especially in interpersonal relationships. We might temporarily fool ourselves that "knowing" has allowed us to control certain situations, but this will unravel over time. Often we use this false knowing to force people and situations to do and be as we wish. But when the unravelling inevitably occurs, the dark energy of our Wound will be waiting to remind us yet again that each and every Fear-Self is merely a mask for the Wound that underlies it.

Exercise 12:   Releasing the Need to Know

To a Fear-Self, important knowledge consists of fears, desires, and hopes. It regulates and believes its world using these vital reference points. Attention will always go to "things" that relate to a fear, desire, or hope. See if you do that in your own life. Observe what really grabs your attention, and see if it generally does not relate to a desire, fear, or hope. Then step back and see what it would be like if these elements did not dominate your attention.

What is it like to live without all that much concern for your desires, fears, and hopes? This is an exercise that is relatively easy to do at times when your level of stress is low. It's a lot more challenging when you're feeling anxious.

As with all of the exercises in this book, the issue at hand tends to operate in a wide psychological dimension, ranging from the very obvious to the extremely subtle. In general, it is in the subtle manifestations of a problem that the Fear-Self most needs to be seen. As we evolve away from our identification with the Wound and the Fear-Selves, energies that were obvious prior to understanding will continue to express themselves, but in ways that are even subtler. Awareness of these energies can take a fair amount of practice. Here is a shortcut: when dealing with their more obvious manifestations, just as a fear-based personality identification is happening to you, try to get a sense of what life feels like when you are free of a Fear-Self. Let that feeling be your guide. Remember that resistance or forcing a mood or feeling is a waste of time. These states must arise without any coercion on your part. All coercion, including self-coercion, is an expression of a Fear-Self. This Fear-Self wears the mask of sophisticated self-awareness. It is always a fake.

Essential knowledge arises in the moment and is not a consequence of a planning and calculating Fear-Self. It takes a lot of trust to really believe that and live your life with that faith. The only necessary preparation is to be alert to the effects of the Wound and its Fear-Selves. Dedicate most of your attention to what is actually happening and devote less attention to the compulsions and projections of a presenting Fear-Self. Understanding that very little knowledge-based preparation is necessary should take a big load off your shoulders. You can release those unnecessary concerns and live with a lot more aliveness in the now.

Using awareness with effort is the act of a Fear-Self because it has an agenda. This exercise has no agenda but to see. The true self has no agenda. It may use agendas when it needs to, but it is not identified with any of them.

Awareness uses the senses, but the true self is not a sense. Our senses are of the body. They change over time. What is underneath never changes.

Living life as a slave to hopes, fears, and desires is the life of a Fear-Self.

The important thing is to see how knowing is used to maintain the Fear-Selves. Nearly all Fear-Selves are "know-it-alls." Raise your arm. Do you really know how you did that? Outside of practical knowledge required by a job or hobby or everyday home maintenance, everything we need to know emerges from the fabric of life as it unfolds.

Exercise 13:   Seeing the False-Knower

Watch the self that seeks to know. Observe from the seat of your unknowing awareness. Let it all just happen. Then see how effortlessly you identify with this "need-to-know" person. If you can see this process carefully, you will witness, firsthand, how our whole identities are co-opted by a Fear-Self. A Fear-Self experiences a need. That need is then linked with a desired goal. Before we know it, we are that needy Fear-Self.

22 - Our Stories

Ultimately, all Fear-Selves are stories we believe about ourselves. For the sake of simplicity, these stories come in two sizes: expansive and micro. Most of our discussion has focused on the "expansive" form of the Fear-Self. This is the big life story we have organized to counter the pain and suffering of the Wound. However, it is the "micro" form of the Fear-Selves that most colors our moment-to-moment experience.

All stories ask us to suspend some element of our critical faculties. This rule applies to Fear-Selves. But, by far, the most subtle element of the "micro" Fear-Self is a belief that nearly all of us take for granted. By understanding this belief, we can obtain the key to experiencing happiness in essentially every moment.

Take a look at what is happening now in your life. Allow your vision to see something. It can be anything. When we see an object, unless it surprises us in some way (beautiful or ugly or unexpected) or relates to the larger story of a Fear-Self, we tend to ignore it. As a result, we ignore most of our sensory elements manifesting in the now.

Why is this so?

We ignore these elements because of a very subtle, micro story. This story is the thought-based I. It is the very story we believe ourselves to be. The story of me is an extremely subtle narrative that is based on memory. It is an artifact of thought. It is not the authentic self; it is the thought self. Of all our personal stories, this one is the most deeply embedded and difficult to discern.

The key element of this story can be captured by the words, "I see _____" (fill in the blank) or "I feel _____". Now look at anything and feel that element of the seeing that is captured by "I." Feel the I that is seeing, the I that is hearing.

Attached to every sensory experience is an I. This is the I of our body, and as such, it is something that can be observed. This I/body is part of everything we do in life. It is the I that loves and hates, that drives to work, that hugs our kids, that was educated at university, etc.

The micro story that underlies all of the Fear-Selves is the belief that who we are is this I/body. We are not. It is simply a reference to the body that is doing the seeing, hearing, moving, or whatever else. It is an essential I, but it is not the being we truly are.

Now let's explore the alternative experience allowing this I/body to hear, see, touch, move, read, whatever. Try getting a sense of the I that is attached to the activity at hand. Allow the activity or object to manifest without the added quality of the I story; it just is. Do the same thing with whatever enters your field of hearing. Allow all sounds to be just as they are without inserting the story of an I that is hearing something. Now try the same experiment with a feeling you are experiencing. Experience the world in the moment; feel what is alive in your moment-to-moment experience.

Try getting a sense of the I that is attached to the activity at hand. Allow the activity or object to manifest without the added quality of the I story; it just is. Do the same thing with whatever enters your field of hearing. Allow all sounds to be just as they are without inserting the story of an I that is hearing something. Now try the same experiment with a feeling you are experiencing. Experience the world in the moment; feel what is alive in your moment-to-moment experience.

We are real—that we know—but we are not a thought-based story. The I that we conventionally attach to every experience is the I that is based on selective memory. It is selective because it is based on the hopes, fears, and desires of a Fear-Self. It is a projected story.

The nature of our reality cannot be captured by thought (ever!). The sense of who we are is morphed by thought into the extremely habituated sense of "I" or "me." As soon as we process our experience through the filter of thought, it becomes dull and predictable. The aliveness of everyday experience is killed by the projection of memory, the "I" that is habit. By seeing the story of "I" and "me" within our moment-to-moment experience, we are, in effect, clearing the debris and dust that clouds our perceived world.

The "micro" thought story has another effect on our life—it separates us from our experience. The story "I" looks at the tree and turns it into an abstract "tree thing." But when there is the pure tree without the filter of thought that imposes habit and projection onto the experience, the tree and you are together, alive as one.

> *The "micro" thought story has another effect on our life—it separates us from our experience. The story "I" looks at the tree and turns it into an abstract "tree thing." But when there is the pure tree without the filter of thought that imposes habit and projection onto the experience, the tree and you are together, alive as one.*

We experience this absence of separation very infrequently in our daily lives. It usually happens when we are surprised or greatly absorbed in what we are doing (the "flow" state). We can access this flow when the story of "I" is extracted from our moment-to-moment experience. One of the most common examples is listening to music you really enjoy. When you listen without inserting the story of "I am listening," you allow the sounds to be just as they are. You are the music.

The "I" and "me" stories are our most intractable personal affects. They will persist until they fall away through an act of grace or are seen through. They do not disappear as a consequence of willpower. Using our will is just another Fear-Self in action. But the more we practice it, the more natural and automatic this process becomes. We do this simply for the sake of obtaining clarity about our authentic natures. Ultimately, there is nothing to "get" or "achieve." Any getting or achieving is the stuff of thought and the Fear-Selves.

Try to see through your "I" story for 10 seconds at a time, and then gradually extend the period. The "I" story will persistently work to reinsert itself into your experience; this is natural. To fully liberate ourselves from our "micro" story, we need to see through the veil of thought and know that the "I" that sees, hears, tastes, and feels is just a thought we use to fill the mystery of our existence. There is a deeper sense of self that is one with everything that emerges within consciousness.

Try to feel for the mysterious sense of self when doing this exercise. It's there! It is pure joy, and if you are feeling this joy when playing with this exercise, then you will have gotten it. This sense of aliveness even manifests with "things" that our "I" story would experience as painful. This is authentic liberation in the here and now.

23 - Background and Foreground

If we observe carefully, we can see that our entire perceived universe contains two discrete but closely linked entities. I call these entities background and foreground.

The background of our experience is everything we subtly sense in the background of perception. It is the perceived environment—diverse sounds, tastes, feels, and moods which make up our experience, but which are outside of the much narrower focus of our immediate attention. We are minimally aware of the background.

The foreground is the much smaller and rapidly shifting zone where our attention is placed. Elements from the background become strong and attract our attention. We extract these elements from the background, and they then become our foreground. As our attention changes, elements that were part of the foreground fall back into the background.

Normally, we have very little feeling for the background of our experience. It's just something that's there. Now here's a key question in reference to our experience: Who are we—background or foreground?

Nearly everyone relates personally with their foreground because they don't really relate much at all with the background, even though it is far more expansive, richer, and diverse than our ever-shifting foreground.

In exactly this way, we identify with the narrowest element of our experience and leave the vast zone of our world behind in the refuse heap of indifference.

How does thought fit into this structure? I would suggest that most thoughts are background energies that fail to attract our attention. They are puffs of energy floating along the stream of consciousness. But a few stronger thoughts and feelings are able to emerge from the vague zone of this background into the foreground and "become us."

Our sense of happiness/contentment and unhappiness/discontent rests in the feeling quality of the foreground self. The Fear-Selves live exclusively in the foreground.

Our Life Force, however, is "grounded" in the background of experience. This is a radical difference. For the Fear-Self, the background is an indifferent environment and everything important happens in the foreground. For the liberated self, the foreground emerges below the background layer; the identity links both the foreground and the background.

Notice how the background is problem-free. It fails to elicit judgment. It is the one place where we are totally accepting. All of our problems, all of our fears occur only in the narrow zone of foreground attention. We don't get rid of a problem or a fear by changing our attention; rather, the way we experience problems and fears changes greatly when we disassociate our core self with the foreground.

When our identity is limited to the foreground of experience, there exists a kind of restive friction with the background of experience. Because we focus exclusively on the foreground, the background is quietly pushed away. From the liberated perspective, the background is the constant zone of identity and the foreground emerges in harmony and balance with it.

Notice that the background is "automatic." It is a place where we have no control. It is a given, utterly calm and in balance. Our whole sense of control and power is centered in the foreground, that relatively small place of self and life story identification.

Also notice how your attention center, the foreground, emerges through the neck and into the head, while the background seems to reside in the center of the chest, in the area of the heart. When the head (foreground) is grounded in the heart and stomach (background), we are content, balanced, and in solidarity with our world. We can allow the head to be embraced by the heart and live nearly every moment of our life in harmony. Our true home is the heart. When we lie on our deathbed having deprived our heart of the life it deserved, we die with the most soul-crushing regret. Don't let that happen to you.

When we lie on our deathbed having deprived our heart of the life it deserved, we die with the most soul-crushing regret. Don't let that happen to you.

Imagine if you were the background. What would that be like? Why not try that idea on for size? As elements of the background capture your attention and become foreground, see such elements as waves emerging from the vast sea of life and being. The waves splash into focus and then, almost as quickly, fall back into the ocean of life and being. There is never a problem. Life and being are effortless.

Try this exercise the next time you go to the dentist or have a bad headache. The pain is still there, but the vigor of our identification with it is reduced. The same applies to turbulent and upsetting emotions. They happen, but our new perspective greatly changes the quality of the feeling. Living this way, we have much more depth and substance.

Identification with the foreground of experience is likely to tug powerfully at your sense of self. This is habit. Let it happen like you would let anything else happen in your world, but experience it with understanding and depth. Ultimately, we are the sea of experience and not its waves.

This is not to criticize the awesome power of thought. The ability, right, and responsibility to think is absolutely essential to our well-being. Using effort to shut off thought is pointless and even irrelevant. Thought and attention are magnificent, and their greatest gift is to allow us to use the instrument of thought with knowledge to make choices that are intelligent and loving. It is thoughtlessness and laziness that have spawned a vast array of brutal wars (with religion and empty patriotism often at their cores). It is thoughtlessness and mindless conformity that makes possible the savage assault of religious indoctrination. It is ignorance that makes it possible for societies to bind women's feet, rage against sexuality, and set one group against another. Quality observation, thought, and action are essential to living a liberated life of balance.

When we seek answers, we hope to find them in the zone of attention. We often fail to find them because our true identity lies in the background of experience. When our identity shifts away from the foreground, everything changes. Habitually we have relied on thought to provide us with all the answers, but in this journey, it is thought which primarily obscures potential revelation. In this journey we look to what contains thought as the answer. That is the key. It is the background from which all thought and feeling emerge. This is the pathway home.

24 - Life and Meaning

The Paradox of Power

Fueled by the Wound, we vainly seek meaning in life through the aspirations of our Fear-Selves. We do this by exerting ourselves to connect with sources of power outside of who we are. This is the way we create meaning in our lives. Without this pursuit, our lives appear lifeless and without meaning. What constitutes "meaning" depends on the Fear-Self type; it could be material success, knowledge, fame, having many friends, or recognition.

But if we are not our Fear-Selves, then what meaning could life possess?

A Fear-Self's favorite mode of thinking is called "either/or." If a Fear-Self hears the message that living life as a compulsive Achiever is a sure-fire way of maintaining insecurity, then the Achiever responds, "But if I am not supposed to achieve, then it would seem that I'm nothing." Through either/or thinking, we are either our insecurity-based identity or we are nothing at all.

In my own life, I have persistently sought to experience security and contentment through intellectual understanding. As a person prone to worry, I used my love of learning (which comes directly from my Life Force) as a way to control my world (which shows how a Fear-Self distorts an authentic state of being by bending it toward the goal of control). In the state of powerlessness, which is a Wound identification, we and our world are out control. Pain is life out of control. When we experience this kind of pain, a Fear-Self will resolutely take center stage and show us the way out of our pain. The Fear-Self becomes the vehicle through which we reduce pain and accumulate power, which is used to control and bring order to our world. It comes in every shape, color, and size. For me, it has often come in the form of knowing more than other people—or believing that I can completely understand myself. If I could understand myself completely, I thought, I could finally conquer my fears and doubts. Life just doesn't work that way.

When I realized that the acquisition of power through knowledge was a dead-end, my Fear-Self instantly moved to its polar opposite. I strove to be one who is utterly unlearned and unknowing, a kind of Zen sage. The efficacy of this new identity was strongly supported within Eastern philosophy. The state of utter unknowing is that of totally uncritical openness to things just as they are. This sounds great, but underneath it's just a variant of the old, all-knowing identity.

The Fear-Self operates through the play of opposites, either/ or. If I'm not this, then I must be its opposite. If I am jealous, now I will cease ever being jealous. If I am violent, now I will be non-violent. If I worry too much, I must never worry. As long as we are operating on the field of opposing identities, no true change has been effected. The me that could "let go" of the need to know more, the me that was utterly unknowing, was just as frustrating and unreal as the me that needed to know everything.

Moving from the me that needed to always know more to the one that needed to know nothing represented a false journey.

The need for meaning arises from a place of apparent meaninglessness. This is the condition of the invalidated person. When we are firmly established in our innate goodness, that is our meaning! We need not search for it elsewhere.

Invalidation obscures the immediate meaning of life. That is why the question of life's meaning haunts so many of us.

Mirroring the life of an individual, when a culture is invalidated, it craves power. It carves out its meaning through its power. This is the state of much of modern Islam. Exploitation from the West has resulted in political disempowerment. A core emotion of disempowerment is rage, and this is why much of the Islamic world feels such immense anger at the West, which it blames for its current condition. This rage is further fueled by its role as an energy source for the very world it condemns.

A disempowered people will be drawn to leaders with whom they can identify; through that identification, they can feel themselves to be powerful once again. Their leaders will revive images from a glorious and idealized past. Thus we have the Al-Qaedas of the world. We also have the angry evangelicals, the crazed patriotism of Imperial Japan, the demonic hate-filled universe of Nazi Germany, and on and on it goes.

This is exactly why the need to establish meaning through power is the source of so much conflict and divisiveness. Seeking validation fuels the potential for conflict and violence. Until we can see through the cloud of our own invalidation and projected powerlessness, we can never experience the power that resides in our own hearts.

The more we strive for meaning and power, the more powerlessness we will experience, and this sense of powerlessness will fuel the drive for power in whatever form it might assume. This is a dangerous path.

Starting now, see the aspiration for meaning and power for what it truly is. It is the life fully manifested as restless and insecure.

Meaning

A meaningful life is one that finds meaning now. There is no meaning separate from immediate life. Our life is our meaning. How different this is from the world of a Fear-Self, where the meaning of life is primarily self-centered and often opposed to life as it unfolds.

A Fear-Self will always be ready to jump into any now colored by its interpretation of what's happening and its agenda for the next moment. Try seeing this habitual process for what it is—a puppet pulled by its strings. It will be full of self-justification. It will come with a boatload of "good" reasons. See it all as just fluff; no matter how affable a mask it might wear, it is just another incarnation of the Wound in our lives.

Fear-Selves seek the meaning of life in their projected future. All conflict is rooted in how life varies from our own version of how it ought to be.

The only need we ever have is to see how falsehood has played out in our lives (the interplay of the Wound with its Fear-Selves) and then to have faith that our Life Force still resides in our hearts.

This is the only faith you will ever need. At heart, you already have all the goodness and love the universe can bestow—as does the rest of life. All "evil" is a consequence of a belief in our own powerlessness and our drive to possess power no matter how ugly and divisive a form it might take.

All things awaken. Know that if your heart is not already awake to your dignity and integrity of being, it will be! This is the sacred dimension of life. This is the life of the liberated Human Being, and it is, ultimately, life itself.

Your meaning is your dignity, your birthright. Know this with all your heart.

The Kingdom of God is connection with your own innate goodness. Deviance from that truth is life separated from its source. If you are truly standing in the light of your own innate goodness, you will effortlessly have the power to forgive everything. Your vision will be the vision of life itself.

The Kingdom of God (if you choose to call it that) is connection with your own innate goodness. Deviance from that truth is life separated from its source. If you are truly standing in the light of your own innate goodness, you will effortlessly have the power to forgive everything. Your vision will be the vision of life itself. The sun shines on all alike. The tree gives to all its cooling shade.

This is the meaning of life.

25 - Conflict: A Pathway to Liberation

Conflict is a fundamental element of life. We ought to be deeply thankful for that. Without conflict, life would be flat and without spice. Thank goodness for our enemies! We can enjoy conflict, as we can love its absence. But we can only enjoy conflict once we have seen through the thrall of our Fear-Selves.

Thank goodness for our enemies!

All conflict with which we personally identify reflects a defensive posture from a Fear-Self. When the desires and needs of a Fear-Self are blocked, serious and emotional conflict will ensue. Fear-Selves hate anything that prevents them from getting their way; this applies to all kinds of situations, from long lines in the supermarket to threats to our loftiest aspirations. Every such obstacle pushes us into the shadow of the Wound, and that means suffering. When there is suffering, a Fear-Self will instantly emerge, full of rage, complaining bitterly about the presenting situation and looking to do something to "correct" it. This is the source of nearly all violence in the world.

If we can see conflict as an obstacle to the needs of a Fear-Self, the struggle is instantly transformed from a source of anger and disappointment to a pathway to our liberation. Because it is emotional, it possesses great power to transform. This is the gift of conflict.

When a Fear-Self is blocked, its intense need to control is thwarted. For a Fear-Self, a block is a direct threat to its survival. A greater gift would be difficult to imagine! Conflict is perhaps the most direct path to profound self-understanding that we have.

Exercise 14:   Working With Conflict

*The next time you experience a conflict in your life—
which, if you're typical of the mass of modern people,
ought to happen sometime in the next 24 hours—stop your
forward momentum toward self-indulgent anger and try
seeing what Fear-Self is dominating your reaction.*

Often I get annoyed when there is a long line at the supermarket, especially when the forward flow is slowed by people fum-
bling with their credit cards. In many cases, these people are senior
citizens, and I can get contemptuous of their ineptness. This is the
Achiever/Expert who disparages the incompetence of others. My
Fear-Self is being blocked by a doddering old person who should be
either dead or safely ensconced in some home for the feeble! How
dare they block me! I remember one very elderly lady who insisted on
paying her bill with spare change. First she had to locate them in her
pocketbook. I watched as her fingers labored endlessly, searching for
individual pennies and then counted them out, penny by penny, for
the cashier. In her enfeeblement, she lost count and had to start over!
I looked on with outraged disbelief. Why was I the one who always
got stuck behind such people? The "vast" expanse of time she spent in
her transaction gave me a terrific opportunity to concoct a whole life
story for this pathetic old person. She probably lived alone; this little
shopping trip, where she bought tiny quantities of things, was probably the highlight of her day. She probably didn't care in the slightest
about the people waiting behind her; she might even secretly enjoy
holding them up. She was probably bitter about her crappy life ,and
this was how she took it out on others, and so on and so forth. Also—
why do *I* always get stuck in these lines? Sometimes I feel I should be
wearing a sign giving fair warning to anyone choosing the line I'm in:

"Stay away—beware." The Fear-Self is a great storyteller. It justified my rage and made me feel shitty (of course). Looking back on it, I had an terrific opportunity to feel my own shame and stupidity by experiencing such thoughts.

If you can see the process *before* the full force of the Fear-Self takes over, it provides an outstanding opportunity for self-understanding. Behold the blocked Spiritualist (annoyed with phone calls as he meditates), Pleaser (who experiences callous indifference from someone for whom she has done a kindly favor), Loner (when the world inevitably intrudes on his safe withdrawal), Expert (whose new book delivery from Amazon never shows up), and Tough Guy (who gets reprimanded for just doing his job from some asshole higher-up).

Conflict is not a problem once we have awakened from the thrall of our Fear-Selves. Liberated, conflict is both an intriguing challenge and a source of good-natured fun. No matter how awful another's behavior may appear, we understand that they are operating from a position of powerlessness seeking power and that underneath the drama is their Life Force. In other words, they are no different from us. We will continue provoking others until we really see through the false projections of the Fear-Selves.

Liberated, conflict is both an intriguing challenge and a source of good-natured fun.

Seeing others as power hungry while experiencing ourselves as power content can make us feel superior to others. The attitude of pre-eminence is, of course, another Fear-Self guise, as it undermines our newfound empowerment. Yet again, *we* have achieved something and are able to demonstrate our ascendance over the crude and desperate behaviors of our pathetic fellow human beings.

This is the danger lurking when we believe that we have evolved to our authentic selves in contrast with the enslaved masses. Liberation is more like returning than getting somewhere. We have found our sense of who we were prior to contamination through invalidation. If you have made it this far in this book and believe that you have evolved to some higher plane of existence, then you have missed the point entirely. Such a belief will operate to validate one's self just as it sustains the invalidation of others. It is a subtle manifestation of an achievement-focused Fear-Self.

Living from our authentic selves has a quality of empathic understanding. It possesses a humility toward ourselves, others, and life in general. When we are in conflict, the sense of empathy does not rest with the other, but with our hurt Fear-Self. We recognize our capacity for our own frailties, which we might also see in others.

The opportunity to see our Fear-Selves in action within conflict never ends, because we are never entirely free of our Fear-Selves. They live as long as we inhabit a body.

True Conflict

Conflict can be real. It is not only the consequence of the actions of a Fear-Self. Perhaps it would be more accurate to say that conflict can be real when we are fighting for things we believe in. It probably wouldn't be much of a dispute if we didn't believe what we were fighting over. But people fight over things they don't believe in all the time. We often call these people attorneys and politicians.

So when we are engaged in serious conflict, we are arguing over something that we believe in.

Let's take a look at another kind of conflict. Couples are often conflicted on issues of parenting. Let's say their son is failing several courses in high school. The father expresses his view that at his age, the boy ought to be taking some responsibility for his actions. The mother asserts that he is having problems related to his adolescence and suggests a short course of therapy. The father responds that the boy would use the therapy as a way to avoid personal accountability. The mother then retorts with a claim that her husband is insensitive to their son's issues.

This is a serious conflict. Both parents appear to be motivated by their son's best interests. It also appears that the conflict ultimately will have a winner and a loser. In such cases, even when a Fear-Self does not appear to be playing a dominant role in the ongoing discussion, when an outcome results in someone winning and another losing, an opening is created for the intrusion of the winner's Fear-Self and the loser's Wound. No matter how it gets resolved, the conflict evolves into the zone of the Wound and its Fear-Self mask.

With this knowledge, we can now look for other options these parents might have. They could engage their son in a way that allows their mutual openness, connection, and love to come first.

When we place these qualities first, everyone is transformed. So the key is to locate an option or options where the disputants can act from love and not what they believe to be the best interests of the subject of the conflict. When we operate from our beliefs, no matter how well intended, we stimulate the background presence of our Wound and Fear-Selves. Games that result in winners and losers ought to be played for fun. When the issue is a serious one, we are asked to reach higher and dig deeper. We are asked to expose ourselves through the field of our vulnerability. This approach might take a little practice.

Most of us are powerfully habituated to assume positions based strongly on our beliefs. Even when a Fear-Self is not
apparent, its presence in the conflict is never far away. This does not
mean that we abandon what we believe to be right (although it does
mean opening up to other perspectives on the presenting problem).
Instead, we are urged to see a pathway through which our beliefs and
position can be mediated by our connectedness and love. This is the
key to creative and restorative problem-solving. Through love, the
presenting issue moves from "it" (in our example the son's academic
problems) to "us." Love is rarely linear. We never know where it will
take us, but we do know that it will take us some place different from
where our habitual judgments and beliefs take us, no matter how well
intended they might be. It is a wholly different journey. Using love as
the path, life becomes the forge for our own personal transformation.
With practice we become instruments of life. We can approach everything on this pathway. As we practice, the dark, self-centered star of
the small self is transformed through the alchemy of conflict. We may
not know where the path will take us, but perhaps for the first time
we are able to trust the journey.

---

*Love is rarely linear. We never know where it will take us,
but we do know that it will take us some place different
from where our habitual judgments and beliefs take us,
no matter how well intended they might be. It is a wholly
different journey. Using love as the path, life becomes
the forge for our own personal transformation.*

In this case, we understand that everyone is feeling the pain of
invalidation and competing beliefs and judgments. The parents need
to drop their own agenda and become open to their son's voice, particularly if it refocuses the anger toward themselves! This could happen if the son rejects both parents' positions. The family Wound is then

brought to light, and powerful healing is energized. Father, mother, and son are now on a wholly new journey. No one knows where this path will lead, but the family's hidden invalidating dynamics will be seen, possibly for the first time, and each person will have an opportunity for understanding and healing. Retreat to an old agenda kills the process, which is why only love can take us through the field of vulnerability.

How does love transform? Transformation happens when we are vulnerable to our Wound. When we stop running away from that which we fear most, the pathway to our own liberation cannot be stopped. That which has the power to terrorize us also has the opposing power to liberate us. This is the gift of conflict and suffering. Nothing else provides us with such powerful opportunities for reuniting ourselves with our Life Force. The only reliable crucible of our authentic being is through suffering and struggle. Our Soul waits for us, but it waits on the other side of grief.

How does love transform? Transformation happens when we are vulnerable to our Wound. When we stop running away from that which we fear most, the pathway to our own liberation cannot be stopped.

When we have the courage to embrace the fiction of our false identities, we are freed of their grip. This is coming home to our true self. We honor the Wound for everything that it is. It is the energetic mass that stands between our Fear-Self and our Life Force. All pathways to our authentic being must travel straight through the heart of its scary darkness.

This is the monster left alive by the Hero Twin Monster Slayer. It was left alive for us.

26 - The Oneness of Self and Other

The Fear-Self lives in a false universe. It is false because it is falsely known.

A Fear-Self understands her world through projection, which disaggregates the dynamic flow of life into discrete and static objects which are labelled good, bad, or indifferent. It ceaselessly judges her experiences and her life based on its own needs and fears. The Fear-Self cannot know anything, although it is obsessed with knowing things—because through knowing, it believes, it can exercise control over life. Living in a universe of insecurity, where threats to our self can manifest at almost any moment, seeking control (in any of the ways Fear-Selves seek anything) is an essential life plan.

The Fear-Self thinks or believes it knows itself through memory, but this knowing is selective, changeable, and predicated on the arbitrary and selective story of the Fear-Self.

This is the universe of false knowing. It is the knowing of a false being, that is, itself, a consequence of insecurity. It is often a reactive knowing not grounded in reality.

This world of false knowing describes a universe of objects that are separate from each other. Things don't just happen; they either happen to me or they don't happen to me. Out there is a tree, then there is me typing on this keyboard, and somewhere in my mental universe, I wish my daughter would find a job. It is a world of fragmentation and disconnection all organized around the fears, projections, and needs of a Fear-Self.

The Problem of Good and Evil

When we label someone or something as good or evil, we are placing a static label on a dynamic and transactional process. A label stops life and turns it into a fixed commodity. We may label a person as "bad" when they steal. But if we were privy to the person's whole story, we might see someone operating out of desperation or hopelessness. This person's thieving might provide us with an opportunity for self-discovery. But labels block understanding.

A number of years ago, a senior at the University of Texas was carjacked and murdered. He was the only son of a single mother. His murder was devastating to her. She petitioned the court to execute her son's murderer, but the judge sentenced this man to life imprisonment instead. In reaction, the woman began a grassroots organization to strengthen the death penalty in Texas. In the ensuing years, she petitioned the court to have this man executed.

Several years passed. Her son's killer became aware of her campaign and requested, through a prison counselor, to meet her. She refused, but the man continued to make this request. Finally, the mother agreed to sit down with the man who killed her only son. She wanted to use the opportunity to express her hatred for this man, to tell him how he ruined her life and how he brutally ended the life of her only child.

When they met, she did just that. She spewed her hatred and sadness at him. She told him that it was her life mission to push for a resentencing hearing that would result in his execution. All the man could do was sit and listen. When she was finally finished, the man looked at her and apologized. He said that he was sorry for what he had done. He told her that he, too, was in agony over her son's murder and that that was why he reached out to her. She didn't want to hear his words of contrition and walked out of the meeting.

Afterward, the man wrote her several letters requesting a second meeting. After about a year she agreed to meet him one last time. At this meeting he told her of the circumstances of his own life. He told her how he was raised in a broken home, surrounded by drug addiction, poverty, hopelessness, and desperation. He made no excuses for what he had done, but he did want some understanding. The killer wanted her to see that each of them were victims. They were connected by grief.

Over time, the man and the mother developed a relationship of mutual understanding. From their pain, a light appeared, piercing the obscuring power of hate and isolation. The mother abandoned her efforts to have the man executed and instead began to support organizations dedicated to ending the death penalty. Although the man is still in prison and will likely die there, she legally adopted him.

Her son's killer is now her only son.

When we label, we seek to exert control in a very complex world. We use our false knowing to give us firm grounding in a shaky reality. But in effect we are only sustaining our own isolation and insecurity within the walls of our own making. When we fail to see the infinite connectivity of life, we descend into our own isolation, desperate for certainty and grasping for security.

Life moves along a polarity. Sometimes it moves to an extreme. Nazi Germany was one such extreme. Remarkably vibrant and creative Athens in the time of Pericles was another. For better or worse, the darkness and insanity of the Nazis made it possible for Israel to be born and to give Jews a nation of their own after 2,000 years of exile. The golden age of Pericles ended with the Peloponnesian Wars that brought to an end the greatness that was classic Greece. This is the great circle of life. The interplay of light and dark is continuous and unknowable.

What we think of as great evil thrives under one of two conditions. When power becomes concentrated in the hands of the very few, the opportunity for immense violence is greatly enhanced. The second condition occurs in the context of a person's perceived powerlessness. When a person is desperate to be seen, he will often use a brazenly violent act to show the world that he is not powerless.

What we know as evil is the essence of invalidation. The profoundly invalidated group or individual must show the world that they are something that others must acknowledge. Germany was massively invalidated after World War I; the University of Texas murderer, like most other desperate criminals, was raised in a universe of invalidation. The only path to living on a firm ground is understanding. We need to understand that harm will always come from invalidation. It has no other place to go.

The Great Flow of Life

Good and evil are subjective fictions of the mind, but invalidation is real. Darkness will always move toward light, and brightness will inevitably, dim.

Life is an ever-present flow in which everything is connected to everything else. The connectivity of things, thoughts, and feelings traverse space and time. My mood is a consequence of my present view of the world, the weather, the physical state of my body, news about the fighting in Iraq, the level of my bank account, and whatever else is happening in and around my life. If I'm in a cranky mood, my feelings will have a powerful effect on everything around me. Moreover, when I'm feeling cranky, I will experience everything around me as irritations. The reverse happens when I'm in a pleasant mood. In either case, a Fear-Self will identify with the mood, blaming the world for not meeting its needs when cranky and pleased for having its needs met when content.

We avoid experiencing the deep connectivity of everyday life anytime we are identified with a Fear-Self.

Incomplete identities are always conceptual as opposed to real. That which is real is alive and complex. That which is conceptual is a mental construct often linked with a sense of lack. The conceptual me, who is a function of lack, wants to be "happy." It has already told itself what it needs to be happy, and it strives to make those things happen. It also knows what will make it unhappy, and it seeks to avoid those things. When we are strongly identified with these rigid thoughts, we become overtly two-dimensional. Our experience is filtered by a single, simpleminded, and false thought. This is a life which is wholly conceptual, non-spontaneous, and unreal. It is the very definition of suffering. It is our hopeless attempt to beat life into a shape that will please us. But like every other behavior that resists the ordinary flow of life, it will result in the opposite of what we want.

The conceptual me, who is a function of lack, wants to be "happy." It has already told itself what it needs to be happy, and it strives to make those things happen. It also knows what will make it unhappy, and it seeks to avoid those things. This is a life which is wholly conceptual, non-spontaneous, and unreal. It is the very definition of suffering. It is our hopeless attempt to beat life into a shape that will please us.

While life loves diversity and complexity, the Fear-Self craves simplicity. When even the most casual observation of life will immediately show the pervasiveness and depth of its connectivity, the Fear-Self stands on the sidelines, isolated and alienated.

When we project that only certain conditions are capable of making us happy, then we place life in a stranglehold. Through the vehicle of the Wound, we crave love to heal the belief in our unworthiness. As we have seen, this rock-hard belief creates the thoroughly conceptual Fear-Self which stalks the world, seeking someone to love her and give her the attention her conceptual belief in happiness demands.

The energy of attention also firmly establishes the ever-present relationship of a "me" on one side of the attention line and another on the other side. This is the way it works even if a Fear-Self is not dominating the mind. This obvious insight will provide us with a way to move away from conceptual self-ideation.

The Fear-Self performs two contradictory actions simultaneously. One, it believes it can control life based on its conceptual knowledge of things; and two, it filters everything as good or bad. How are these actions contradictory? No matter how much self-understanding we might have, all of us have painful thoughts and feelings, and we encounter situations in life that we would dearly prefer not to face. While most Fear-Selves "know" that they cannot completely control what happens in their lives, they don't realize that they also cannot control what thoughts and feelings manifest in their experience. If the Fear-Self had real control, it would not produce painful thoughts and feelings in the first place. Yet they happen to even the best adapted Fear-Self.

The meditating Spiritualist is experiencing a particularly bliss-ful session when someone with a boom box decides to enjoy his music outside his open window. The meditator thinks, "Fuck—I hate when that happens. Who is this asshole?" Then he might have the sec-ondary thought, "I shouldn't be having such an angry thought. I guess I'm a loser as a meditator." The Body Person gets sick and can't get to the gym, then thinks, "In no time I'm going to look like shit." The Ex-pert is shamed in public by someone who knows his field better than himself and thinks, "I'm a failure. I don't know squat." In each case, the Fear-Self is projecting its narrow demand on the world, and the world just doesn't cooperate.

Now let's go through the same set of scenarios, but this time remove the conceptual demand for happiness and control. You will note that there are no simple answers, because life is rich and diverse and usually allows us to have a range of responses. The Spiritualist could take a break from his mediation, he could get pissed, he could enjoy the music, he could see how fixed and narrow he is with what he believes he needs to be happy, he could see how meditation encour-ages a type of self-centeredness. The Body Person could get irritated with her "bad luck" in getting sick, she could use it as an opportunity to see how compulsive she is, she could tell herself that she could use a rest, or there could be a combination of responses. There are many possibilities, but when we project our well-being and happiness onto a narrow concept, which usually has little to do with the real nature of life, we guarantee ourselves a life of isolation, resistance, and suffer-ing. We might appreciate the few "breaks" that happen to come our way, but then bemoan the vast stretches of monotony and bad luck that characterize the rest.

In these cases we have noticed how the energy of attention creates our relationship with life. When attention is framed by our concepts, it serves those concepts. Driven by self-centered and fear-based beliefs, it cannot relax and "smell the roses." As Fear-Selves, we restlessly scan our environment, seeking things, feelings, and ideas that will serve the narrow needs of a Fear-Self. It is a horror to realize that most of us live much of our lives this way. The Fear-Self feels particularly alive when it shops, when it sees itself in a mirror, when it is in a place of worship, when it is waiting for a potentially serious medical diagnosis, when it is embroiled in conflict and in all of those situations where it can draw attention to itself.

This is the unreal life. The Fear-Self desperately wants to feel good. It exploits its attended world (which represents a very thin sliver of its potential experience) to obtain those feelings. Our beliefs organized around what will make us happy and secure are concepts. They are not real.

Exercise 15:   Living Free of Concepts for an Hour

What would it be like to live without concepts about what makes us happy or unhappy? Try to free yourself of any concept of good or bad for the next hour. Just do what you would ordinarily do, but let go of any concept of what is necessary to make you happy or unhappy. Notice how your concepts almost immediately work to reassert their dominance in your life. When we are in the trance of a Fear-Self, we are unaware of the pervasiveness and power of these concepts to run our lives. Also, get a feeling for what it's like to just be and do what needs doing in life without the dominance of these conceptual thought patterns. Get a clear sense of this feeling. This is a step in self-liberation.

Happiness and unhappiness have very little to do with any concept. They are just energies that happen in our lives, and they will happen with a lot more frequency when we cease demanding that life serve our conceptual needs. Think of concepts as blinders. When we are dominated by thought-based concepts, we are essentially blind to the rich diversity of life.

Relatively free of concepts, we are an integral part of the flow of our life. We are open to the sensuous pleasures of simple things. Instead of worrying about looking great six months from now, we can be open to the pleasure of an Oreo cookie right now. We are alive to the moment. We can still try to win that big case and make big bucks, but we can also enjoy the primal joy of cuddling with our dog or cat. Instead of spending another hour wrapped up in the latest book that will help us further our expertise, we can feel the magic of a spring breeze as it mysteriously lifts leaves and raises the attention of birds. We have no idea of the beauty we can experience when we attend with wonder and appreciation to things that previously might never have even entered our awareness. We are transformed utterly by the quality of our attention when it is liberated from the grip of a conceptually based Fear-Self.

Eventually, as our concepts of good and bad, happy and unhappy, lose their meaning to us, an entirely new universe of meaning opens up to us. For the first time, we can feel a oneness with life exactly as it is without the corrupting influence of false knowing. That is the delicious mystery of our authentic being operating with spontaneous wonder and appreciation for the ever-unfolding movement of life. See this for yourself. Let your concepts drop off like old clothes, and feel your senses come alive to the mystery of this moment. Feel your dignity in this moment as equal to anything else in this wide, wide universe.

Ahab's Tear

Recall from our earlier reference to <u>Moby Dick</u> that just prior to his final encounter with the White Whale, the solitary and melancholy Ahab peered over the bow of his ship, the Pequod, and a single tear fell from his eye and mixed with the waters of the Pacific Ocean. Herman Melville informs the reader that "nor did all the Pacific contain such wealth as that one wee drop."

Our own worth is no different from the one wee drop that fell from old Ahab as he leaned over the Pequod as it sailed closer and closer to its demise. The inexorable passage of the Pequod reflects the madness of Ahab's Fear-Self.

Why was that "one wee drop" worth more than all of the Pacific? Why was it not just equal to the Pacific? It was worth more because its very existence represented the magisterial moment of awakening, and such moments are transcendent. When that happens, we feel effortlessly lifted up by a force that has been missing in our life. In that moment we <u>are</u> life. Thus, not all the vastness of the Pacific could equal the worth of one of Ahab's tears.

Why is that moment expressed as a tear? The tear is born from our opening up to the other side of the Wound. All our efforts to escape its terrifying visage have ceased. For the first time we turn around in humble understanding of our very young selves who primitively sought a safe harbor through our assumed victimhood and created the lie of their own failure as human beings. Bringing the light of understanding to that Wound arouses the deepest and most profound melancholy, and so even in mad Ahab, a single tear forms and unites him with the vast and mysterious Pacific which holds both Moby Dick and himself in its primal immensity.

Turning back and honoring that very young person is the most direct way to self-understanding. We can only do that when we have seen through the illusion of our dominant Fear-Selves. It is a process that can't be rushed. Your liberation will unfold at a rate proportional to the seriousness of your commitment to understanding and the courage you possess to challenge your most accepted notions about yourself and your world. Every thought you hold dear needs to be seen in the glow of understanding and the willingness to let it go even if you have believed it to be your sole (soul!) protector at the times of your greatest fear. It never protected you from anything. That is not the purpose or capacity of any thought. All that was protected was a Fear-Self.

When that "one wee drop" forms in Ahab's eye, the reader rejoices. He sees that transformation can happen, that even mad Ahab can save himself from his obsession and ceaseless suffering. Our heart goes out to his terrible anguish. Were we there, we might extend a hand to help him remove the metaphorical cross that he so painfully has carried from his earliest memories. But it is not to be. Despite the depth of his realization, Ahab's fierce Fear-Selves return; in that very moment, the White Whale, Moby Dick, is sighted, and Ahab's magnificent awakening doesn't have the chance to be nurtured. The whale, nature, the object of his fury (for the Fear-Self can never be joined with nature), finally emerges, and Ahab's liberated self collapses under the weight of his hate and fear.

Let Moby Dick be your guide away from taking the path of death and despair, but instead to coming alive to your shining within the extraordinary flow of life.

27 - Can We Be Free of the Wound and the Fear-Selves?

The short and long answer to this question is—no. Wishing the Wound and Fear-Selves to go away forever is the voice and desire of a Fear-Self. This is the self that needs freedom from pain and complexity. More to the point, this is the self that wants to be perfect. If we forget the lesson of honoring our Wound and Fear-Selves, we will never be free of their power to dominate our lives. We need to continue to honor and respect them. They are a part of who we truly are.

The purpose of <u>Liberation</u> is to see and understand. Only the voice of self-contempt is motivated to kill our own story. This is the story that life gave you and only you. Unless you treasure that story, you will continue running away from your authentic self.

Besides, you have no choice in the matter. These forces will be a part of your life for as long as you live. You can continue to resist the Wound and live as an array of Fear-Selves, or you can turn back and embrace your Life Force. It is as simple as that.

We dishonor life when we fail to treasure every element of ourselves. When you know that, you will have the capacity to see through the fear of everyone else in your life and honor their stories as well as your own. That is true love.

In doing this, we also honor our parents who knew no other way. We thank them for making this journey possible. We thank our enemies for making this awakening as beautiful as it is. It was all as it was meant to be. No matter how long and hard the journey has been, we offer thanks to it and say, "This has been my journey; nothing like it has ever happened in the whole history of this universe." Nor will it ever happen again.

The Problem of Self-Love

When we have not experienced enough love and safety in our very early years, we are likely as we grow older to fail to establish enough strength in self to be whole. The trauma of separation results in focusing our identity in a place that is, in part, fear-based.

We have talked in great detail about the Wound and its corresponding Fear-Selves, but there is one more idea that needs discussion: the idea of "self-image." When we are not centered in our Life Force, when we do not trust ourselves or our world implicitly, we need to have an "image" of ourselves and of others. This "image" is, essentially, a form of a Fear-Self. It is the thing that we believe we need to be or that we are without choice.

Often the image we have of ourselves is unconscious. Let me try to make this clear by describing my own experience with image.

Over the last 10 years, I have thought of myself as a very good person: honest, funny, accepting, intelligent, interesting, a little moody, politically passionate though somewhat detached emotionally, and, deep down, very kind. Yet despite all these "pluses," I noticed that many people tended to like me a lot at first but over time seemed to grow emotionally distant from me. In some cases, people became outright contemptuous of me. I could not understand what was going on. I applied my analytical skills to the problem and reflected deeply on it. I questioned everything. I even wondered whether I was misinterpreting the whole situation and perhaps it was I who had become emotionally distant from others.

Then, one day, a question popped into my head: "Do I have an inflated concept of my own intelligence and insight? Does that inflated sense of self act to push some people away from me?" I had to respond honestly and whispered a somewhat hesitant, "Yes, I do think I'm more intelligent than most people—but I only think that some of the time." I immersed myself in this issue, and it came to consciousness that when I spoke with people, I often found that much of what they had to say, which I assume had to be important to them, I found boring and predictable. I tended to find my own "story" a lot more interesting and fun—so much so that I felt that even they ought to find me more interesting than themselves!

I was really in love with myself. Because I read a lot and have a very wide range of interests, I can hold court on an array of subjects, from major league baseball to economic theory.

Underneath all of the kindness, knowledge, humor, etc., I had an image of myself as smarter than most people. When I met someone new, I would often say something like, "She's a nice person, but not so smart," or "She's not only pleasant, but also very intelligent," as if intelligence were the most important quality a person could possess.

My own sense of intelligence has nothing to do with "book learning," which anyone can achieve, but is a kind of quick and nimble intelligence that can separate the "wheat from the chaff" with speed—the ability to just see through things. What I failed to see was the effect my own image was having on others. I often asserted my image and implied that I was smarter than other people. I would actually say things like, "You know, I had an incredibly brilliant insight yesterday." Such remarks were meant to be funny, but others linked them to my core image and found them offensive. I have sought to counter this behavior with self-effacement. In my own mind, everything is pretty much absurd, so why should anyone take anything I say all that seriously? But this has its dark side. I didn't ask questions of others because I just wasn't that interested in their answers. Also, I might inwardly laugh at others just as I laugh at my own pronouncements. I might not find that offensive, but others do. As a pontificator, I was very much like some of the people I find most contemptible.

Here is the point: As a result of not having enough love and support as a young person, I unconsciously created an image of myself that needed to assert its intelligence. It might have started out as raw bragging, but over time it became a lot more refined. Images evolve. I needed to connect with this image. I needed to be seen as a person worthy of respect. The image, whether "negative" or "positive," is designed to bring attention to one's self. It is a form of self-inflation.

> *As a result of not having enough love and support as a young person, I unconsciously created an image of myself that needed to assert its intelligence. It might have started out as raw bragging, but over time it became a lot more refined. Images evolve. I needed to connect with this image. I needed to be seen as a person worthy of respect. The image, whether "negative" or "positive," is designed to bring attention to one's self. It is a form of self-inflation.*

If I read in a self-help book that I need to love myself, what might I find to love? All that I could find was an image! If there is a "you" doing the loving, then there must be *another* you that needs to be loved. In the absence of a solid core, we can only love an image.

This is the problem of self-love. For it to be valid, it needs to be real, and as long as it is connected with an image, it cannot be real.

In the absence of a solid core, we can only love an image. This is the problem of self-love. For it to be valid, it needs to be real, and as long as it is connected with an image, it cannot be real.

We may "see through" the Wound and many of its Fear-Selves, but as long as an "image" of ourselves is there to judge, we have barely taken the first step to self-understanding.

What is it like to be alive and yet have no image of self and others? That way of life can itself quickly morph into a new image. We are so accustomed to living life as a set of images that we tend to regress back into images, because that is all we know, and we depend on this brittle knowing to construct the world within which we live.

Exercise 16:   Finding Your Image

Find your own image. If your image is unclear, it can be identified by exploring the question, "How do I want to be seen by others?" You also need to investigate what you find most contemptible in others. The negative side of your image is often projected externally. For me, it was ignorance in the face of "facts." I really can't stand this characteristic in others.

Watch how your image plays out in your life. It is really your most dominant Fear-Self. Then explore who you are without the need to have others feel a certain way about you. Conversely, investigate how you impose your nega-

tive image onto others when they fall into your "reject" image container.

It is likely that your dominant image is profoundly well-justified by your habitual thought stream. This is not an easy exercise to perform. It is also your core Fear-Self, so it is an identity to which there has been a long and very well established addiction over many years.

It should feel really different being in the world without your core self-image. If it doesn't feel different, then you haven't found quite the right self-identity. I would suggest that you continue working on identifying your primary image.

What is the difference between one's image and a dominant Fear-Self? A Fear-Self is a sustained life story personality. It can be expressed as an image. In contrast, an image is situational, particular to the current context. For example, in a business meeting, one might need to appear "authoritative" even if she is not an Expert or Tough Guy Fear-Self. A situation often requires us to project the particular image that is expected of us within that particular context. The distinction is an important one. Image-seeking is a potent and common way to avoid feeling bad about ourselves through contact with our Wound. Understood in this way, it is a more temporal variant of a Fear-Self.

When no other source of security has been dependable in our lives, we seek to find security in our images. They are, after all, who we *need* to be. They provide us with a center to our life. When we finally break away from our images, we release our grip on the last holdouts of the false self. It can be a scary time.

The most powerful attribute of primary images is their ability to take us over in an instant. What makes matters worse is that they feel so familiar that they manifest below the horizon of our awareness. They fill us up and we do their bidding before we know what has happened. They make time come alive because they are concerned about what is happening to give them life—the presenting stimulus—and what needs to happen to remedy the situation—the immediate effect.

When we live connected to the now, there are no causes and effects of a psychological nature at all. Released from their psychological grip, we are made free. But our Fear-Selves do not live in the here and now. They live with an agenda that has an explicit future, which their actions are designed to effect.

There is simply no escaping the fact that profound security is indifferent to images and self-saving thinking. We are the security of life that comes before any thought or concept. We are the integrity of life prior to the experience of lack. That is the place of our Life Force. That is a place, a spirit, an energy, and a being all at once.

Like the Wound and Fear-Selves, the core self-image never really goes away, but its impact in our lives can be diminished greatly.

Your image is the you that needs to be. It is based in our belief in our inadequacy. This image ceaselessly says, "Look at me; look how smart, good-looking, interesting, different, spiritual (take your pick) I am." The image can also say, "Look how sad and depressed I am. I am more sensitive than most people. I cannot escape the pain and suffering of this earth bound life." This is the you that came to be in the absence of love. But now you know that it is all right to be just as you are without the crutch of the self-image. Find out who that wonderful person is. Feel that energy underneath the weight of the compulsive and overbearing self-image. There you will find all the love you will need in this lifetime. The only person who needs to "love herself" is she who believes she is not adequate, sufficient, or worthy in the first place.

When we discover our essential beings—the energy that has absolutely no need to inhabit a Fear-Self or project an image—we get a taste of a wholly different way of living. We still need to "do" in life. That which interacts in life is our body. On the level of our thoughts, feelings, and emotions, this body will continue expressing elements of our Wound and Fear-Selves. Our doing will always be "personality"-centric. The difference between the liberated you and the imprisoned you is understanding. Through understanding, we stop believing that we are, in essence, our Fear-Selves. What was serious becomes playful. What was fearful becomes interesting. Liberation moves us from living an insecure and compulsive life to one that is ultimately a life of play and depth.

28 - Understanding Fear and the Ending of Fear

When I was in my 20s, I read Flaubert's magnificent <u>Madame Bovary</u>. I can remember the sense of terror as I followed the main character's inexorable descent into poverty and ruin because of, in my view, unnecessary spending. I was literally seized by anxiety as I read her tragic story.

Flaubert's story of financial ruin keyed directly in to my own Wound-based fears. Poor and abandoned, I would be nothing. Poverty-stricken, no one would notice me and I would descend into the most horrible collapse. <u>Madame Bovary's</u> story became my story.

This is real fear. When our Wound is stimulated, our fears rise into consciousness with immense vigor and we begin weaving stories about how awful life is likely to become. In these stories, we are alone, vulnerable, disconsolate, and lost. When I read <u>Madame Bovary</u>, these very distant fears were brought to my immediate consciousness. Most of the time our fears hover in the background of our experiences, but life will reliably provide us with experiences that bring the Wound to palpable reality. The images and stories they arouse are so terrifying that our life becomes one vast plan to avoid them.

This is the Wound in action. In response we do two things. First, we resist fear by fleeing it. In <u>The Wisdom of Insecurity,</u> Alan Watts describes this process with particular insight: "Running away from fear is fear, fighting is pain." Examine this sentence carefully. The very resistance to fear is fear. We fight fear in so many ways, through therapy, meditation, self-help, and being phony (false bravery, or *machismo*). Can you see how you do this in your own life?

Watts continues: "If the mind is in pain, the mind *is* pain. The thinker has no other form than his thought. There is no escape. But *as long as you are not aware of the inseparability of thinker and thought, you will try to escape.* The absence of any resistance brings about a way of feeling pain so unfamiliar as to be hard to describe. The pain is no longer problematic. I feel it, but there is no urge to get rid of it, for I have discovered that pain and the effort to be separate from it are the same thing. This, however, is not an experiment to be held in reserve as a trick for the moments of crisis. It is a way of life."

That pain is the Wound in action. Our hopeless attempts at escape are based on the false belief that we are separate from the Wound. And yet, the person we believe ourselves to be *is* the Wound! It is the Wound that keeps our stories going. Our psychological fears are linked directly with our Wound of invalidation. Observe this in your own life. Much of our lives are organized around avoiding fear. Seen with this understanding, we can realize that the Wound is the dominating influence in our lives. We are lost in the cloud of the Wound. It spawns the false life of the Fear-Selves. Fleeing from fear through the machinations of a Fear-Self is the secondary form of the Wound.

The challenge is to find the part of yourself that has no relationship with fear and the flight from it. This is your authentic self.

Who we are is not a project that we need to work on. Nor is it something we can conceptualize with a thought, feeling, or any combination of words. It is, in fact, something that was completed long before its emergence within our personal consciousness. That is why it's impossible to "find ourselves" through thought or hope. As long as we keep alive the story of us "getting better," the endless drama will continue. That false belief needs to be questioned and, eventually, relinquished.

The you that you believe yourself to be cannot overcome this problem.

We must cease believing that we need more power. Instead, we need to come alive to the remarkable power we already possess.

Who we believe ourselves to be—the object within our consciousness—can be thought of as a container waiting to be filled with thought and feeling. When it is relatively empty, this object will generate a feeling of boredom. It needs thoughts and feelings to continue feeling alive. This container is useful in connecting with the everyday requirements of living. But it is not who we are—it just feels that way. Try getting a feel for your container which needs thoughts and feelings to stimulate itself. It is the you that is like a hamster on a treadmill. Whenever it is consumed by thoughts of inadequacy, it is driven toward a hasty retreat into a Fear-Self, including any form of self-improvement or search for Nirvana-like awakening.

This is the life of fear. Fear is Wound avoidance. It is the search for more power. It is the search to be taken care of. It is the search for a "final solution."

We must cease believing that we need more power. Instead, we need to come alive to the remarkable power we already possess. This is the capacity to experience anything. Is that not power enough? It is the capacity to provide a space for life to unfold as it does. We can only allow this to happen when we stop identifying with inadequacy, which always needs more power to secure its utopian fantasy of endless security. All the horrible violence in our world is a consequence of the urge for more power from a position of insufficiency or powerlessness.

Identified with insufficiency, we cannot love—we can only need.

29 - The Healing Process

To read a book or listen to a talk in order to grasp some new knowledge is useless; it is a waste of energy. However, there is immense value when you read to confirm your own observations.

~ Manuel Schoch

To begin healing, we need to have a clear understanding of our own invalidation and the fear-based adaptations we have created to respond to the Wound. This is a process that cannot be rushed. We need to really delve into our personal histories and the identities we have developed to tell our story to ourselves and others.

We also need to address our feelings and judgments associated with:

1. Invalidation, by understanding how our contempt for the vulnerable reflects and recreates our own invalidation;

2. Our invalidator(s), by understanding how our contempt and/or unquestioning admiration for the powerful recreates and reflects our relationship with our invalidators; and

3. Our Fear-Selves, by releasing our need to impress others and ourselves in order to counter our belief in our inadequacy, insufficiency, and worthlessness (our belief that we are undeserving of love).

This is not a one-shot, cures-all process. Rather, it is living from the understanding of the origin and manifestation of our suffering and thereby discovering a state of being which underlies the Wound and our Fear-Selves.

Step One: Understanding Our Own Invalidation Through Our Contempt for the Vulnerable

Ask yourself what you really hate in people you see as vulnerable or weak. Be ruthlessly honest with yourself, and focus on the contempt you have toward people who appear weak, lazy, needy, or pathetic. For example, do you really dislike people who are helpless or who act entitled or spoiled? Do you really resent "cry babies"? Do you hate people who are always complaining but don't assume responsibility for what bothers them? Find out what vulnerable type you really dislike. Do you hate cowards, or do you hate fearless, pretentious fools?

Once you have settled on what vulnerable type you really can't stand, write down the specific content of this visceral contempt image to really nail it down. Then consider the following: The vulnerable type you hate the most is the personification of your Wound. This is the wounded self. It is the you that you believe yourself to have been prior to its covering by a Fear-Self. The contempt you project outward toward the weak and vulnerable is the repressed hatred you have for yourself but cannot contain. See every vulnerable type you hate as yourself. See that the brutal judgment you make of others is no different from the brutal judgment you made of yourself at a time before you could even speak. See the "lazy," the "spoiled," the "obnoxious," the "self-centered" as yourself as you experienced your original invalidation trauma. Feel their pain as your own pain about yourself which you could not contain. Feel your heart break for them, for they are you.

Our original invalidation occurred prior to memory. We can only know it through our projections, which is the purpose of this exercise.

Some people may need to modify this exercise somewhat. People with stronger "feminine" (as opposed to more overtly aggressive "masculine") characteristics tend to be more empathetic toward the vulnerable and may have more difficulty perceiving their contempt for vulnerable types. Women and men who don't have much conscious disgust for the vulnerable might instead consider what they really can't stand about adult members of their same gender. Thoroughly immerse yourself in what you hate about others. The details of this contempt should give you a clear understanding of your personal Wound.

This doesn't mean you ought to "approve" of the slovenly, the rude, the self-centered. That would suggest a kind of imperial superiority, where you are the judge and jury and have the power to tolerate others because you're such a great and loving guy. This is much more radical—it's not that you need to abide these people; you *are* these people. Your condemnation, your rejection precisely mirrors your own self-rejection. When you reject, when you judge, you are simply replaying the trauma of your own Wound.

Step Two: Understanding the Invalidators through Our Contempt for the Powerful

Again concentrate on what you hate, but this time consider what you despise about those who are powerful. You may hate those who use their influence to bully people, or those who are arrogant, or those who are manipulative, or those who intimidate the defenseless. It could be that you hate all of these. When you have identified what you hate about the powerful, write down a detailed description.

The powerful people you hate are mirrors of your original invalidators. These are the people who made you feel bad about yourself. If you are a compliant Fear-Self, it may be difficult to locate this hatred, but if you are a rebellious Fear-Self, it ought to be quite easy.

Experience your hatred on a visceral level, then think about yourself when *you* have invalidated others. You may believe that you are not nearly as horrible as those you really hate, but no one is entirely innocent of invalidating and negating others and making them feel bad about themselves. If you have been a parent, you have certainly invalidated your children, even though you may be loath to admit it. Remember that we invalidate our children when we ignore their cries in the most formative period of their life. Lack of action can invalidate as easily as action.

When you see those you hate as yourself, feel your hatred drop away as you replace it with understanding and compassion. We are interconnected beings; these people are us. They are not the "other." Reach out to those powerful people you hate and say, "I am no different from you for I have also invalidated the people I claim to love most in my life."

This morning, I was listening to an interview on public radio with an eminent linguist. His tone was vibrantly enthusiastic and extremely informed. Despite the fact that I found what he had to say interesting and I respected his knowledge, there was something about his tone that I resented. I did not like his self-assuredness. It sounded a little "over the top." Then I realized that he sounded just like I do when I'm pontificating. I was able to find my own Expert Fear-Self laughable. The person I was resenting was *me*—how ironic!

Step Three: Releasing Our Identity with Our Fear-Selves by Seeing that They are No Longer Necessary for Our Safety and Well-Being

This is the most difficult step in the healing process. Where Step One and Step Two involved understanding and compassion, Step Three asks us to surrender our most desperate dreams and place them on the vast rubbish heap of the false. Yet Step Three is the only act that will fully free us from the Wound.

What is your most dominant Fear-Self? By now you should have a pretty clear idea. Remember that a Fear-Self exists only to counter the awful weight of the Wound and that this is exactly what prevents us from experiencing our Life Force.

Now is the time to give up completely on the dreams of your Fear-Self. If you have dreamed of becoming enlightened and living a life as a saint, know that your dream is a disease—it is not you; it is a false, fear-based identity. If your dream is to be beautiful and cease-lessly attract the jealous and desirous stares of others, release that dream, for it is a reflection of a lie. If you are a Terrified One, see all of your anxiety as the horrible fears of a little one who never got over her invalidation but now can step out into the light of life, secure in your connections and needing no psychological safety net. If you are a compulsive Achiever, let go of the need to impress others of your worth and become free to live what you love.

These fear-based aspirations live in a future that is wholly inse-cure. You are not responsible for your future; that is the responsibility of life. Forget the future and live your joy now.

Release everything you associate with your dominant Fear-Self. Release all of the images and ideas through which you define this identity. You are no longer the Expert, the Tough Guy, the Body Person, the Loner. In truth, you never *were* this person. Feel the immense relief as you understand that you will never again be compelled to realize any fear-based dream you possess for yourself. You are free of your false dreams and are able to live the life that gives you dignity now.

Know that this means you are releasing your hopes for yourself. Your hope for a better you is exactly what keeps you dissatisfied with yourself. You may hope for a sick child to get well, you may hope for peace in the world—that is different. But stop hoping for a better you. She has already arrived—you just haven't noticed her yet.

Step Four: Celebration

Feel the person who sees the vulnerable as her wounded self. Feel the person who sees the corrupt and powerful as her invalidators just as she is that invalidator. Feel the person who has released the dreams of a solitary, needy being. This feeling is the perfectly secure manifestation of life itself! You are carried by life and are life, all at the same time.

If you can't quite pull this off, try to see how your judgments play out in your life. See yourself living as your dominant Fear-Self. When you reject yourself as you are and follow a false identity, ask yourself, "Is this what I really want to believe about myself and my life? When I am on my deathbed, will I have any regrets about pursuing an identity that sought to ceaselessly prove my worth to others and myself? Is this how I want to live my life?"

Know that we define ourselves by what we reject and hate and what we aspire to. If these dreams are, in any way, based on a need to prove ourselves for purposes of impressing others, then they are false. Such aspirations are always based on a belief in our fundamental inadequacy. When we give these qualities up, it may be hard to say who we truly are. Who are we outside of our harshest judgments and loftiest aspirations? This discovery process is part of the adventure. Embrace the moment and have fun—you have just received your "Get Out of Jail Free" card!

Exercise 17:   Situation Exercise

Apply all four steps to situations and not just people. Situations in our life arouse feelings of contempt and hatred, just as people do. When you experience those feelings, connect them with your own personal Wound and the origin of your own invalidation. Hatred is a wonderful resource for self-discovery. Don't reject it!

Exercise 18:   Connecting

Most of us experience our sense of self in the muscles of our face. It is in this part of our body that we separate ourselves from the rest of our sensed environment. We also feel it in our shoulders, hands, and feet.

Try this: As you look out into the world, feel the place of immediate connection in your face, shoulders, feet, and hands. See these parts of your body as the bridge that connects you with the rest of the universe. Feel your face merge with all of your sensed reality. Feel your feet merge with the earth. Feel the absence of a dividing line between the tactile universe and your fingers. This is all about dissolving boundaries between your body and the world. Now experience your feelings as also merging with the world. Draw your heart into the whole of the experience. Don't force bliss; that can be faked, and appeals to the ever-desirable drama of a Fear-Self. Just softly feel your way through this exercise and explore what happens as you do it. Silently do this exercise with members of your family, people in your workplace, and even strangers you see on the street. Feel the absence of any boundary that isolates you from the sensed universe.

Don't misunderstand—you are not supposed to be in connection all of the time, that is impossible. The purpose of this exercise is to allow for its possibility. It is a portal to a new experience of being.

Exercise 19: Connection 2

Connection happens prior to thought. Look out your window and feel your connection with the world without thinking about it. That connection is real and vivid. Any line of separation is absolutely arbitrary!

Try this exercise with another person. Feel the connection prior to thought. It is only thought that imposes lines of separation. Thought is an overlay we place on reality.

We might believe that we use thought to "make sense" of reality. Is that true? Haven't all of us been misled by our thoughts as often as they have appeared to be true?

Our Life Force is our dynamic connection with our world. When we live from our unencumbered authentic being, those connections have primacy over thought. When we are most spontaneously happy and secure in ourselves and our world, thought becomes irrelevant.

Thought only becomes primary when happiness and security have ebbed away. What does this say about thought? We can see that the purpose of thought is to analyze. In the immediacy of life, its role tends to be greatly overrated.

Exercise 20: Giving It All Away

When we are born, we are whole. Once we are trauma-tized by negation and develop our array of Fear-Selves, we and our environment have acted to cover our inte-gral being with a kind of pain-forged armor. Another approach to healing is to give it all away. Everything we want, desire, fear, and experience—let it go. To whom do we give these things? We give them to whatever we believe is the creative force of the universe. You may call it Tao, or God, or Krishna. It only matters that you give it all to the universe, without exception. You no longer need knowledge, wisdom, or experience. Whatever comes your way with respect to knowledge, wisdom, or experience is yours only in the moment. Enjoy everything you sense in the moment, but then let it pass to that which receives everything.

Once you experience your authentic core, you know that you no longer need any knowledge or experience. There is an energetic source of being that thrives irrespective of what we sense and know. This is our Life Force.

It is awareness flooded with pleasure. It is complete and flows perfectly with life as it unfolds. Emotion is transformed. What was in-tense, self-engulfing anger becomes a momentary response to frustration. What was deadly serious becomes play. The hardness of the Wound and its attendant Fear-Selves softens greatly, and the loving light of our Life Force grows in strength and vitality. The need for external validation dies completely as we access our personal wholeness. What was struggle changes into love for the ongoing wholeness of life itself. What was a focus on "me" becomes a focus on "us."

30 - Living a Life of Trust

Be faithful to that which exists in yourself.
~ *Andre Gide*

Life free of the dominance of the Fear-Selves and their underlying source, the Wound, is a life liberated to discover its own voice. The voice of the liberated person is quite different from that of the person living in the shadow of the Fear-Selves.

This life possesses far less anxiety, stress, and compulsiveness—these are Fear-Self qualities. But just as important, the liberated person has the capacity to see and understand these qualities in others. With this understanding, we are far less likely to take either slights or accolades personally. We are finally able to be truly gracious with others and not just pretend. Authentic graciousness does not feel superiority over others; it feels warmth and compassion for them. This is the compassion of equality. We now understand that our own suffering and struggle are little different from the sufferings and struggles of everyone else. (Of course, these struggles may be exacerbated by the social conditions of class, gender, sexual preference, and race. Social prejudice and intolerance deepen invalidation.)

Graciousness and compassion are two sides of the same coin. We cannot be authentically compassionate without grace, and we cannot possess authentic grace without compassion. This also means that we see through the veil of "specialness" in others. No one is special. Once someone is labeled as special, someone else must be relegated to the category of "unspecial." This is the core material of the Wound, which resonates throughout the excessively competitive nature of our society.

Although we are not special, we are unique. Each of us has her own individuality and journey. We can either embrace our uniqueness or seek to hide in the shadow of illusory sameness. Either way, the journey will be unique. That's the irony of the absence of specialness and the fullness of uniqueness. It cannot be avoided. A snowflake cannot will itself to be identical to another snowflake. Each person is distinct no matter what her personal predilections might be. Embrace your uniqueness and embrace the glory of our diversity.

The liberated life is one of passion, resilience, and vigor. Just as life allows anything and everything to manifest, so does the liberated self.

First, let's make an important distinction. Whether we occupy the position of a Fear-Self or the liberated self, for each there is a "story." The tale of the Fear-Self is one marked by the compulsive need to achieve in a way that refutes the Wound. It is a story that unfolds within the pained interplay of the Wound and its array of Fear-Selves.

The story of the liberated self, on the other hand, is based on the absence of compulsion. It does seek to prove anything. It is aligned with life itself. It is not set in stone. If certain hoped-for achievements occur, good; if not, then that's OK, too. Our identity is shifted away from the need to succeed to the pleasure of just being and doing. The liberated person allows everything and anything to happen without resistance. He loves to just feel the experience. This is a sensuous form of existence that is responsible only to itself.

The story of the liberated self, on the other hand, is based on the absence of compulsion. It does seek to prove anything. It is aligned with life itself. It is not set in stone. If certain hoped-for achievements occur, good;

if not, then that's OK, too. Our identity is shifted away from the need to succeed to the pleasure of just being and doing.

Because the liberated person honors the Wound, she is deeply connected to the sufferings and challenges of others everywhere in the world. Their struggles resonate in her heart as her own. Because she understands that life happens only now, she is responsive to the moment, even if that moment means that she cannot respond on account of her limited capacity. We are not here to be saints. We are human beings defined as much by our frailties as our strengths. But when we are freed from the dominance of concepts, we are much more alive to the situations that arise in the ordinary unfolding of any day. Where the person dominated by a Fear-Self experiences interruptions that block her needs with exasperation and anger, the liberated person takes such events as part of the fabric of life.

While the Fear-Self is tightly attached to its self-centered dreams and needs, the liberated person is involved in life as it happens. This is the core of resilience. He does what needs to be done without losing touch with his own dreams. When we are free of the severe goal-setting of the Fear-Self, energy is allowed to flow to the ordinary activities of everyday life.

It is an act of great strength to see through the aspirations of a Fear-Self. It cannot be done until the lie of our inadequacy and insufficiency is thoroughly exposed. As an appendage of the inner Wound, the Fear-Self is a compulsive goal achiever. With the liberated self, energy is placed on the doing instead of the agenda. The end will take care of itself. This is the liberated heart of the Life Force—we stop running after what we believe will make us feel safe and do what makes us feel good. Outcome is based not on thought, but on life just as it is. Thought has nothing to with it. That is the gift of trust. We trust our own goodness and allow life to take care of the other details. This is the world view of the hunter-gatherer, and it is available to each of us once we have seen through the dance of the Wound and the Fear-Selves.

The Self-Image and Achievement

What if you were to know, beyond any shadow of a doubt, that no happening had an impact on your authentic self? This means that attaining or not attaining any achievement has no effect on your authentic being. How might absolute certainty of that knowledge influence your life?

When we "do" something, we are using our bodies. This means that we use our minds and our physical beings to the best of their abilities. In many situations, our bodies' actions are deemed "success" or "failure" through the assessments of others who have their own images and agendas to live up to.

Bodies perform certain tasks better than others because bodies differ. I have some ability at statistical analysis, but could not cleanly lay a brick if my life depended on it. Some bodies love yard-work; my body does not care for it. Each body has its own strengths and weaknesses.

Now consider this much larger question: If who we believe we are is the complex actions of our bodies and their various interactions with other bodies, then does a personal, separate psychology exist at all? Since psychology is fundamentally about explaining the self after its inevitable invalidation and helping that self cope better in an invalidating social and cultural environment, it becomes largely irrelevant from the authentically liberated perspective. Free of the psychological need to achieve or not achieve, free of a needy or despotic self-image, free of all our images of others, we are truly free.

Freedom is liberation from all our fear-based selves. Understanding this idea and living its reality in our daily lives is the whole purpose of this book. Free of images, we are, utterly and totally, liberated.

Exercise 21:   Discovering the Joke Behind the Fear-Self

All images are crude generalizations. More importantly, they are untrue. The word "tree" creates an image in our minds, but it is not a tree. Images are two-dimensional thoughts. The next time you stake your identity on any image of yourself or someone else, try to see the humor and absurdity of it. Bring all of what you have read in this book and your own testing of these principles in your everyday life to see, in a way that is crystal clear, that image thoughts are false. They are the self-preserving ideas of a Fear-Self that has co-opted your self-identity. Every time you pin your identity to an image you have taken one big step backwards. Try seeing the humor in it and then move on, free of any image.

Or, as a fun alternative, go ahead and play out your images—just know that you're playing. Ultimately, you will come to understand that there is no escaping images— that's just how our minds operate in the world—but you don't have to believe them. When we play with images, we divest them of their seriousness. We can play serious, but we don't need to be identified with seriousness.

Life can appear quite serious, but our guide can be the liberated heart and not a psychologically conditioned image.

Seeing the play of image with humor is of vital importance. The expression of the Fear-Self is, nearly always, serious. When a Fear-Self appears humorous, it is using this quality to either minimize itself or minimize others. Fear-Self humor is, often, quite miserable. Fear-Selves also use their cleverness to impress others. This can be done in the spirit of fun, but it often is just another of the innumerable cloaks of the Wound. You should be able to observe this in yourself and others.

At the core of image-seeking is comedy. It is, after all, a Fear-Self operating seriously in the world, and that is ultimately a kind of joke. The Fear-Self can eventually be seen as a fool operating with a simplistic set of rules in a world cut off from the actual flow of life. If you can see the humor in this, then you have made a giant step toward your own liberation. When you can really laugh at yourself, you've made it.

Exercise 22: Who Are You?

The next time you think you need something external to yourself to feel good, try saying this to yourself: "I am not this person. Knowing with absolute certainty that I am not this person, then who am I?"

The purpose of this exercise is to get a sense of your authentic being which is always there beneath your identification with desire and need for external validation. Do this exercise any time you feel that you need something outside yourself to provide you with a sense of completion. When we are free of this compulsion, we are altogether free. Remember that the *desire* to be free is another mani-festation of a Fear-Self. You *are* free prior to any desire.

The feeling of neediness is a temporary appearance of a Fear-Self. It is an object of consciousness, like anything else in the universe, no different from the chair you're currently sitting on. It's just another thing of which you are aware. When we can see the global projection of inadequacy, we are free to experience our own reality, free of any belief in who we are or are not. The most exalted realities are those created with humor and bigheartedness.

Trust

The hunter-gatherer lived a life of trust. She never doubted nature's capacity to take care of her and her people. For thousands of generations, human beings lived with this great well of trust. It may be hard to believe, but we can live that way as well.

You are not your Fear-Self who is ceaselessly needing to run to the next moment, who lives exclusively in the "what's next?" mode, constantly pursuing something to make you feel better, turn you on, make you secure. See that person as everything that is false and anxi-ety-inducing. It is a shallow vapor of a person. Try to stop personally identifying with this habitual energy, but don't try to think your way out of it. Life goes on exactly as it does without any thought from you. See how thought drives the process.

Now try settling into whatever is happening in your life. Just get interested in that. Note that as you see, hear, touch, or taste some-thing, that object has already manifested in the moment you notice it. Look out the window and see what's outside without any intention to get anything out of the experience (that's the "what's next" energy doing its thing). Try not to experience any feeling (that's the phony spiritual energy doing its thing). Just be with what is happening, and let things be just as they are. That is trust.

Everything you experience has already happened! Perception lags just an instant after an object manifests. It is always slightly behind. We can never know the instant things happen, because we are always ever so slightly catching up to them. This might sound like splitting hairs, but it's really important. Because everything we notice has already happened, it cannot be changed. The "what's next" energy dismisses the now because it thinks that it already knows it and is eager to move on. The now is boring, because it is already known. The "what's next" modality feeds on the concept of new and exciting. It is not real. It is merely the energy of need filling its perceived dead zone of the now.

But we can never know what's next because what's next isn't now. What's next never happens except in the imagination of a Fear-Self. The time from our birth to our death can only happen in the now, and even the now has already happened. Neither are we the person who doesn't know the now. We are neither knower nor not-knower. We just are.

But we can never know what's next because what's next isn't now. What's next never happens except in our imagination.

Get the feeling of placing your trust in the now. In this way you trust yourself utterly. It is insanity to deny any element of the now. As you say "yes" to whatever happens, a whole new you is born. This is the you that can be trusted but never known. You can only know the false you.

If you have scary things happening in your life, like a divorce, serious illness, or financial problems, watch the terror conjured up by your "what next" energy. Watch how horrible it makes you feel about yourself and your life. Then try relaxing into the reborn you that completely trusts the ceaselessly changing now. It really is beautiful. Hear the rain or the cries of your child; feel how your body/mind is in this moment. Without applying any unnecessary effort, just whisper a resounding "yes" to this wondrous, magical now exactly as it unfolds. Join the great river of life. Feel the immense power as life buoys you up.

Do what you need to do to address the challenges of life, but just trust implicitly the vast flow of life.

The fears your imagination conjures up are happening to a being that is not you. They are thoughts happening to a thought.

Even feel the resistance of the "what's next" energy as it inevitably re-enters the now and you regress into a Fear-Self.

One last proviso: One of the most subtle manifestations of a Fear-Self is the meaning it invests in objects and situations. When we live in trust, those meanings melt away and all objects and situations are seen anew, not just as worn-out versions of their previous manifestations in your life. Life becomes boring and oppressive when you categorize your experiences into old containers. That is the way of the Fear-Self.

Identification

The Fear-Self is our most narrow and self-centered identification. It is the greedy, selfish, and ignorant self in action.

The narrower our identification, the more prone we are to conflict, suffering, and insecurity. As Fear-Selves, we are like rats fighting over a very small piece of cheese. Everyone is a potential adversary. This is life as struggle. Even the Spiritualist aggressively attacks himself and life as he pines for enlightenment and transcendence. This is the life that is ultimately isolated, desperate, and lonely. This is the life that is firmly rooted in the soil of the Wound.

Is this the life you want?

Try returning to Exercise 5. When we are rooted in life, which asks us to center our awareness on life as it unfolds in the moment, we are free of all apparent identities. This exercise aligns us with life. It frees us from the confines of any self-image or self-impoverishing, invalidating belief. It frees us from seeking refuge in any new belief in order to spruce up our sense of self. We are just part of life, like the bird merrily chirping outside the window, like the breeze rustling the leaves and like the galaxies gliding through the universe.

We have a choice. We can continue living through complex mental concepts that insist on imposing a rigid story on life with its "good days and bad days," or we can be life. We are free to play with our dreams—and "play" is the operative word. Freedom is play.

Thought and Feeling

Nothing is ever wrong with the Wound, the countering Fear-Selves, or any thought or feeling. As they present themselves, they are exactly as they ought to be.

As long as we resist any thought or feeling, we are still inhabiting a Fear-Self. Thoughts and feelings are aspects of the body/mind and are as much a part of our beings as our heart, hands, and brain.

Thoughts and feelings emerge within a person's consciousness and then fade and disappear. They come in all sizes. Some seem mightier than a great mountain, others are like wispy feathers lighter than air.

As long as we resist any thought or feeling, we are still inhabiting a Fear-Self. Thoughts and feelings are aspects of the body/mind and are as much a part of our beings as our heart, hands, and brain.

Thoughts and feelings enter our consciousness just as our physical body parts do. Most of the time we are unaware of our bodies. Our hands, mouths, hearts are simply *there*, and only come into focus when life thrusts them into our awareness—we smash a thumb with a hammer, we taste a delicious flavor, we feel our heartbeat quicken when we are frightened. But quickly enough, they fade away into the background again. Similarly, thoughts and feelings shows just happen. We can't know them ahead of their manifestation because they are not predictable. We might anticipate a certain feeling, whether scary or wonderful, but the experience of anticipation is always different from the actual experience of the thing anticipated. This is the mystery of thought, feeling, and life itself. None of it can be known.

We don't need to fear thoughts and feelings. If we do fear them, we give them power. and when we give something power, we make ourselves proportionately powerless. There are truly fearful elements in life, but most of our fear-based thoughts are the product of an anxious imagination, and they are likely to be the consequence of a Fear-Self. This is life out of balance, as we cower in the shadow of thoughts and feelings. When we possess the courage to reach out to even the most terrifying thought or feeling, we heal our powerlessness and are proportionately empowered.

The bridge to that healing is greeting all our thoughts and feelings with heart-felt welcome. Since we are never separate from our thoughts and feelings, when we open up to them, we are made more whole and balanced. The fearful identity with which we previously identified departs us, and we gain a greater sense of our complete self.

There is no escape from the part we are called to play in life's drama. We can play it with gusto, tears, joy, and thoughtfulness, balanced on our own two feet resting on the solidity of the earth. Or we can nurture our fears and live a false life in the shadow of our invalidation. The gateway to joy is found in the recognition of that which is false; there can be no true joy without understanding. We need to pass through the portal of grief and mourning before our Life Force lets us enter its primal fields.

There is no escape from the part we are called to play in life's drama. We can play it with gusto, tears, joy, and thoughtfulness, balanced on our own two feet resting on the solidity of the earth. Or we can nurture our fears and live a false life in the shadow of our invalidation.

It is never our responsibility to provide "solutions." A life devoted to finding solutions is the ultimate egotistical gesture. A belief in solutions is a belief that if you don't win, you lose. The mythic world of solutions is the stuff of man the superhero, man the conqueror, man the pontificator, man the perfectionist. Solutions are the path of false authority, and only the small mind, the invalidated mind, the bitter mind seeks them. Indeed, there *are* no solutions—there is only play and process. Liberation is only an invitation to the play … the play without purpose …the play for its own sake. There is only play, play, and more play. The play may be tragic, heart-rending, hopeless, ruinous, but, ultimately, it is still play ... play ever leading to more play ... till the end of time.

Solutions are the path of false authority, and only the small mind, the invalidated mind, the bitter mind seeks them.

The issue of solutions could fill an entire book of its own. Seeking permanent solutions to obtain happiness, contentment, and well-being occurs when we believe that a thought can trump the mystery of existence. It's not coincidence that the Nazi term for the extermination of the Jews during the Second World War was the "Final Solution." Fascists, zealots, and fanatics are enamored with solutions.

We can be free, but the cost of that freedom is relinquishing any belief in the existence of final solutions. This means we will never know who we are and why we are here. We will never know the meaning of life or death. We will never know how to find happiness. We will never discover a reliable path to any human goal. It's all process, and we have no clue where it leads. All we can say is that it leads somewhere, and I'm here to experience the ride. In the glorious spirit of not having a clue as to my identity, I will love and hate, work and play, live and die.

This means we will never know who we are and why we are here. We will never know the meaning of life or death. We will never know how to find happiness. We will never discover a reliable path to any human goal. It's all process, and we have no clue where it leads. All we can say is that it leads somewhere, and I'm here to experience the ride.

It is the mind that craves certainty. When a mind is told that it cannot be certain of anything, it then thinks, "Then I must be uncertain." But the thought of "uncertainty" is equally unreal—it is just the mind-state opposite of certainty.

The same principle applies to the thought/concept of "security": If I'm not secure, then I must be insecure. Yet they are both just opposing thoughts. They are walls erected against the vast flow of change.

The other night, my partner was worrying about her daughter's departure for college. She was busy imagining the disasters to come and experiencing her failure as a mother. I asked her, "Are you grateful for Van Gogh and all the great art he produced?" She answered, "Of course." "I don't think his mother was," I continued. "Here is her beloved son, made in her image, and he can't get a regular job, becomes a second-rate artist, shacks up with other artists—and then things get worse. He cuts off one of his ears to show his love to some floozy, and then kills himself. Could it get any worse?"

It's all relative.

When we can see our hopeless striving for certainty and solutions for what they are, we are freed of all our painful cravings. Life rarely, if ever, matches our worst imaginings. We can count on it to be vastly different from our thoughts.

When we stop seeking certainty and security and see through the falseness of their opposites, we are free completely. And best yet, we have a lot more energy for what we love. We are free to be playful and creative. This is the big payoff, the golden ring, the grand prize.

You may fear that if you divorce yourself from your ceaseless search for solutions, you are in danger of falling into nihilistic meaninglessness. But this is not so. When we see that we are connected to everything and everything is connected to us, then we experience the fundamental equality, integrity, and dignity of all beings. That is the very essence of meaning. There is no greater joy than the joy of our shared destiny. This is life at its most basic and mutually responsible level.

Death

All life's journeys lead to death. While our beings are unique, our destination is not. With every passing second that we spend identifying with a False-Self, the gap with the inevitable grows shorter. I cannot imagine a more pathetic fate than reaching the end and looking back on a false life. But that is the fate for most of us.

This is life unlived. It is the life of regret. It is full of "coulds" and "shoulds." But even if you have just one day left, there is still time to find and live through your authentic self.

If nothing else, the purpose of life is to find and speak with our real voices. Those voices will remain hidden as long as we live our lives in rapt belief of our self-crucifying lie, the Wound. The time has come to undo that self-negating error before it's too late.

Too many of us die before our bodies give out. Now is the time to stop dying and start coming alive to whom you really are on the other side of the Wound. Who is that person who no longer needs to draw attention from others to feel good about life? Who is that person who no longer strives for happiness based on achievements that need to be noticed, if only by one's self? Who is that person who has seen through the false promise of personal enlightenment?

Who is that person who no longer needs to draw attention from others to feel good about life? Who is that person who no longer strives for happiness based on achievements that need to be noticed, if only by one's self? Who is that person who has seen through the false promise of personal enlightenment?

On the other side of the Wound there is the being and energy one possessed prior to invalidation. It is someone we barely know. It is the source of wisdom independent of books, patience independent of goals, love independent of romance, and fun independent of winning or losing.

Let this person reawaken. This is not a project—it is a happening. It has nothing to do with feeling good about yourself through an act of will or the repeating of a mantra. It is who you are outside the concepts of mind, the compulsions of the Fear-Self, and the belief in your own inadequacy.

Ultimately, who you are is a being without effort. Your authentic identity, your Life Force, is the effortless state of being that underlies all acts of the body and the universe. When we seek to understand our being through effort, we are in the world of the Fear-Self, the world where we need to *do*. The pressure of feeling the need to do makes us exhausted and rigid.

Get a feel of the effortless being that comes before any doing. It is both the source and the destination. We do nothing to arrive. We see through the false promise contained within desire and knowledge.

The Mystery

"Life cannot be held back. It will find a way," says Dr. Malcolm after hearing of the very logical and linear plans behind the creation of "Jurassic Park" in the movie of the same name.

Our philosophies, our morality, our plans, our identities, our beliefs all are approaches to understanding and controlling life. They all fail. Life will always find a way to show us its real meaning and the true value of our most sacred beliefs—which is to show each and every one of them to be false.

Life cannot be contained. It cannot be known. It cannot be controlled. That is the first part of the mystery.

If life cannot be controlled or known, then you cannot be controlled or known. There is nothing we can do, simply because anything we contemplate doing would be based on an idea that is false, a lie. The only liberation is that which gives up on knowing or seeking to control.

When you vainly try to impose knowing or control onto life, that too is part of life. It is just another happening. Anything can happen in the next moment utterly without reference to any knowing we might think we possess. Stars explode, animals become extinct, and I need to go to the bathroom.

Everything we do to know and control is merely the throwing of rocks into a moving stream. They make white water, excitement, and sound, but little else. Ultimately, they are just a small part of the stream.

We can throw those rocks with the purpose of control or the spirit of play. Consider the difference.

We know all too well the person who is seeking to know and control life. But we don't know the person who can live with and live as the mystery that is life. That is the second part of the mystery.

Who is that person who can finally release his grip on all false knowing and control? That is the person we want to get to know.

31 - Examples of the Liberation Process

This book was written for many reasons, but one reason a person might read it is to get help with problems that bring them emotional pain. This kind of pain seems so complex and unresponsive to healing that is sustainable. We can see a therapist for years, meditate, take medications, endlessly read self-help books, and still feel, at the end of the day, that we're just spinning our wheels. That lingering pain and upset is still there.

Words are a very small and largely ineffectual subset of "reality." The words of this book present a theory. That means they are, primarily, descriptive of a process. They are a way to help us understand why we are the way we are. Terms such as the Wound and the Fear-Self are just labels that describe a process. But if the theory is accurate, they can provide us with a different way of responding to emotional turmoil.

The theory of <u>Liberation</u> is as deep as we would have the capacity to take it. The following summary applies its understanding to examples from everyday life.

Through invalidation we become wounded in the very depths of our being. Our most enduring emotional pain is connected to invalidation. We are invalidated on the levels of self-image, body, gender, race, class, ethnicity, and age. We naturally develop Fear-Selves to cope with emotional pain. The Fear-Self is the identity we believe ourselves to be. It promises us completion and well-being but can never deliver. It is only a porous wall that is erected around the Wound. It is a Band-Aid. Some Band-aids are better than others, but no Band-aid is part of our intrinsic selves. The Band-aid metaphor breaks down because, when our body is wounded, it recovers naturally. But when we identify with a Fear-Self, we effectively block the body/mind from ever recovering. The Wound festers underneath an object (the Fear-Self) which prevents light from ever reaching it.

The Wound and the Fear-Self are actually one and the same. The invalidation experience creates the Wound. The Wound creates the Fear-Selves and the Fear-Selves lead us back to the Wound.

Now let's apply this understanding to our daily lives.

Let's say that speaking in public terrifies you. Anytime you get in front of an audience, you freeze with fright. This fear is the living expression of the Wound. Your original invalidation under-mined your sense of yourself; now your handicap manifests any time you are put in front of an audience. The thought, "How could anyone respect what I have to say," is a replication of your early invalidation experience. Your very young self's interpretation of the absence of love and support evolved to the belief that you possess insufficient worth. So when you experience emotional pain, the drive to shield yourself from the pain automatically kicks in. You cover it up by being brave, putting on a false front, or just agreeing with the thought and organizing your life to avoid any experience that allows contact with your Wound. Your Wound can make you a hermit, a person scared to really live.

Our liberation comes when you do absolutely nothing when you are overcome with fear and emotional pain. After all, you know, in the very depths of your being, that there is nothing you can do to overcome this fear! Instead of shielding yourself against the pain and turmoil, open yourself to whatever terror life brings. So there you are, in front of a large audience. The old terror returns. You notice it and say something to yourself like, "Welcome, terror—nice to see you again." Then you do nothing—you don't make a big deal of it, you don't give it undue and unnecessary attention. You just go on doing whatever you need to do. Feel the pleasure of not needing to do anything about it. Do what you need to do with grace and refuse to pay any special mind to the belief in your low worth and inadequacy. Perhaps, to your surprise, you discover that you are just fine!

Our liberation comes when you do absolutely nothing when you are overcome with fear and emotional pain. After all, you know, in the very depths of your being, that there is nothing you can do to overcome this fear! Instead of shielding yourself against the pain and turmoil, open yourself to whatever terror life brings.

It's important to distinguish between doing what we need to do and doing the "right" thing. In the public-speaking example, the person who needs to focus on the terror is the very identity that is identified with insufficiency. The person who needs to work on himself is the inadequate self. See the need to fix yourself as precisely the expression of the insufficient self—it can be nothing *but* insufficient. When you really know that, the terror is not a problem; it is only a problem to the insufficient self. And you are able to do what you need to do—go ahead and give the speech.

This is different from the person who must do the "right" thing, the egotistical personality who must attend to what he believes needs fixing and the false spiritual self who takes pride in that insight. See that identity as a form of refined egotistical behavior. Just as with the terror, refuse to give it any attention; don't give it the prominence it wants for itself.

Instead of fixing yourself, instead of feeling pressured about doing the "right" thing, feel the effortless pleasure that emerges when you live from your true core. This is the authentic self revealed when we see and undercut the story of the inadequate self. Liberation is liberation from the need to run here and there, busily repairing what is not even real.

One proviso regarding egotistical actions: Any effort used to suppress them is also egotistical action but in its inverse form. The actions of the ego change only with understanding and experience. We will continue the actions of the ego as long as we believe we need to. They will cease on their own accord when they have lost their meaning to us.

So the nervous public speaker just speaks. You might hesitate, you might stumble, but you do what you need to do in the moment. Thinking about how awful you sound, how pathetic you are, how inferior you are to other public speakers are all thoughts of the Fear-Self. Speak, and when you speak, make sure that each sentence, each word is heard. Don't rush just so you can finish faster and lessen the pain. Don't look down and mumble so your audience will fall into accord with your belief in your own inadequacy. Instead, be the person you want to be. Be that person now and forever, irrespective of the inclination of a fear-based self.

Many of us are defensive about our bodies. We will always be defensive about anything with which we personally identify. When we say something is "ours'" or that it belongs to us, we are investing our identity in it. Nearly all of us believe that we are our bodies, so when our appearances do not meet our standards on how we should look, we are flooded by an undercurrent of shame about our very being.

The experience of shame is one the most common manifestations of the Wound in our lives. Images of how bodies should be abound in our culture. We must be youthful, slim, vibrant. Few of us are those things, and many of us feel shame as a result.

When we experience some shame about our bodies, we are likely to impute negative labeling to others. Our Wound is brought to the surface, and great suffering fills our sense of self.

Liberation from shame asks us to respond to that emotion just as was described in the first example. We recognize the Wound as its source. We recognize how we have created Fear-Selves to respond to this pain. We open ourselves to the pain with welcome. We no longer resist it. We feel for ourselves with an open heart and a sense of preciousness. If dieting or exercise can help our bodies respond better to life, we may select that path. But first we want to feel a welcoming sense of our physical selves.

Many of us let ourselves go in order to justify a self-hating Fear-Self. Explore that possibility in your own life. Many of us are our fiercest invalidators. A neglected body is often a sign of self-invalidation.

Ultimately, when we welcome the shame about our bodies, we enter a much deeper level of realization. That which can welcome the world of shame and struggle is, obviously, not the body. It is the authentic self. When we are able to welcome the universe of the Wound into our lives, we are able to see through all of the identities we have assumed to be true.

When we feel shame about our bodies or our minds, we identify with the body and the mind. They are who we believe ourselves to be. But when we understand what is really going on and are capable of welcoming the Wound into our lives, we can see who we are not. That which can see through the Wound is our true identity. When we fully realize this, we are living in truth. There is such immense beauty in this realization. We can love everything and everyone. That which can understand and welcome is our true home and our Life Force. We have lived our whole lives in the veil of shame, and now the veil can be cast aside and we can allow the light of truth into our lives.

When we feel shame about our bodies or our minds, we identify with the body and the mind. They are who we believe ourselves to be. But when we understand what is really going on and are capable of welcoming the Wound into our lives, we can see who we are not. That which can see through the Wound is our true identity. When we fully realize this, we are living in truth. There is such immense beauty in this realization.

So, just as the body is not our authentic self (no matter how great it might look now!), neither are our incidental thoughts and feelings who we are. We believe they are who we are only when we claim ownership of them. When we see such ownership as false, as merely an echo of the Wound/Fear-Self dyad, we are free.

This realization cannot be faked. Until we can welcome shame and fear, we will identify ourselves with shame and fear. We are liberated from shame and fear when we see, with absolute clarity, that we are not those emotional beings. This is the core of liberation.

Notice how unforced awareness welcomes absolutely everything, whether it is a hair growing in an unwanted place or the massive horror of the Holocaust. This energy evades nothing, absolutely nothing. It never needs improvement.

If you integrate this concept into your own life, a new identification may emerge which has primarily a sense of pride or accomplishment. This is just another, highly refined Fear-Self assuming the gold ring of achievement. That too needs to be understood and seen through. Self-inflation is the flip side of self-negation.

For most of us, identification with the mind—its thoughts, feelings, opinions, and fears—is far trickier terrain to negotiate than identification with the physical body. When we take pride in an accomplishment, such as seeing through the self-veiling elements of the physical body, the self-identity may transfer to the mind. But the same insights and understandings that we have applied to the body can be applied to the mind. When we can welcome any thought without identifying ourself with it, no matter how painful it might be, we have broken through identification with the mind.

The truth of who we are is the vastness that encompasses our perception of our body and our experience of our mind. From that "placeless" place, a thought, any thought or feeling, can be experienced with joy and pleasure. It is only when we personally identify with a thought or feeling that they can have the power to make us miserable. We can take pleasure in our achievements, but we don't need to personally identify with them. When we do, then the fear of loss will haunt us to the end of our days. We are much more than any thought or feeling.

It is only when we personally identify with a thought or feeling that they can have the power to make us miserable. We can take pleasure in our achievements, but we don't need to personally identify with them. When we do, then the fear of loss will haunt us to the end of our days.

Let's look at another example.

Many of us are motivated to "do good" in the world. We might volunteer to feed the homeless, we might feel awful about missing church or temple, we might believe that we should work harder to save the environment. We might not exactly feel "bad" about not doing enough, but we would like to do a lot more for the world, for the less fortunate, and to make our community a better place in which to live. This need to do good becomes our identity.

Please allow me two short digressions.

In the 1870s, after the "Indian Wars," Easterners, particularly Quakers, wanted to do a good deed to the defeated and despairing Native Americans. At that time, nearly all Indians (having worked with Indians for many years, I learned that there is a preference for the term "Indian" over "Native American") lived on relatively large Federal Indian reservations. The traditional way of life was either gone or in its death throes. Yet many Indians lived in traditional ways, in tipis on the Plains and in hogans and wikiups in the Southwest. They lived as communal groups, with no concept of individual land ownership. In the spirit of doing good, these Eastern Quakers created legislation that would give Native people a productive purpose in life. They created what was to become the Dawes Act. This law provided Indian heads of households with the right to own 160 acres of land. The purpose was to shape these "primitive" nomadic hunting people into proud individual landowners who could take the energy they previously devoted to hunting and redirect it to farming, just like white folks.

People much more cunning than the naive Quakers saw immense opportunity in the Dawes Act. They understood that the government could sell these deeds to Indians, and then white entrepreneurs could purchase the land from the Natives for pennies. So, what was Indian land promised in perpetuity by treaty with the U.S. government became, almost overnight, land owned by whites. Not only were nearly all reservations vastly reduced in size in a matter of a few short years, but even federal reservation land was transferred to white ownership. That means that the Lakota or Cheyenne or Blackfoot reservations now denoted on U.S. maps are actually made up of land largely owned by whites. Moreover, the shrewd whites bought only the very best land. The Indians ended up keeping the most eroded and empty land granted to them by treaty.

By seeking to do good, the well-intended Quakers produced a catastrophe. The Dawes Act accomplished what no military campaign ever did: It displaced Indians from well over half of their land in the United States in a single stroke.

For centuries, Christian missionaries have traveled through much of the non-Western world to spread their faith. They believe that they are saving people they describe as pagan or heathen. They assume that their faith is better than any other, that it is in fact the only truth. So they go off with the purpose of converting the savages of the world, to make them proper, God-fearing Christians. They believe in their hearts that they are doing good. They are on a mission; hence we call them missionaries.

The societies targeted by these missionaries are fragile. Their very limited exposure to and knowledge of Western civilization make them vulnerable to the razzle-dazzle of technology, Coca-Cola, metal pots and pans, and all the rest. But when they lose their connections to their cultural roots, they collapse into an abyss of alcoholism, violence, child abuse, prostitution, suicide, and utter despair. Missionaries are a big part of the civilization package. Those who convert oftentimes have been lured to accept tacitly the intrusion of outsiders into their world through offerings of food and medicine, and they are the most vulnerable, already defeated. The utter destruction of these age-old cultures and communities is a core part of the Christian missionary package.

Whenever one group claims that it is better than another, that it knows the only truth, violence and despair must ensue.

Just as the Dawes Act became the final, all but lethal blow to Native American culture, missionaries play a similar role in the cultures they invade. Often, in "doing good," we actually produce the most acute despair and hopelessness. We fail to see the massive ego that lies at the core of these efforts.

The urge to do good often originates in a belief in our insufficiency. We seek to do good in order to heal our own self-contempt. When we seek to do good in order to feel better about ourselves, we are operating from the position of ego and a Fear-Self. Instead of doing good, we are far more likely to spread our own poison.

When we seek to save another, we assume that we know better than this person. We must be brutally honest with ourselves any time we believe that we know better than another what is best for them. For the most part, we are acting from the position of a Fear-Self, and our efforts are more about ourselves than about anyone or anything else.

When we seek to save another, we assume that we know better than this person.

The sorrow we feel for others is often a projection of the sorrow we feel for ourselves. This is tricky territory, because those motivated to help others can be doing exactly what the world needs. But the *compulsive* need to do good is likely the refined masquerade of a Fear-Self.

Any time we act from a position of inadequacy and insufficiency, not only are we likely to fail to provide something of value to another, but we also perpetuate a belief in our own flawed self.

The language of formal religion is full of this toxicity. We speak of Original Sin, of seeing ourselves as sinners, of seeing others as sinners, of seeing ourselves as spiritually superior to others … and on and on it goes. All of it is the language of insufficiency. This is the language of violence to self and others.

We are conditioned to believe that we need to do good. On the surface this sounds fine. But first we need to understand who we truly are. We need to experience the absolute equality of beings, including non-human beings. We need to understand that the journeys of others are <u>their</u> journeys, and that we are not responsible for them. Even when we are thoroughly grounded in the truth of our authentic beings, we can only speak for ourselves.

The ego is our response to inadequacy. It may sound harsh, but the person who goes to therapy to make himself "better," the person who meditates to get enlightened, and the person who reads endless self-help books are each operating from their identity with inadequacy.

Whenever we experience emotional pain and then seek to repair it, we are doomed to fail. "Fixing" is an endless, perfect loop, which, like every Fear-Self, only promises fulfillment and completion in the future but can never deliver.

When you experience emotional pain, take note of it, but refuse to give it undue importance. Only a fixer does that. Welcome it, as we welcome any truth in our sensed universe. Our authentic selves are the very spirit of welcoming. Wanting to fix *is* the pain. We can understand that desire to fix as pain and no longer seek refuge in it. We can feel the pleasure that inevitably will arise when we are liberated from this compulsive loop and we take the next step. We might fear that same old voice telling us how good or bad we are, but we also know it to be the voice of ego, and give it scant attention. Life carries us and everything else forward in its vast current, and we are seated in our place of self, ultimately mysterious and ineffable.

If there is an ultimate key, it is this: The inadequate self has an idea of happiness that is at variance to whatever is happening in his life (except at those times of unselfconscious happiness). Life is labeled "inadequate." The self is labeled "inadequate." The *idea* of happiness trumps everything. As a result, the whole of one's unhappy identity is subsumed by a negative idea. Through the ghost of our invalidation, we insist on pursuing an idea of what will set ourselves and life right. This is the lie. See this lie as it operates in your own life. Stop the drive for self-improvement, for enlightenment, for wellness that is driven by this one nefarious idea. Remove this toxic projection from life; remove all of the false stories it spawns. Be free.

32 - Life

Forget self-help, forget meditation, forget Buddhism—forget it all. They are all distant provinces in the land of thought.

When we cling to these secondhand, borrowed notions, they become desperate thoughts imported from the fields of fear.

When we seek answers from external sources, we turn our back on ourselves. Cease seeking and find yourself. Find yourself without needing to seek.

If we stop seeking, what is HERE?

What is here is Life. Each of us is the light that shines on it and makes Life possible. That is the ultimate act of love. Love IS.

Life is ALWAYS there, and it is there for only one person—YOU.

Life never forsakes us, but we so aggressively forsake it. We forsake it for dreams that are always just past the next moment, just a little farther along the road of meditation and self-infatuation and self-rejection. We run from Life, thinking that there is always something better, something looming in the distance, that if we could only touch it, we could then *possess* it.

Life cannot be possessed. Instead, be possessed by Life!

When we feel trapped and hopeless, it is there—LIFE … LIFE with all of its potential, its mystery, its opportunity to connect—with its opportunity to TOUCH you and for YOU to touch IT.

Dance with Life … DANCE with all your HEART … dance with Life that is vast and Life that is small. For there is something out there that is indeed looming, and that thing is DEATH—your death, the death of your parents, the death of your husband or wife, the death of your children, the death of all that you hold dear.

Know death, and through knowing it—its inevitably, its HERE and NOW—see that every moment is dear. it is your love and understanding that make it so. Do not let Life down with your seeking for something better. There is something out there. You don't need to seek it, for it will surely find you.

In that gap between now and the now that ends all nows, dance with all your heart. Life is your partner, Life is your center. Let it touch and caress you with its carelessness, with its ripe abundance.

It's time to leave the shore and dive in. Be as life.

Life IS. Love IS. But they are lonely without YOU. Life needs YOU and only YOU. You exist for it and it exists utterly for you. Life made you for itself.

Do not let Life down. It's NOW or never. Cowards run from Life seeking something better. They run and they run.

It's time to walk away from that race, where winners only die, exhausted and spent after Life has passed them by.

Be brave and let Life TOUCH you. Be brave, and reach out in the smallest way and touch IT.

And … don't feel bad if you just need to give up, for that too is life … LOVE knows that, and LIFE knows that sometimes you need to lower your head and go no further.

But in that lowering, in that heavy-heartedness, in that mourning, all beauty still unfolds before you. This beauty is so very patient. She waits for YOU, she waits only for you, because she loves you and only you. She knows your pain and your sadness. All the patience you may lack, she possesses in limitless abundance. She waits at your doorway, waiting for you to open your eyes, to open your heart, to let the LIGHT in.

She will always be there to invite you to the dance. She will be THERE and HERE and EVERYWHERE. She is outside and she is inside … She IS you, if you only knew that.

The Hero Twins, Part Two

The task of Born for Water and Monster Slayer was to make the world safe for human beings. Monster Slayer went out into the world and killed nearly all of the fearsome monsters who, in those primal times, inhabited this small, fragile planet. The Hero Twins succeeded in their mission. They made it possible for First Woman and First Man to start the first family, and we are their descendants.

But even mighty Monster Slayer could not kill all of the monsters. Depression, Lack, and Hunger survived his onslaught. These are the monsters that still inhabit our lives.

Liberation is about finding our own Born for Water and Monster Slayer in the deepest recesses of our hearts. They are there, just waiting for the call. This book has been one such call.

A traditional Diné healer told me several times that to live a good life, one first must know and be stabilized within the esoteric, then all things will follow in balance. This is the way of Beauty. Being centered in the esoteric allows Life to flow unimpeded, like a mighty river.

Feel the power of Born for Water and Monster Slayer as the power and passion of your own self. This is your authentic birthright.

33 - Conclusion: Liberation

When all is said and done, liberation is not easy. Identified with our fears, we prefer the safe haven of arbitrary identities. We embrace our national and religious associations and choose to fight to the death to defend them. Our shared humanity is very rarely a source of harmony and connection. An Israeli is a Jew and a Palestinian Arab a Muslim before they are human beings. They may acknowledge the mutuality of their humanity, but their group identification trumps their equality. Even when we are able to embrace our collective humanity, we still separate ourselves from the "non-human" parts of life and posit ourselves as superior to them.

We are frightened of the realization of authentic freedom as equal beings, despite being warmly receptive to its rhetorical expression. If history teaches us anything, it is that people are driven to abdicate their unique individuality and prefer the safety of their ideologies and beliefs which are not intrinsic to their nature. All such associations are based on fabrications designed to empower the specialness of their "membership."

True freedom means that we are finally free to be who we are, without any compulsion to adopt identities that are arbitrary and based on our fear of aloneness and powerlessness.

When you can see through every belief and live through your own self, you discover that you're not part of any club. When we identify with our gender, religion, political affiliation, or anything else, we continue to hold onto some idea or image of who we are. We are always free to join any club that appeals to us, but that identity is not who we are. Rather, we can join a club for the aliveness it provides us.

We can join our power to it, rather than depend on it for the power that we lack.

When we identify with our gender, religion, political affiliation, or anything else, we continue to hold onto some idea or image of who we are. We are always free to join any club that appeals to us, but that identity is not who we are.

The only true freedom is the one that lives with the I AM of existence. We ARE, and as active elements of our own being, we are responsible for how we are in the world without needing to consult any book of rules. The right action relates only to the presenting circumstances, and no new rules are created as a consequence of these actions. Freedom is contextual; it is in the moment.

Freedom is no cakewalk. We will need to understand our lives through what is real as opposed to what is taken on faith, fear, or hope. Our only reality is the reality we have experienced directly. The American poet Theodore Roethke said, "I don't know a thing, except what I do." That's it. We "do," but hopefully we don't do within the isolation of an ego pitted against a world that is always potentially threatening. Instead, we do within the far larger context of the many connections that manifest simultaneously. We are not alone in the world. Rather, we are our world.

We are called upon to use our brains and our hearts in a way that brings honor, dignity, love, and light to our experience. We must take hold of our own power and be mindful of the legitimate power of others, including such life-sustaining entitites as the air and water. When we identify with the whole of the world, we really are a friend to ourselves. As Lao Tzu said, "Surrender yourself humbly; then you can be trusted to care for all things. Love the world as your own self; then you can truly care for all things."

Until we identify our self with the world, we will continue fighting one another, ceaselessly striving to possess more and be more (as in enlightened!) while we kill our planet. We need to place every identity with nation or god into the trash heap of failed civilization.

We learn that happiness is a consequence of giving up the struggle for us and the world to be different.

We are together in all of this. The rapidly disappearing rainforests, the coral reefs, the wetlands are together with us. The living earth thrives without human beings, while human beings die off without a natural world. This is the most basic of all lessons, yet, based on our actions, if not our words, it is a lesson few take to heart.

No man is an island, no god is better than any other god. Only the living truth, what we actually experience, is real. You and I are real—that much we know.

Now is the time to embrace your own living presence, which is the world.

At the end of the day, all our efforts to escape fear merely keep it alive and strong in our lives. Indeed, we survive just fine even under fear's most intense assault; there is a part of us that is utterly untouched by fear

The enduring question is not how to end fear, but how to see, once and for all, that it was a fiction in the first place. It is the core part of the illusion that keeps the whole monstrosity of false belief alive. "There is nothing to fear but fear itself"—how wise were those words. For when we finally see through fear, we also see through the whole soul-killing apparatus of organized religion, ruthless secularism, and empty capitalism.

We are then free to be with the world as equals … laughing together at the joke.

Afterword

For millions of years people lived quietly as hunters and gatherers. They left no tracks or monuments, for their touch on this Earth was very light. Explorers described their exuberance, full-hearted happiness, and generosity. They lived in harmony with their environment, and both the wild world and they themselves prospered. They sang their songs and laughed and loved.

The key element that allowed such cultures to function was trust. They trusted utterly in the world. They knew that nature would take care of them. They returned this blessing with their ceaseless appreciation for and wonder at the abundance of this caring world. Their abiding trust allowed them to live with hearts open to the mystery of existence.

With the development of city-states and empires, a new era dawned. As trust in the world collapsed, people had to deal with considerably more fear in their lives. They feared starvation and their covenant of trust in the world was severed, then and forever after. We are still haunted with these same fears.

This book has focused on the issue of lack as a primary motivator for fear-based behaviors. This same sense of lack lies at the very core of our post-industrial culture.

The dark shadow of lack is cast over all social classes. The well-off have created a vast security industry to protect their possessions. They can never be safe enough. Many live in walled communities, protected by private police. Their children grow up overly pampered and are sent to the most privileged schools so they can attend the most elite universities and extend their power and position across generations.

The middle class emulates its social superiors and fights for the same prize, but with fewer resources. They live with the fear of job loss, loss of medical insurance, and loss of social standing. An immense advertising industry goads them to buy more and better. They cope with these pressures through booze, recreation (itself a massive and often polluting industry), drugs (legal and otherwise), and self-help books and classes. The lower middle class fears dropping down into the lower class, and the upper middle class works ceaselessly to enter the higher realms of the social elite.

The poor grasp at the few strands of power accessible to them. They latch onto the lower ends of the vast illegal drug empires and seek at least to rule the streets of their distressed communities. Their social and economic pressures are much more reality-based than those among the middle class and the wealthy: Will I have enough to eat? Will I have a roof over my head? Will I be shot on the street?

This is the age of insecurity. We have all but sacrificed the planet in our vain attempts to deal with our fears. Our failure is palpable. The battle for the world's last remaining oil and gas fields has just begun, and can only become much more intense and destructive in the future. Looming beyond that is the battle for water, which is already becoming a scarce commodity in many parts of the world. Meanwhile, the environment continues to deteriorate at an alarming rate.

We have become estranged from the world that gave us birth. The world that we human beings trusted for eons has now become our victim. We strike violently at her very heart as we desperately try to ensure our own survival. We are at war with the very entity that gives us life.

This is the challenge of our era. The greater the challenge, the greater the need for vision and capacity for personal and collective transformation. The responsibility for change does not lie with our corrupt governments or technological engineers; it lies with each and every one of us.

The flip side of our society based on limitless consumption can be seen in the world's vast population continuing to live without the "fruits" of industrialization and advanced technology. Billions of people live in utter squalor and destitution in places like the slums of Lagos and Calcutta, the newly barren deserts of Sudan and Kenya, broad swaths of Africa, Asia, and South America. They live in a world of brutal crime and victimization, of poisonous water, of civil wars without end, of wrecked families, of HIV, of hopelessness.

Underneath our world of glittering consumption lives this other, crushed world.

Is this the world we want? Can we live happily indifferent to this truth? Can we live with soul in a world where crass consumption is all that seemingly matters?

Is this what _you_ want?

Concentrations of enormous wealth come at a very high price. The cost is a world of depleted people and depleted environments. The cost is ever-present resentment between those who have and those who do not. The cost is war or the threat of war between countries which are always jockeying for more power and control. It comes at the price of children raised in a world where we do anything we can to shield ourselves from the chaos and destruction that thrives in the wake of our voracity. It comes in the need to sedate ourselves so that we can deal with the trivial pressures that we, as individuals, face compared with those fighting for crusts of bread in Nairobi or Rio or Dhaka.

This is a world tormented by division. We have indeed been cast out of the Garden of Eden. We are divided by religion, by race, by gender, by economics, and by sexual preference. We assume that all of this is "natural." In one sense it is.—it is natural in that it accurately reflects the way of the world now. But it is certainly not typical. Humans have lived for nearly 150,000 years. It is only since the creation of intensive agriculture and political states that have we fomented so much violence against one another, and it is only in the last 500 years that we have fomented so much violence against the planet itself.

We have lost our center and replaced it with insecurity. We have lost our innate sense of trust in our world and have replaced it with fear. We have taken the burden of survival away from the abundance of the world and imposed it on our own minds. In much the same way, we have lost our individual selves in the maelstrom of modern life and have dutifully accepted the frantic burden of survival onto our own machinations.

We have lost our center and replaced it with insecurity. We have lost our innate sense of trust in our world and have replaced it with fear. We have taken the burden of survival away from the abundance of the world and imposed it on our own minds. In much the same way, we have lost our individual selves in the maelstrom of modern life and have dutifully accepted the frantic burden of survival onto our own machinations. We are driven by fear because, for the vast majority of us, this task is overwhelming and ultimately soulless. We have sacrificed our souls to consumption. We have sacrificed our planet to this same end.

Do we want to live in walled cities and nations bristling with weapons? Do we want to live on the precipice of environmental catastrophe? Do we want to live in a world where billions suffer squalor and malnutrition so the rest of us can buy cheap clothes at Wal-Mart? Do we want to live in the cold blue light of our television screens, secluded from the warmth of our neighbors and the natural world? Is this living by the light of our heart?

While looking out at the world can fill us with dread and despair, it also can show us our capacity for vast compassion. People are wired to express compassion where there is need. The world offers us two distinct lessons: one, no trend continues in the same direction forever; and two, seeing the pain that flourishes in places both rich and poor can motivate us to great change.

One of the key understandings of traditional wisdom is that nothing is permanent. We may believe that we live with permanence, but life tells a very different story. Everything is in ceaseless flux. We might use the language of stasis, but that is not actuality. All suffering, all pain leads to counter-energies. This is the time to see the pain and suffering in the world and in us, and to look inward to discover the authentic source of transformation. It is within each of us.

We need to identify the root of the problem in our culture and in our own hearts. The purpose of this book has been to describe the root as well as gateways to self-understanding.

Know that the root is existential fear. It is the hollowness we feel in the very cores of our culture and our psyches. The bad news is that it is has spawned an empire of wealth and decay; but the good news is that the core of lack within ourselves is, itself, an illusion. It is a fiction we have assumed to be real. Because we take it to be real, we live our lives motivated by fear. To whatever extent we strive to soothe our fears is the same extent to which we sacrifice our authenticity.

This book is a call to discover our authentic voices amid the din of avarice and technology. It is the journey back to our true selves.

This is not the New Age promise of limitless abundance if we only believe it for ourselves, where everyone can be very rich and have a Porsche and swimming pool. That is poison, one of the most worthless spectacles of mindlessness expressed in the modern world. To the contrary, the planet has been all but bled dry to satisfy our relentless diversions.

This is not the New Age promise of limitless abundance if we only believe it for ourselves, where everyone can be very rich and have a Porsche and swimming pool. That is poison, one of the most worthless spectacles of mindlessness expressed in the modern world. To the contrary, the planet has been all but bled dry to satisfy our relentless diversions.

Everything we create, everything we manufacture must all eventually be discarded. The unseen trash of our civilization is in the air we breathe, the water we drink, and the communities of the economically destitute. Our culture is brilliant at hiding its waste. But that doesn't mean it isn't everywhere. It is killing even the planet's seemingly inexhaustible oceans. Environmental scientists tell us that life in these oceans may disappear in as little as 60 years. How could things have gotten so out of balance?

If we speak of abundance, speak of the abundance of the human heart that is still here and still thriving. Our abundance is one of spirit. One of the keys to experiencing this abundance is to understand our world. The greatest connector is our shared need. We need to be in this together. We need to extend our hearts and hands to all our brothers and sisters as we put together a world without the inequality that demeans us all and without the inherent destructiveness of our failing civilization. This is the abundance of spirit and caring we need to bring to the forefront of our individual and collective lives.

This book is about reconnecting with this abundance of the heart. It is a call to wake up from the nightmare of lack, fear, and insecurity. We cannot look to others to wake up for us. This task is ours alone.

This book does not suggest that we should or could return to our tribal roots. That phase of the human journey is over. The message instead is that we can see how our choices are often motivated by fear and the compulsive drive for personal security, and that we can be secure without a compulsive need to achieve—which is the very drive that thwarts our security in the first place. The drive for security is the most destructive choice we can make. There are alternatives, but they cannot enter our consciousness until we see how the individual and collective egos operate.

With understanding comes transformation.

It is a journey of finding our true selves without the cruel burden of constant striving. It is a journey of unlearning, of unpacking most of the bags we carry on our tired backs. It is a journey of reclaiming what is our rightfully ours.

What is rightfully ours?

It is our right to live with integrity and vision. It is our right to live in honor of ourselves and our neighbors. It is our right to trust the universe to take care of everyone and everything. It is our right to love as our hearts guide us. It is our right to discover our own voices in our own way.

You are only responsible for yourself. You are not responsible for anyone else, and certainly not for the entire world. Allow the world to do as it does. The task of finding and expressing our authentic voices falls only to those who choose to take this journey. It is a task which, unlike many others in our lives, possesses not the slightest element of coercion.

Get a feel for the confidence that is within you. If you can't feel it at first, just close your eyes and breathe in a way that yields a sense of pleasure. Then guide yourself to your source of confidence.

That is the starting place. Open your heart to that place. Feel the smile forming on your face. Discard your seriousness. The process of liberation calls for the loving, smiling heart of your true self. This person is secure; she loves the feel of blood and oxygen running through her body. Begin to sense your connection with the vast cosmos around you. This is your authentic body. It is whole and confident. This is where the journey begins and ends.

4185249

Made in the USA
Lexington, KY
31 December 2009